The Social Life of Kimono

Annette Lynch, *Dress, Gender and Cultural Change: Asian American and African American Rites of Passage*

Antonia Young, *Women Who Become Men: Albanian Sworn Virgins*

David Muggleton, *Inside Subculture: The Postmodern Meaning of Style*

Nicola White, *Reconstructing Italian Fashion: America and the Development of the Italian Fashion Industry*

Brian J. McVeigh, *Wearing Ideology: The Uniformity of Self-Presentation in Japan*

Shaun Cole, *Don We Now Our Gay Apparel: Gay Men's Dress in the Twentieth Century*

Kate Ince, *Orlan: Millennial Female*

Ali Guy, Eileen Green and Maura Banim, *Through the Wardrobe: Women's Relationships with their Clothes*

Linda B. Arthur, *Undressing Religion: Commitment and Conversion from a Cross-Cultural Perspective*

William J.F. Keenan, *Dressed to Impress: Looking the Part*

Joanne Entwistle and Elizabeth Wilson, *Body Dressing*

Leigh Summers, *Bound to Please: A History of the Victorian Corset*

Paul Hodkinson, *Goth: Identity, Style and Subculture*

Leslie W. Rabine, *The Global Circulation of African Fashion*

Michael Carter, *Fashion Classics from Carlyle to Barthes*

Sandra Niessen, Ann Marie Leshkowich and Carla Jones, *Re-Orienting Fashion: The Globalization of Asian Dress*

Kim K.P. Johnson, Susan J. Torntore and Joanne B. Eicher, *Fashion Foundations: Early Writings on Fashion and Dress*

Helen Bradley Foster and Donald Clay Johnson, *Wedding Dress Across Cultures*

Eugenia Paulicelli, *Fashion under Fascism: Beyond the Black Shirt*

Charlotte Suthrell, *Unzipping Gender: Sex, Cross-Dressing and Culture*

Irene Guenther, *Nazi Chic? Fashioning Women in the Third Reich*

Yuniya Kawamura, *The Japanese Revolution in Paris Fashion*

Patricia Calefato, *The Clothed Body*

Ruth Barcan, *Nudity: A Cultural Anatomy*

Samantha Holland, *Alternative Femininities: Body, Age and Identity*

Alexandra Palmer and Hazel Clark, *Old Clothes, New Looks: Second Hand Fashion*

Yuniya Kawamura, *Fashion-ology: An Introduction to Fashion Studies*

Regina A. Root, *The Latin American Fashion Reader*

Linda Welters and Patricia A. Cunningham, *Twentieth-Century American Fashion*

Jennifer Craik, *Uniforms Exposed: From Conformity to Transgression*

Alison L. Goodrum, *The National Fabric: Fashion, Britishness, Globalization*

Annette Lynch and Mitchell D. Strauss, *Changing Fashion: A Critical Introduction to Trend Analysis and Meaning*

Catherine M. Roach, *Stripping, Sex and Popular Culture*

Marybeth C. Stalp, *Quilting: The Fabric of Everyday Life*

Jonathan S. Marion, *Ballroom: Culture and Costume in Competitive Dance*

Dunja Brill, *Goth Culture: Gender, Sexuality and Style*

Joanne Entwistle, *The Aesthetic Economy of Fashion: Markets and Value in Clothing and Modelling*

Juanjuan Wu, *Chinese Fashion: From Mao to Now*

Annette Lynch, *Porn Chic: Exploring the Contours of Raunch Eroticism*

Brent Luvaas, *DIY Style: Fashion, Music and Global Cultures*

Jianhua Zhao, *The Chinese Fashion Industry: An Ethnographic Approach*

Eric Silverman, *A Cultural History of Jewish Dress*

Karen Hansen and D. Soyini Madison, *African Dress: Fashion, Agency, Performance*

Maria Mellins, *Vampire Culture*

Lynne Hume, *The Religious Life of Dress*

Marie Riegels Melchior and Birgitta Svensson, *Fashion and Museums: Theory and Practice*

Masafumi Monden, *Japanese Fashion Cultures: Dress and Gender in Contemporary Japan*

Alfonso McClendon, *Fashion and Jazz: Dress, Identity and Subcultural Improvisation*

Phyllis G. Tortora, *Dress, Fashion and Technology: From Prehistory to the Present*

Barbara Brownie and Danny Graydon, *The Superhero Costume: Identity and Disguise in Fact and Fiction*

Adam Geczy and Vicki Karaminas, *Fashion's Double: Representations of Fashion in Painting, Photography and Film*

Yuniya Kawamura, *Sneakers: Fashion, Gender, and Subculture*

Heike Jenss, *Fashion Studies: Research Methods, Sites and Practices*

Brent Luvaas, *Street Style: An Ethnography of Fashion Blogging*

Jenny Lantz, *The Trendmakers: Behind the Scenes of the Global Fashion Industry*

Barbara Brownie, *Acts of Undressing: Politics, Eroticism, and Discarded Clothing*

The Social Life of Kimono

Japanese Fashion Past and Present

Sheila Cliffe

Bloomsbury Academic

An imprint of Bloomsbury Publishing Plc

BLOOMSBURY

LONDON • OXFORD • NEW YORK • NEW DELHI • SYDNEY

Bloomsbury Academic

An imprint of Bloomsbury Publishing Plc

50 Bedford Square
London
WC1B 3DP
UK

1385 Broadway
New York
NY 10018
USA

www.bloomsbury.com

BLOOMSBURY and the Diana logo are trademarks of Bloomsbury Publishing Plc

First published 2017
Reprinted 2017

British Library Cataloguing-in-Publication Data
A catalogue record for this book is available from the British Library.

ISBN:	HB:	978-1-4725-8553-0
	PB:	978-1-4725-8552-3
	ePDF:	978-1-4725-8554-7
	ePub:	978-1-4725-8555-4

Library of Congress Cataloging-in-Publication Data
Names: Cliffe, Sheila, author.Title: The social life of kimono : Japanese fashion past and present /
Sheila Cliffe.Description: New York : Bloomsbury Academic, 2017. |
Series: Dress, body,culture, ISSN 1360-466X | Includes bibliographical references and index.
Identifiers: LCCN 2016030443 (print) | LCCN 2016030936 (ebook) | ISBN9781472585523 (paperback) |
ISBN 9781472585530 (hardback) | ISBN9781472585547 (epdf) | ISBN 9781472585554 (epub)
Subjects: LCSH: Kimonos. | Clothing and dress–Social aspects–Japan. |
BISAC: HISTORY / Asia / Japan. | DESIGN / Fashion. Classification: LCC GT1560 .C59 2017 (print) |
LCC GT1560 (ebook) | DDC391.00952–dc23
LC record available at https://lccn.loc.gov/2016030443

Series: Dress, Body, Culture, 1360-466X

Cover design: Sharon Mah
Cover Image © Okumoto Akihisa. Model: Tamura Nodoka.

Typeset by Integra Software Services Pvt. Ltd.
Printed and bound in Great Britain

I dedicate this book to Graham, Kaz, Misha, and Natasha
because you all bring much joy into my life.
You are my greatest blessings.

Contents

List of Figures

List of Charts

Preface

When I first came to Japan in 1985, I knew extraordinarily little about the place. This was to be a month-long summer vacation trip. I never considered that I might actually stay. However, I discovered kimono and the rest is my history. I often considered myself handicapped as a kimono wearer because I have no memories of family members wearing kimono, nor have I worn kimono on Japanese ceremonial occasions when kimono is de rigueur. In addition, I have not had a kimono collection bequeathed to me by a grandmother, mother, or aunt, so I have started mine from scratch.

In other ways, I have been very privileged. Although my Japanese was negligible, the teachers in my kimono dressing school classes responded with enthusiasm to my hungry spirit. I asked more questions than all the other students put together, probably in almost incomprehensible Japanese, but they would explain with infinite patience the ways of the kimono. At that time it was a teacher who taught me about kimono. Later I realized that it was the kimono that was teaching me about Japan. The more I viewed images, looked at kimono, wore kimono, spoke to sellers and makers, the more I became aware of the depth and subtlety of the kimono and its dressing system.

At the beginning it was because of, and not in spite of, my being a tabula rasa, eager to soak up everything I could find out about kimono, that my eyes were not blinkered when something new started to happen. I was in Japan, looking, learning, exploring at the moment when the kimono renaissance began. I was trawling the book shops, kimono shops, department stores, and flea markets making discoveries by asking questions and examining fabrics and garments, so I was on the scene to witness the birth pangs of the revival.

So why another kimono book? As I enthusiastically digest anything written in English about the kimono, I feel the need to explain why this book has come into being. It came into being because it wasn't there. This is the book that I was looking for and could never find. Minnich's *Japanese Costume and the Makers of Its Elegant Tradition,* a comprehensive history, was written over half a century ago and Dalby's *Kimono: Fashioning Culture,* an insightful social history, over twenty years ago. Both are excellent texts, and I reference these writers, but I do not cover the same ground. These were not the books I was looking for. I wanted a book that sold me kimono how it really is now, kimono as fashion, a book that would explore the relationships between the Japanese and their kimono. I wanted a book to make me fall in love with the cloth and the characters whose lives are wrapped up in it, because in the end it is the kimono's interconnectedness that is so fascinating. Kimono fashion is not fast, not anonymous, and not without location. It is a wonderful example of an embedded fashion.

During the writing of my Ph.D. and this book which has developed from that research, I have witnessed and worked in two areas of Japan completely devastated by tsunami and earthquake. In both cases I have seen the demise of many kimono. I have also had the privilege of talking to earthquake and tsunami survivors. It is not unusual for them to mention kimono alongside photograph albums, family ashes, Buddhist tablets, and identity cards as items that they would like to be rescued from devastated housing. They are living in jeans and sweatshirts, but rather than such items, it is the kimono that they desire. The kimono speaks of continuity, people's weddings and celebrations, coming-of-age, and graduations. Often they belonged to other women in the family, and sometimes they were specially commissioned. I am reminded again about the power this garment has for Japanese, and how many meanings are embedded into it.

With this personal dimension, and connectedness in mind, I have respected the wishes of the interviewees and used their names in their chosen order and have not capitalized when they prefer not to have names capitalized. It is my hope that the reader will come to find these people, whose lives are wrapped up in kimono, to be as fascinating as I have found them, and come to love both the garment and the world built around it.

Acknowledgments

This book was made possible with generous grants from:
The Society of Authors' K. Blundell Trust Awards
Jumonji Gakuen Women's University

Special thanks to: Hannah Crump and everyone at Bloomsbury Publishing Plc, Advertising Museum Tokyo, Akira Times, arecole, Bunka Gakuen Costume Museum, Chichibu Meisen Kan, Dai Maru Goufuku Ten, Todd Fong, Fujioka Hiroharu, Naomi Hormozi, Ishibashi Kouichi, Ishioka Kumiko, Lyuta Ito, Kento Itoh, Anna Jackson, Lyuba Johnson, Jotaro Saito, Linda Kentie, Kidera Masaru, Kikuchi Sae, Kimono Times, Kitagawa Sachi, Kitamura Kumiko, Kobayashi Tomohisa, Kodansha, Koiso Art Club, Magdalen Méan, Mitsukoshi Isetan Holdings, Hosono Miyako, Morioka Masahiro, Nagasaki Iwao, Nagata Lunco, Nakagawa Michina, Nakayama Asako, Nasu Sachio, Nishiwaki Hisae, Nishiwaki Ryuji, Okano Yoshimi, Okumoto Akihisa, Berber Ostenbrug, Otomo Chisato, President Inc, Shibasaki Rumi, Shirataki Mikio, Shiseido Art House, Helen Stewart, Sugino Costume Museum, Suzuki Kiyoko, Suzuki Yasuko, Tanabe Keiko, The Victoria and Albert Museum London, Yuuki Yukari.

To all the encouragers in real life and on Facebook who helped me along the way, I could not have done it without you.

Introduction

This book is a social analysis of the kimono in both the past and present. It explains why the kimono can be considered to have fashion and not only tradition and outlines the differences and similarities between the kimono system and the western fashion system. In the course of writing this book, wanting it as contemporary as possible, I have conducted over thirty interviews with kimono craftspeople and makers, businesses, and magazine publishers as well as kimono wearers. I am grateful for their trust in me and their desire to tell their stories. I have also found pockets of resistance. There are those who would rather not contribute and tell their stories, although being known is probably key to saving some varieties of kimono. The kimono must be viewed to be appreciated and indeed has often been considered to be art for wearing. Therefore color photographs are an essential part of this work.

Of necessity I have concentrated on artisans and brands in the Kanto area, or those who came to Tokyo, and I could meet. Whole books could be written about textile artists in Kyoto, Okinawa, or other outlying areas in Japan. As many other dyeing techniques such as *sarasa*, chintz, *Edo komon,* small dot stencil dyeing or *shibori,* tie-dyeing exist along with weaving techniques such as *minsa,* from Okinawan Islands, *Oshima tsumugi,* from islands near Kyushu, and *ojiya,* from the west side of Japan, and other new brands such as *Mamechiyo, Modern Antenna,* or *Double Maison* that are fascinating and are bringing in the new. My research shows a sample across a broad range of producers.

Chapter 1 is a theoretical one, which defines the terms fashion and tradition used in the book, providing a framework and an essential background for those who study fashion. Chapter 2 looks at two important periods in the history of kimono, showing evidence for trends, and discussing these in regard to fashion, and the social and political factors of the periods, concluding with evidence pointing to a full economic fashion system in place by the Edo period. Chapter 3 covers changes in the modernist period, after western clothing arrived in Japan, discussing the takeover by western dress and concluding that such a takeover has never been as complete or definitive as has been assumed. It highlights the evidence for a continuing love of kimono among Japanese. Chapter 4 examines kimono in the media by introducing historical pattern books and kimono in advertising, and also by discussing English language kimono texts and Japanese magazines which demonstrate change over time in printed media. Chapter 5 considers the impact of new technology on makers and marketers. New developments have affected not only production but marketing and distribution too. Internet communication has significantly altered the kimono world. As kimono is no longer the default clothing in Japan, usually a special reason lies behind someone choosing to wear it. In Chapter 6, wearers inside and outside Japan are introduced, and the meanings that kimono embodies for them are explored.

In Chapter 7, I suggest a possible future for the kimono. Through the internet and a rise of interest in Japanese popular culture, kimono is being spread beyond Japanese borders. That it is possible to learn *kitsuke,* dressing, outside Japan, without even understanding the language, has implications for kimono schools and businesses. As with all fashion, what kind of kimono will emerge in the future is unknown.

Only once imagined in a designer's mind can it be born. Some worry that kimono loses its kimono-ness, something of its essence, as it interacts more with western fashion. But if we look back 1,200 years and remember that the inveterate observer and diary writer of the Heian court, Sei Shonagon, was complaining about the high clogs of young guys and the wonky back seams of fashionable courtiers, we realize that these worries are probably as old as fashion itself. The kimono of tomorrow will not be the kimono of yesterday, which is a great thing because no one wants to be "yesterday."

Bibliography

Dalby, L. (1993) *Kimono: Fashioning Culture*. New Haven, London: Yale University Press.

Minnich, H. (1963) *Japanese Costume and the Makers of its Elegant Tradition*.

Shonagon, Sei. Trans. Morris, I. (1967) *The Pillow Book of Sei Shonagon*. London: Penguin.

1 Think Fashion or Tradition?

Fashion and Orientalization

Kimono lovers may question the necessity for this chapter at all. Why does it matter if kimono is regarded as fashion or tradition anyway? It matters because the West in general, and France in particular, have claimed the center of fashion as their own and still retain a hegemony in fashion discourse. Even at a fashion technology conference at the most prestigious fashion school in Tokyo in 2014, I heard two Japanese professors referring to Paris as the center of the fashion system. In spite of increasing calls to reexamine the position of the West in fashion theory, such opinions and biases continue to be prevalent and to be published.

According to the conventional wisdom of fashion theorists, a seemingly traditional garment from a non-European country would not qualify as a fashion item. Until relatively recently, it has been almost universally assumed that fashion is a product of western social conditions, and that it started in Europe. Bell (1976), Barthes (1966, 2006), Hollander (1993), Lipovetsky (1994), Baudot (1999), Entwistle (2007), Evans (2003), Kawamura (2006), and Barnard (2007) all locate fashion in the West. A western location is also implied in the work of Veblen (2003), Laver (1986), and Baudrillard (1983). The hegemonic centrality of Europe in fashion theory has been justified variously by its economic system, its flexible social system or, in the case of Hollander, through the fact that its clothing changes in shape (1993).

Non-western, in particular eastern, cultures have been considered in this discourse to be static, love tradition, and produce clothing that is unchanging. Eastern clothing systems have repeatedly provided a foil against which western progress and fashionability are measured. Lipovetsky assumes that those countries outside Europe have "unchallenged ancestral legacies" which produce conservative modes of being. He declares that stability was characteristic of China, India, and other Asian civilizations and that the Japanese kimono remained unchanged for centuries (1994:19). Bell's example of unchanging fashion is China, Hollander's is "Eastern countries or the ancient world" (1993:357), and Entwistle's is "contemporary cultures where society is rigid" (2000:44). This is expressed, she says, in traditional dress such as the kimono or sari, both of which are characterized by continuity with the past.

Barthes describes history as having three timescales which overlie each other. There are events which are short; situations that are longer than events called conjunctures; and there are structures which are long term. All three of these affect change in fashion. The longest timescale covers "archetypal forms of clothing in a given civilization." He characterizes this timeline by the example of the Japanese kimono. Hollander (1993) divides clothing into western and other non-fashionable clothing, which has the function of maintaining tradition and custom and expresses certainty and a fixed cosmology. After discussing social mobility and economic systems, Entwistle concludes that "the evidence for treating fashion as a historically and geographically specific system of dress is overwhelming and convincing" (2007:47). She continues by saying that fashion requires social mobility, specific kinds of production and consumption, and a system of regular and logical change, all of which are found in European societies. Whether or not these elements are also present in non-European societies is not examined. Neither does this body of literature provide any evidence of the supposedly static social systems, or the unchanging clothing that they produce. This study of the kimono contests the necessity for social mobility based on evidence found in Japan.

A critical reading of fashion theory with non-European clothing in mind leads to the conclusion that this body of literature has serious problems. It produces arguments which essentially erase clothing development and history from non-western nations and generalizes, simplifies, and contributes to the othering of non-western clothing systems. Why have such orientalizing positions continued to thrive? I suggest here three contributing factors.

The first reason for the persistence of these ideas must be the lack of evidence garnered from non-European nations to refute them. Diachronic data, collected over a long period of time, are necessary in order to detect evolution and trends or fashion change. As Welters and Lillethun (2007) and Riello and McNeil (2010) argue, there has been little research on fashion systems to date, beyond Europe. Lack of such evidence has led to other systems of dress being easily dismissed as unchanging and conservative. It has been assumed that change happens in response to outside circumstances rather than innovation. For example, Rovine (2011) believes that African local dress has been wrongly excluded from discussions of fashion and believes that it has incorrectly been associated with tradition, statis, conservatism, and even primitivism, ignoring a history of innovation and creativity. This, she says, is partly because of a lack of data to show change and partly because of the orientalism described here. She argues that the study of African artistic expression is not complete without attention being paid to its fashion, which is a key element of African expression. Africa has not only a long history of indigenous fashion innovation but has also been a source of inspiration for global fashion (2015:7). Hansen and Madison (2013) agree that seeing fashion as a one-way process responding only to external stimuli hides the heart of African dress. "In Africa, 'traditional' dress was always a changing practice, remaking itself in interaction with other dress styles, with garments of western commercial manufacture and the West's fashion system" (2013:4). Rovine emphasizes the ability of fashion to tell stories and demonstrates how innovative African fashion and dress reveal political alliances, cultural exchange, and a complex history full of cultural meanings. Her project aims to decentralize Paris in the consideration of African dress. Paris is only one of many significant centers when considering the fashions of Africa.

A second reason is that the factor signifying fashion in western countries is, as Hollander has said, *change in shape*. Western eyes are trained to look for rising and lowering hems and waists, narrowing and widening of sleeves and trouser legs, and changes in collar shape, all of which signify a change in style. Hollander writes:

> Sometime during the thirteenth century, the aesthetic impulse towards significant distortion and creative tailoring, (as opposed to creative draping and trimming) arose in European dress and established what has become the modern concept of fashion (1978:17).

A change in pattern or color would be construed perhaps as a seasonal trend but would not be seen as significant in the way that change of shape would be significant. Though it is systematic, the choice of shape as a signifier is, however, completely random. There could be clothing systems where the main factor is not change in shape but in color, pattern, texture, thickness, even smell. Changes in these areas would not be detected as fashion change by western eyes, as the signifier of fashion change for western eyes is the shape or silhouette. While outsiders from countries where change in shape signifies fashion change might regard only a change in shape as constituting fashion, those from countries where a change in pattern represents a change in fashion, insiders will recognize the fashion change that comes with change in pattern. Again to refer to the African case for an example, Kirby writes that not the silhouette, but the embroidery motif and color change yearly and previous years colors are shelved at the top and bottom, rather than the easily seen middle shelves of the store (2013:68).

A third reason for orientalizing discourses must be seen in the history of clothing studies. The nineteenth century saw ethnologists and anthropologists studying different cultures and countries around the world and bringing back data which were used to create hierarchies and taxonomies according to new Darwinian theories. The agenda was to prove difference between western culture and other cultures. Puwar (2003) describes how the Pitt Rivers collection in Oxford exemplifies the Eurocentric framing of knowledge, with other countries being measured against Europe. The agenda not only proved difference but superiority, as the European culture became the measuring stick for other cultures. Puwar also explains how women's dress has been appropriated to teach about traditional roles and rituals, and interpretations are often framed as dichotomies, where modern is progressive, rational, democratic, and enlightened, but traditional is fixed, ahistorical, spiritual, and mythical. In particular according to European standards, a perceived lack of clothing was framed as primitive and savage by western standards.

Paradigm Shift

Increasingly, fashion theorists have begun to problematize definitions of fashion because of their exclusive nature which refuses admittance to non-western systems of dress. It has been suggested by Craik that our definitions of fashion be expanded to include all kinds of fashioning, which literally means making, and all kinds of bodily adornment and decoration (1994). This would enable clothing from all countries to be considered as fashion. This viewpoint recognizes that fashion is found in all the things that humans make, and that dress includes not only clothing items but also all kinds of bodily practices which contribute to appearance, such as bodily modifications, painting, scarring, or tattooing for example. Desires for beads, furs, feathers, or other such ornaments among non-western people are evidence of fashion in other civilizations. Craik argues that not only modern but preindustrial, industrial, colonial societies all engage in a dynamic play between traditional and fashionable uses of dress.

Eicher and Evenson have made a classification system for dress, dividing it into various modifications to body parts, and supplements to the body which can be hung, wrapped, suspended, or pre-shaped, and also attachments to the body itself or to the enclosures, including hand-held objects. This system provides an objective tool for examining dress, so that unbiased assessment can be possible. Once meanings are added, culturally specific ideas come into play, and it becomes impossible to make impartial evaluations about body modifications. An example would be tattooing, which carries many different meanings to different people. Being condemned by a tattooed number on a forehead, tattooed as a cultural ritual, choosing a tattoo for fashion, or being tattooed to signify your membership of a gang in Japan embody very different meanings although they all employ the same practice. The meanings ascribed to the practice are cultural, and Eicher and Evenson emphasize that dress is material culture that is related to nonmaterial culture, "especially beliefs, values, and patterns of social interaction" (2015:31).

Eicher and Evenson also divide sociocultural systems into tribal (kinship based), imperial (with a central government and hundreds of thousands of people), and commercial (with commerce being the main activity and transnational interactions and economic systems). This is dynamic, and as more and more countries are involved in the third kind of system, the world is increasingly globalized, but tribal and imperial systems still exist inside larger sociocultural systems. In this milieu, the choice of dress becomes an important way both for establishing identity and demonstrating allegiances and is therefore a political as well as an expressive tool. Change in dress which is material signifies change in nonmaterial culture. "Dress…can be an extremely powerful, symbolic, ritualized way of expressing and reinforcing subtle values, relationships, and meanings in human cultures" (2015:123). A feature of the commercial system is the proliferation of computer and internet technology, which enables the transference of huge amounts of information, linking people and economies worldwide and creates the possibility of multiple authorship and global markets for all kinds of products, services, and ideas.

The First International Non-Western Fashion Conference was held in Morocco in June 2012. *The Berg Encyclopedia of World Dress and Fashion* was first established in print in 2010 and then went online as a part of the *Berg Fashion Library* in 2011. These are major steps forward in the redefinition of fashion theory. In fact, it seems apparent that a paradigm shift is occurring in the field at the time of writing. This shift is from a hierarchical reading of fashion with western values embodied in western styles in the central, top, or dominant position, toward a more fluid reading which recognizes a wider definition of dress, variety of cultural interpretations, and innovation from multiple sources both technological, advanced, commercial, and local, hand-crafted and culturally rooted items.

Because this is a period of flux, and it is easier to see where we have come from than where we are going to, many ideas are contested. There are many theorists who would not agree with my interpretation of the kimono as a fashion garment. It is possible to frame fashion only in terms of economy and mass production. It is also possible to maintain that it is about change in shape, as Hollander does. In the light of all the recent research published on non-western fashion, my own definition could be considered to be very conservative. However, I consider this to be a plus point, as even when using a relatively narrow or strict definition of fashion, the evidence that I found points to the presence of a fashion system in Japan, at least as old as that in Europe.

Defining Fashion and Tradition

Kimono is not fashion because I happen to think it is beautiful, cute, or stylish. It is fashion because it fulfills the definitions and functions of a fashion system. I have constructed a five-stranded definition of fashion here, from the body of fashion theory. I devote this chapter to fashion theory and Chapters 2 and 3 to kimono's fashion history, demonstrating with examples throughout the history, that the kimono, generally thought of as Japan's national costume or traditional clothing, is also fashionable. If the core elements of fashion can be identified from fashion theory, and then extensive diachronic data on clothing systems gathered, a clothing system can be evaluated in terms of whether or not an economic system of fashion, change over time, form over function, group-based clothing behavior, and personal clothing behavior exist. Fortunately, in the Japanese case, there is plenty of data in the form of written historical records from and about Japan, some images, and in recent history extant clothing items. Here the terms of fashion and tradition are examined, and the history of the kimono is detailed in Chapters 2 and 3 in the light of the definitions of fashion that emerge from the theory. This approach provides a model which could be utilized in the study of other non-western systems of dress, where such kinds of data are available.

Although there is much discussion about fashion, tradition is often assumed to be understood. It is thought to be the opposite of fashion and is self-evidently non-fashion. Tradition speaks of the unchanging or static. Lipovetsy (1994) describes it as having "rigidity," and he also invokes the phrases "principle of immobility" and "repetition of models from the past." In tradition, the old is thought to be better than the new, whereas in fashion the opposite is true. Fashionable clothing changes fast. Some fashions may last a matter of weeks, some may last a period of years. Polhemus coined the term *antifashion* in 1978, and Davis used it in 1992 to refer to clothing that is not considered to be fashionable, clothing of the poor, or counterculture groups. Interestingly a Google search on the phrase "traditional clothing" will bring up sites related to regional or national dress such as Japanese, African, or Greenland's costume. On Wikipedia, the phrase will lead to the "folk costume" page. Eicher (1995) notes that ethnic dress is not static but shows "significant changes in form and detail," so relating it to a static tradition is problematic. Tradition turns out to be complex and difficult to define. For our purposes, I have chosen the following definition: **"Traditional clothing is clothing that is relatively static, functioning to maintain customs and social order, valorizing the past."** According to this definition, clothing that expresses rank, conservative dress, or uniforms would be considered traditional when used in the manner for which they were designed. There is much evidence to show that uniforms do change over time, but relatively slowly and they are usually considered to be conservative clothing functioning to maintain social roles or order.

Defining fashion is very difficult because theories show little consensus. All theorists agree that fashion is about some kind of systematic change over time, realized in a series of trends, but beyond this there is little agreement, and fashion emerges as a highly contested area. Here are outlined some of the main theories, grouped into five categories, according to what could be considered to be the fashion driver in each theory.

The first group of theories is class- or economics-based theories which started with Simmel (1904) who proposed that one class imitates the styles of the class above it by copying their sartorial behavior. The styles diffuse downward from the upper classes and gradually lose their newness and value as they become older, or they are made in cheaper materials. Consequently, the upper classes adopt a new style to maintain their social distinction. Simmel's model has come to be known as the trickle-down model of fashion diffusion. It was challenged by Blumer (1969) who considered that Simmel's emphasis on distinction of class through expensive clothing was not the cause of the fashion system, but rather a result of it. He believed it was because they recognized the potential fashionability of a design, that they started wearing it, and that gave the design the elite approval. Crane (2000) also casts a critical eye at Simmel's ideas for simplifying the fashion process and the extent to which lower classes are actually able to adopt the styles of the upper classes, which varies greatly according to both occupation and location. She also argues that the clothing of the upper classes was difficult to adopt by working women because it was difficult to work in. Veblen (1899) believes that dress was a convenient way of marking social rank as it was on display the whole time. For the wealthy, a garment's purpose was to reveal that one did not have to work, through its cleanliness and impractical nature. Top hats, white linen shirts, and high heels are examples of such clothing. Ideally, they had to be changed each season in order to demonstrate conspicuous waste. Conspicuous waste is still relevant today, with celebrities wearing outrageously expensive clothing and the rest of us regularly discarding clothing that is still fit to be worn.

Other directions of fashion flow have been suggested, which challenge the top or trickle-down pattern suggested by Simmel. People are not so clearly defined by class, as by different lifestyles now, and in 1963, King (2007) suggested that fashions trickled horizontally across groups with similar lifestyles, which could be class or other types of groupings. Bourdieu (1984) suggested that people with a similar "habitus" or upbringing showed similar tastes, values, and behaviors, explaining horizontal fashion flow. Examples of such flow could be styles that develop among a specific class, group of workers or ethnic group, or among students in a particular school. Since the 1960s' birth of youth culture, however, it has been suggested by various people that fashions actually spread up from the street. Hebdige (1979) believes that street styles are a "symbolic form of resistance" against a society that promised equality but left working class, immigrant, or underprivileged groups behind. Polhemus (1994) calls this the "bubble up" model and argues that in a postmodern world full of surface and hype, the value of authenticity from the street is more attractive than promises of wealth or power.

Today, it is impossible to explain the diffusion of fashion entirely from Simmel's theory as diffusion happens in different directions, but this does not mean that the theory did not explain fashion flows in the past. Kawamura (2006) sees the economic system as an integral part of the fashion system. She welds the economic and symbolic aspects together in what she calls "Fashionology." The system produces not only items of clothing but also the concept of fashion in people's minds. Fashion, she believes, is not the clothes but this system that gives special symbolic meanings to the clothes. Welters and Lillethun cite market economy as one of the necessary components in society for a fashion system to develop.

> Certain components are necessary for a society to have a fashion system. These include a market economy that provides wealth, adequate technology to make apparel items, a distribution system that disseminates both ideas about fashion and the products themselves, and a system of fashion innovation and adoption. (2007:xxi)

Economic theories are limited by being discussions of only western cultures. Other regions of the world are either never mentioned in such discussions or are summarily dismissed for an absence of fashion. If Japan could support a market economy, had wealthy people to buy clothes and dress up, technology to make apparel items and a distribution system, then it had the economic conditions for a fashion system, in just the same way as Europe.

A second group of theories about fashion are those that concentrate on its newness. These can be considered postmodern theories. That the new is more important and overrides the old is the essential feature of these theories of fashion. For Lipovetsky, fashion is novelty and play and a "way out of tradition and the negation of the age-old power of the traditional past" (1994:4). Newness and play, for Lipovetsky, are the purpose and end of fashion. He sees this as fashion democratizing as we no longer have to imitate the upper classes but are free to be ourselves, as does Polhemus (see online blog). Barthes utilized the structural linguistic methodology of Saussure to demonstrate that clothing works likes a language with grammar structure and rules. He showed that it is a semiotic system where clothes carry meanings. The clothes, which are not only garments but carry symbolic information, he calls "*signifiers,*" and the meanings that they carry are what is *signified*. Baudrillard (1983) sees western society as having now gone beyond the semiotic stage as described by Barthes. He divides western cultural history into three stages from the renaissance to the present day. The first stage he calls "counterfeit," and in this stage, which is from the renaissance to the Industrial Revolution, appearances reflect reality. The second stage he calls "production," and in this stage appearances mask reality. He believes that we are now in a third stage, which he calls "simulation," where appearances replace reality. The signifiers, as described by Barthes, no longer signify an underlying reality but are free floating. Signs refer only to other signs, and there is no depth, only surface. The system becomes self-referential and is about artifice and play rather than form or style.

Tseëlon (1994) applied Baudrillard's tripartite division to fashion and theorized it as similarly passing through three stages of development. These can be mapped onto Baudrillard's counterfeit, production, and simulation phases. Tseëlon calls them "classical" (which is God given), modern (which embodies the social and the class system) and all the different identities that people developed through work and different public and private situations, and finally a postmodern stage, where there is a crisis of representation and a rejection of tradition. Though Baudrillard sees all signification being annulled, Tseëlon argues that even in such a system there are ways to create meanings. Looser signifier and signified systems do not necessarily mean the complete end of the code, and there is plenty of evidence available to show that signification is alive and well, and clothes still communicate. Tseëlon's explanation allows for evolution in the fashion system in a way that traditional theories do not, and is therefore dynamic and more satisfying than more established explanations.

If newness were the only factor in fashion though, we would expect there to be more variation than there actually is. In reality, people dress within certain constraints and seek a similar kind of newness. Uniforms and formality continue to be important in many situations. Newness is not the only factor in fashion, but change and the rate of change are also of importance. How fast change has to be in order to be conceived of as fashion is undetermined; some fashions are short lived, while others survive for longer. Waists have been high in Japan for at least twenty years and do not show much sign of coming down. Entwistle (2007) acknowledges that clothing in non-European countries changes but does not consider that it is fast enough to qualify as fashion.

For fashion to be present, there has to be noticeable change rather than slow change over many generations. Macro trends are often worldwide and are a slow evolution that is realized in retrospect. Micro trends are seasonal or short-term trends that might affect only certain small groups of people. This kind of change is considered to be fashion. The rate of change in eastern clothing has been problematized by theorists. If kimono has changed on a macro level, just as western clothing has, then we must ask the question of whether it has also changed on a micro level. It is possible that newness and novelty in other clothing systems have been overlooked or misunderstood by those who regard fashion as change in shape.

A third group of theories are gender based and are concerned with eroticism. These theories recognize that many of the forms of clothing cannot be explained by the functional explanations of protection, modesty, or adornment as described by Storm (1987). Much fashionable clothing is manifestly impractical. Often form is more important than function, for example high heels or corsets. Psychology has sought to find explanations for this type of clothing. Flügel, bringing Freudian psychoanalysis to fashion (1930), argues that men gave up their right to dress up in the eighteenth century in the "great masculine renunciation" and made women the vehicles of display. Fashion was about the tension between modesty and display. Laver (2003) observed that the areas of women's bodies which were exposed or covered moved around, and he proposed that the changing shape was caused by shifting erogenous zones. As women had no political or social power, he saw the shifting erogenous zone as a way of keeping the attention of males. Fashion shapes had to conform to the zeitgeist or feeling of the age, but they would also uncover the erogenous zone which was no longer of interest, and cover up a new one, which was. Thus fashion is about erotic display.

Steele (1996) argues that covering raises sexual curiosity which explains the changing shape of clothing, and that this area must move around to maintain curiosity. While eroticism is the driver for fashion in these explanations, they all assume, as Hollander does, that fashion is about *change in shape*. Hollander believes that changing shape is fashion's defining factor. For her, changes in hairstyle, accessories, color, and trimming are not fashionable changes. Change in shape is privileged over other kinds of change as it is the signifying and systematic factor in western fashion. It would be hard for western eyes to understand change in surface design as a fashion change, as western eyes are trained to read fashion change as change in shape. If shape and eroticism are connected in western fashion, there must be other ways of showing eroticism in fashion systems that are not about change in shape.

A fourth way of looking at fashion is that it is fueled by identity ambivalence which leads to identification with groups. Davis (1992) says that if fashion were only about marking class status, then it would not have enough to say and would have died out as class has become less important over time. He says that we are ambivalent about age, gender, physical beauty, and race, and it is these ambivalences in our identity that lead us to certain groups of people, who are usually like us in some of these aspects. These groups of people tend to dress in certain distinct ways. Market researchers divide consumers into types according to lifestyles and values, and psychology is also used to group consumers by personality type. Dressing in similar ways provides a sense of security and marks one as a member of a cultural, ethnic, belief-, or age-based group. Fashion is therefore symbolically meaningful group-based behavior. This can be seen easily in style tribes, but also in uniforms, work clothes, and trends for similar kinds of sports shoes or jewelry among groups of people of a similar age, or a similar taste in music, for example. These groupings are evidence of horizontal flows of fashion.

The last way of defining fashion is actually a contradiction to the one just described. While fashion is obviously group based, it is also about the individual and the personal choices that he or she makes.

Paradoxically, humans have a need to be both a member of group, which provides security and also distinguish themselves from the group and assert their individuality. Evans (2003) describes fashion as a "style book of the self." Tseëlon (1992) takes a psychological approach and examines both Goffman's Symbolic Interactionist Theory and Impression Management Theory in her discussion about whether or not presented selves are sincere. Impression Management Theory argues that the private self is sincere, but that public selves are false and insincere. In the West, fashion has often been considered superficial because it is only concerned with outer surfaces and therefore artifice. Goffman (1959) argues that selves are more like roles that we play like actors, and that we are fragmented, but each self is interconnected. While different selves are manifested in different roles, he does not see them as fake or "put on" selves, rather as different aspects of one self. Western philosophy has constructed a self comprising an inner essence, which exists independently of surrounding circumstances. We think of our inner self or our true nature, which is in the universe but separate from it. This is a very culturally based set of values. Miller (2010) found that though academics at Cambridge "looked rubbish" and were considered to be concerned with deeper things, people in Trinidad who had hardly enough to eat would have twenty pairs of shoes, enjoy making fashion shows, and spend three hours getting dressed because the surface, style, and the performance are so important. They have no depth ontology, where what is deep is important, and the surface is shallow. It is obvious to Trinidadians that the truth is on the surface where it can be seen, and that falsehood or lies could be hidden inside. The self is transient and constructed.

Rosenberger (1992) argues that Japanese selves are situationally constructed and are not considered as inner essences. The self is found in the roles one performs, such as mother, sister, wife, etc., and there is no self apart from this situational, interrelated self. This is much closer to a western postmodern conception of self, which is performed on the surface, than it is to a traditional, deep, Cartesian one. Dressing up or dressing for success could be considered superficial in the West, and loosely related to the deep self. Self presentation, clothing, and surfaces are considered to be very important in Japan however; because it is on the surface, where the self meets the world, that dressing occurs. Fashion is therefore considered important, and closely bound with the self. Far more Japanese are interested in dressing up than are their British counterparts. Fashion helps an individual to stand out from a group and make a personal statement.

A Working Definition

From the theory reviewed, five factors have been drawn out that appear to be defining and essential aspects of fashion.

1 An economic system: It is necessary to have a market economy, adequate technology for making apparel items, and a distribution system for fashion items and ideas.

2 Change over time: Fashion evolves on not only a macro, but a micro level, valuing newness and novelty over tradition and age.

3 Form over function: Fashion is often manifested when form is more important than function.

4 Group-based clothing behavior: Fashion is collective, symbolic, sartorial behavior.

5 Personal style: Fashion is concerned with the presentation and care of the self.

These definitions may not be exhaustive. However, they provide a tool for the study of clothing systems. We have seen that western fashion theory has primarily assumed that only the West has had the conditions for fashion to develop, with strong class systems, social mobility, and an economic system that would produce fashion goods. We have seen that non-western clothing systems have just begun to be studied in terms of fashion. I take the definition above and use it to establish whether or not kimono can be considered to be a fashionable system of dress.

The following chapters unwrap some of the layers of this complex kimono—literally "thing to wear"—using diachronic data to establish the presence of the factors of fashion identified here. I continue the investigation of kimono as fashion using synchronic data obtained from makers, marketers, publishers, and wearers to determine how kimono continues to evidence fashion. Japanese fashion was not imported from the West but fulfills the same functions as fashion in the West. It also embodies Japanese cultural values and aesthetic sensibilities. As a national dress, the kimono is deeply symbolic, but as a fashion system it is also concrete and economic. To its wearers it is full of meaning. As fashion and kimono continue to metamorphose, this can never be a truly completed project. Just as our social selves are complex combinations of many roles and situations, a series of connecting and interconnecting threads, so the story of kimono is a complex, interwoven tangle of threads. I have chosen to collect these together, across past and present, in an attempt to explain the social life of the kimono.

Bibliography

Barnard, M. Ed. (2007) *Fashion Theory; A Reader*. Oxon, New York: Routledge.

Barthes, R. (1966) Interview Published in *Echanges. Oeuvres completes*. Vol. 2. pp. 121–5.

Barthes, R. (2006) *The Language of Fashion*. Sydney: Berg.

Baudot, F. (1999) *A Century of Fashion*. London, Paris, New York: Thames and Hudson.

Baudrillard, J. (1983) *Simulations*. New York: Semiotext(e) Columbia University Press and http://www.naturalthinker. net/trl/texts/Baudrillard,Jean/simulations.html (Accessed December 2012).

Bell, Q. (1976) *On Human Finery*. London: The Hogarth Press.

Blumer, H. (1969) "Fashion: From Class Differentiation to Collective Selection." *Sociological Quarterly*. Vol. 10. No. 3. pp. 275–291.

Bourdieu, P. (1984) *Distinction*. Cambridge, Massachusetts: Harvard University Press.

Carter, M. (2003) *Fashion Classics from Carlyle to Barthes*. Oxford, New York: Berg.

Craik, J. (1994) *The Face of Fashion*. London and New York: Routledge.

Craik, J. (2009) *Fashion: The Key Concepts*. Oxford: Berg.

Crane, D. (2000) *Fashion and Its Social Agendas: Class, Gender and Identity in Clothing*. Chicago, London: Chicago University Press.

Davis, F. (1992) *Fashion, Culture and Identity*. Chicago and London: The University of Chicago Press.

Eicher J. Ed. (1995) *Dress and Ethnicity*. Oxford: Berg.

Eicher J. and S.L. Evenson. (2015) *The Visible Self: Global Perspectives on Dress, Culture and Society*. London: Fairchild Books.

Entwistle, J. (2000) *The Fashioned Body*. Cambridge: Polity Press.

Evans, C. (2003) *Fashion at the Edge*. New Haven, London: Yale University Press.

Flügel, J.C. (1930) *The Psychology of Clothes*. London: Hogarth Press.

Goffman, E. (1959) *The Presentation of Self in Everyday Life*. New York: Random House.

Goffman, E. (1969) *Strategic interaction*. Philadelphia: University of Pennsylvania Press.

Hansen, K.T. and D.S. Madison. Eds. (2013) *African Dress: Fashion, Agency, Performance*. London, Delhi, New York, Sydney: Bloomsbury.

Hebdige, D. (1979) *Subculture, The Meaning of Style*. London, New York: Routledge.

Hollander, A. (1993) *Seeing through Clothes*. Berkeley, Los Angeles, London: University of California Press.

Johnson, K.K.P., S.J. Torntore, and J.A. Eicher. Eds. (2003) *Fashion Foundations*. Oxford, New York: Berg.

Kawamura, Y. (2006) *Fashion-ology*. Oxford, New York: Berg.

King, in Lynch, A. and M.D. Strauss. (2007) *Changing Fashion*. Oxford, New York: Berg.

Kirby, K. (2013) "Bazin Riche in Dakar, Senegal: Altered Inception, Use, and Wear." In K.T. Hansen and D.S. Madison. Eds. *African Dress: Fashion, Agency, Performance*. London, Delhi, New York, Sydney: Bloomsbury.

Laver, J. (1986) *Costume and Fashion, A Concise History*. London, New York: Thames and Hudson. (Original 1937, 1969).

Laver, J. (2003) "Fashion as Change, Some Conclusions." In K. Johnson, S. Torntore, and J. Eicher. Eds. *Fashion Foundations*. Oxford, New York: Berg. pp. 114–18.

Lillethun, A., L. Welters, and J.B. Eicher. (2012) "(Re) Defining Fashion." *CSA Forum, Dress*. Vol. 38. No. 1. pp. 75–97.

Lipovetsky, G. (1994) *The Empire of Fashion*. Princeton: Princeton University Press.

Miller, D. (2010). *Stuff*. Cambridge, Malden: Polity.

Polhemus, T. (1994) *Street Style*. London: Thames and Hudson.

Puwar, N. (2003) "Exhibiting Spectacle and Memory." *Fashion Theory*. Vol. 7. No. 3–4. pp. 257–74.

Riello, G. and P. McNeill. Eds. (2010) *The Fashion History Reader; Global Perspectives*. London, New York: Routledge.

Rosenberger, N.R. Ed. (1992) *Japanese Sense of Self*. Cambridge, New York, Melbourne: Cambridge University Press.

Rovine, V. (2011) African Dress. "Fashion and the Meanings of 'Tradition' in Senegal." In J.B. Eicher and R. Doran. Eds. *Berg Encyclopedia of World Dress and Fashion*: Vol. 1. Africa: Berg.

Rovine, V. (2015) *African Fashion Global Style: Histories, Innovation, and Ideas You Can Wear*. Bloomingdale, Indianapolis: Indiana University Press.

Simmel, G. (1904) "Fashion." *International Quarterly*. Vol. 10. pp. 130–55.

Simmel, G. (2003) "Fashion." In K. Johnson and S. Torntore, J. Eicher. Eds. *Fashion Foundations*. Oxford, New York: Berg. pp. 104–107.

Steele, V. (1995) *The Corset: A Cultural History*. New Haven, London: Yale University Press.

Steele, V. (1996) *Fetish*. New York, Oxford: Oxford University Press.

Storm, P. (1987) *Functions of Dress*. New Jersey: Prentice Hall.

Tseëlon, E. (1992) "Is the Presented Self Sincere? Goffman, Impression Management and the Postmodern Self." *Theory, Culture and Society*. Vol. 9. pp. 115–28.

Tseëlon, E. (1994) "Fashion and Signification in Baudrillard." In D. Kellner. Ed. *Baudrillard: A Critical Reader*. Cambridge, Oxford: Blackwell Ltd. pp. 119–34.

Veblen, T. (1899) *The Theory of the Leisure Class*. New York: MacMillan.

Veblen, T. (2003) "Dress as the Expression of the Pecuniary Culture." In K. Johnson, S. Torntore, and J. Eicher. Eds. *Fashion Foundations*. Oxford, New York: Berg. pp. 132–6.

Welters, L. *Non-Western Dress in the West*. Presentation. 2nd International Non-Western Fashion Conference, London. November 2013.

Welters, L. and A. Lillethun. Eds. (2007) *The Fashion Reader*. Oxford, New York: Berg.

2 Tracing Trends in Heian and Edo

Early History

It is probably impossible to pinpoint a moment or location at which fashion started. Chapter 1 outlined five defining aspects of fashion from a body of fashion theory, and now we return to the story of kimono, in the light of those five aspects. References to clothing used in functional ways or to uphold customs, traditions, or the status quo are to be expected, so here the search is for deviations from such norms. The search is for any shreds of evidence of clothing used in fashionable ways, any records that demonstrate the five factors identified are significant. Social mobility has been assumed to be a prerequisite for a fashion system to develop, which is one reason given why it is thought to have developed in Europe and not in other countries. The reason for this theory is yet to be examined. The Japanese social system was not flexible, but was a caste-like system, which according to such theories would negate the emergence of fashion. If evidence for the five factors of fashion is found, this would mean that such theory needs rethinking.

How far back should one go? The people of the Jomon culture; hunter-gatherers and fishers who lived in Japan from 13,680 BC to 410 BC were known to have made bark clothing and also woven with hemp and nettles. They made red clay figures with strange tattoo-like markings on them, so it is likely that these people tattooed their bodies. Clay earrings, necklaces, pendants, hairpins, and bracelets have been found at archeological sites. It is probable then that the story of dressing fashionably goes back much further than is shown here. For the purposes of this text, the exploration is of the kimono as far back as we can know it, as a dressing system. Some previous kimono histories have tended to concentrate more on the shape and materiality of clothing at particular times at the expense of explaining context. Munsterberg (1996) and Kennedy (1990) have focused largely on theater costume, which tells us little about clothing of the everyday. Dalby (1993), Minnich (1963), Kondo (1980, 1985, 2002), Murayama (2007, 2008, 2010), Nagasaki (2006, 2009), and Milhaupt (2014) have written detailed social histories which are referenced here. For two specific reasons in this historical study, two periods are examined; Heian (794–1185) and Edo (1603–1868). First, these periods are thought by the Japanese to be high points in their cultural history and to be particularly representative of it, and second, during these periods, Japan chose largely not to interact with other countries, so that changes at these points are particularly concerned with what is happening domestically, rather than with outside influences. This makes Japan an interesting case for studying clothing development, though Screech (2002) argues that the isolation of the Edo period was not as complete as we are led to believe.

Heian (794–1185)

Sources

The Shoso-in is a treasure storehouse standing in Nara, built in the seventh century. Remaining unopened for centuries, the items inside have been almost perfectly preserved. Among its treasures, it housed thousands of ancient textile samples. Most are thought to be domestic, but others come from as far away as China, India, Iran, Greece, and Egypt. These textiles testify to a lively relationship with other cultures. Being at the end of the Silk Road, Japan was the ultimate eastern destination. These textiles give us hints about trade and relationships with other countries, but it is impossible to put together a story from them because we cannot know how they were used or worn. For that we need some kind of written documents. Such documentation is available from the Heian period. *The Tale of Genji* is said to be the world's first novel. It was written by Murasaki Shikibu, a female courtier of that period, and it tells of the romantic escapades of a beautiful prince. Another woman of the court, her contemporary Sei Shonagon, whose name literally means minor counselor, wrote a detailed diary about court life. It is full of sharp observation and wit and is therefore a valuable resource to find out about sartorial behavior. There are also some painted scrolls extant, in which the clothing of courtiers can be observed. These are illustrations for *The Tale of Genji,* the originals of which are held by the Gotoh Museum and the Tokugawa Art Museum.

The Tale of Genji and Colored Layers

During the Heian period, Japanese arts of the noble classes were considered to have reached their highest development. In an environment that cultivated beauty, houses, gardens, lacquer ware, woodwork, paintings, and musical instruments were all turned into fine works of art. Making incense and writing calligraphy were important skills, and courtiers enjoyed *sadame,* judgment games, when they would compare different people's calligraphy or perfumes to find the most exquisite ones. Morris (1969:183) says, "Artistic insensitivity damned a gentleman of the Heian court as fatally as did a reputation for cowardice among the nobility of the West." Of all the artistic achievements of the period, it is the clothing system that stands out as the most admired. Looking at the illustrations in *The Tale of Genji,* we realize that kimono worn by courtly women at that time were quite different from kimono that are worn today. Immediately this contradicts those who say that kimono has remained unchanged for generations. Essentially, the kimono of the era is of a triangular shape, unbelted, relatively unrelated to the human form and with some kind of a train coming out behind it. The garment, called *junihitoe,* literally twelve layers (though there could be more or less) consists of multiple gowns worn on top of each other, see Figure 2.1.

The kimono today is a tightly wrapped tube, following the line of the body much more closely. The kimono shape has changed, but this change could be on a slow, macro level, not necessarily indicating the presence of a fashion system. The complexity of the Heian-period system of dress increased over several generations. The dressing system has been studied by Nagasaki (1996), Kondo (2002), Dalby (1993), and numerous others. Nagasaki's (1996) study shows 120 two-layered color combinations, 33 six-layered ones, and 58 eight-layered ones. As the layers were very thin and gauzy, they made new colors when worn over each other. Kondo (2002:36) says that it would have been almost impossible to walk in this dress. Women would have had to shuffle on one knee. In order to permit them to move, and to accommodate all the layers, the clothing gradually widened. Logically, one would also assume that larger layers would be worn over smaller ones, but in fact the upper layers were cut narrower in order to show the inner layers at the edges. The garment was at least as debilitating as European hooped skirts. Women were literally cocooned by all the cloth and only their head and long black hair would have shown—except that they did not. Heian courtly women lived a closeted life, remaining behind bamboo screens in dark inner rooms. On the rare occasions when they went out, they were protected from people's gaze inside ox-carts, which had similar bamboo screens across the windows. A reconstruction of a *junihitoe* showing the various garments is shown in Figure 2.2.

Figure 2.1 Reconstruction of junihitoe, Heian-period women's court dress made for a lady in waiting at an imperial ceremony in March 1928.

Source: Property of Sugino Costume Museum.

Photo: Sugino Costume Museum.

How can such a debilitating clothing system be explained? If the layers were for heat regulation, then presumably men would have worn them too, but men's clothing did not develop into complex layers. Neither were the gowns to show off the wealth of husbands as marriage was a very loose affair, and women commonly remained in their parental home. As noble women were not permitted to walk around outside, they were not for public display. All functional explanations for the layers fail, so we have to look for another explanation for this complex system of dress.

There were several clearly defined uses of color at this period. One of these was to represent ranks in court for males. There were light and dark versions of colors, where deeper colors expressed a higher rank, as dyestuff was expensive. The selection of colors used in noble women's robes was far from random. The color combinations represented seasonal plants. From the Momoyama period (1573) onward plants are represented by plant motifs, but in this period plants are represented by the use of specific combinations of colored layers. These combinations had romantic names such as "under the snow," which included a layer of green for leaves, several layers of pinks and white on the top representing snow. In one old

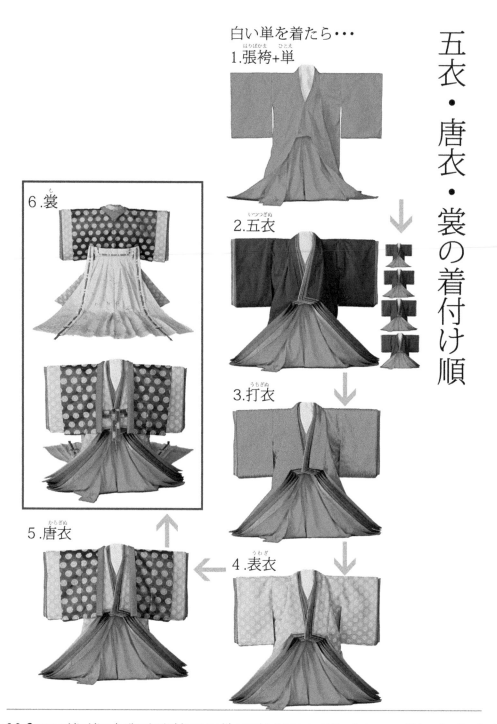

白い単を着たら・・・

1.張袴+単
はりばかま　ひとえ

2.五衣
いつつぎぬ

3.打衣
うちぎぬ

4.表衣
うわぎ

5.唐衣
からぎぬ

6.裳
も

五衣・唐衣・裳の着付け順

Figure 2.2 Over a white hitoe (unlined robe) is worn: (1) a hari bakama and hitoe (a trouser skirt and unlined robe), (2) itsuzuginu (five colored gowns), (3) uchiginu (an over gown), (4) uwagi (a jacket), (5) karaginu (a brocade over jacket), (6) mo (a train).

Source: Property of Sugino Costume Museum.

Photo: Sugino Costume Museum.

calendar system, there are seventy-two seasons of just a few days each, and gowns were changed as the seasons changed. To be behind nature was to be a boring and uncultured dresser but to be in the height of style was to wear the layers slightly before the real flowers actually bloomed, encouraging nature to bring on the next season. It was important to be seen as an innovator rather than a follower, not only among other people, but in relation to nature itself. Though the combinations were prescribed by the seasonal plants there was still leeway for personal taste, and to be beautifully presented was one of the most important accomplishments for a courtier. Although the representations in the color combinations would be opaque to us, they would have been easily read by the Heian courtiers. In this way, noble women became literal representations of flowers in the house.

As women sat behind bamboo screens hanging from the ceilings, only their lower bodies, hems, and sleeve edges would show. Thus the layers and edges represented not only flowers but also the face of the woman herself. Dressing was a serious business because noble women in Heian Japan were obliged to try to keep their lovers' attention, as it was a polygamous society. If a woman failed to maintain her partner's interest he would stop visiting her. Kondo (1985) says that the clothing functioned to maintain the erotic interest of the male. In western clothing, according to Flügel (1930) and Steele (1995) eroticism is about covering and uncovering certain areas of the body, but in Japanese clothing everything was covered. The layers of color which draw attention to the edges were erotic because edges point to what is hidden underneath, deeper layers, and ultimately the body itself. The Japanese word *chirarisumu,* which means to show a glimpse, expresses this phenomenon, and it is still an important part of the contemporary kimono system and indeed, of all Japanese aesthetics. The glimpse draws attention to the hidden unseen part. Today's fashionable young girls utilize this by shortening their school skirts so that their underwear is almost visible, and kimono linings are sewn to show by about 2 mm at the edges of the hem and cuffs. These are examples of the same principle at work, and the contrasting kimono lining is probably one of the last remainders of the complex layering system.

The use of colors to represent rank and seasonal plants was well established but in *The Tale of Genji,* Murasaki, the main female character, is known for her talent at choosing dyes for cloth and for selecting beautiful shades for clothing. In the text, she and Genji, her husband, are selecting cloth from their store-house for use as gifts. Murasaki makes a revolutionary suggestion, which Kondo (1985) suggests would be easy to miss, because today this idea is commonplace. She advises Genji:

> If I may make a suggestion, would it not be better to think whether the stuffs will suit the complexion of their recipient rather than whether they look nice in the box? (Shikibu 1986:463)

To ask "Does it suit me?" is a matter of course now. However, at the time of writing to think of using color in relation to the complexion of the wearer was completely new, revolutionary, and unique. Through her character Murasaki, the writer Shikibu was adding a new element to color usage as an expression of personal taste.

The Pillow Book of Sei Shonagon and Observing Trends

Although the *Pillow Book of* Sei Shonagon is called a dairy, in reality it is a record of court life. It consists of three kinds of writings: songs, descriptions of events, and *Sei Shonagon's* personal reactions to the people and things around her. Morris's English translation is made up of the second and third categories of writing. Almost 50 percent of the entries in the diary mention dress in some context, showing the importance of clothing in court life. From *The Pillow Book,* it is possible to determine many of the ways in which clothing was used. Most of these could be considered traditional. Clothing was given as payment to messengers who functioned as a postal service; it was used as taxes and was gifted at New Year. While faces are never described at all in these ancient texts, clothing is described in great detail. Women, from behind the safety of their screens, enjoyed a kind of voyeurism as they could see but not be seen themselves. Sei Shonagon takes great delight in describing the colors, layers, and luster of cloth, even to the layers underneath that she could just glimpse.

> He looked magnificent as he came towards me. His resplendent, cherry-coloured court cloak was lined with material of the most delightful hue and lustre; he wore dark, grape-coloured trousers, boldly splashed with designs of wisteria branches; his crimson under-robe was so glossy that it seemed to sparkle, while underneath one could make out layer upon layer of white and light violet robes. (Sei Shonagon 1971:94–95)

Sei Shonagon was very particular about timing. While a plum combination of reds and whites was beautiful in February, it was depressing if seen in April. White summer robes should not be seen in August, when presumably early autumn shades would be appropriate. She was rather conservative about clothing and complained about some popular practices. She really disliked seeing a crooked back seam in a robe, or *hakama,* trouser skirt, worn with high clogs, a fashion she observed among groups of young boys. She also reminisced about chamberlains who used to visit their lovers at night. They used to wear long green robes and wring them out if they became wet with rain. Nowadays, she complained, they just wear short green robes, which fails to create the same effect. She also complained about a fashion that was all the rage among courtiers, which was to have sleeves cut of uneven width creating a lopsided effect. Morris explains that this fashion grew from the need to identify oneself when riding in an ox-cart. As bamboo blinds covered the windows, this was done by pushing a sleeve out of the window. Those who rode on the right side of the ox-cart would have the right side sleeve cut larger than the left, and those on the other side would have the left sleeve cut larger. When not riding in the ox-cart, the effect was to create a very lopsided garment. Sei Shonagon argued that this fashion was unsightly and most inconvenient.

Heian Fashion: Comparative Considerations

Referring back to the five aspects of fashion identified and listed at the end of Chapter 1, four of them are already evident in the dressing system of the nobles of Heian-period Japan. There is evidence of faddish fashion or micro trends among certain groups in society, such as young boys wearing high clogs and fashionable courtiers wearing inconvenient asymmetrical gowns. These new fashions were fast enough to cause psychological discomfort to the writer. Form over function is evidenced in a gender-based system with elaborate women's clothing that made it almost impossible to walk, but kept the erotic interest of the male, through the use of colorful combinations of edges. The wearing of such robes was group behavior, practiced by all courtly women, and it also provided a form of self-expression. *Murasaki's* idea of matching colors to complexions is also evidence of fashion used for self-expression, as well as being a new and original way of using color. The only factor that cannot be identified at this point in time is a fully blown economic system of fashion. There were probably only a few thousand people who lived like this, confined to the court circle in Kyoto. Outside court life we have no records to indicate that such dressing considerations existed.

Although the kimono fashion system and the western fashion system are manifested in clothing that looks completely unalike, clothing usage in the two systems evidences striking similarities. In addition to the similarities identified here, there are three significant differences between the Heian and western fashion systems. First, in Heian Japan, representation of plants is not through motifs, but through a series of colored layers, a system comprehensible to the Heian courtiers. Second, the Japanese system is much more deeply connected with nature than is the western fashion system, in which flowers can be worn randomly at any time of the year. The Japanese woman must constantly be aware of the progress of the seasons, in order to dress fashionably. The marking of the season in western dress is largely limited to the thickness of the cloth and whether or not the garment has long or short sleeves, though there may be seasonally popular colors. Third, erotic interest in Japanese fashion is achieved through a series of edges, which suggest inner layers and point to unwrapping, hidden surfaces, and three dimensionality, whereas in western clothing, eroticism is achieved through the covering and uncovering of certain areas of the body and is manifested in clothing changing shape. The Heian fashion system is unique to Japan and is marked by sophistication in its relation to both the natural world, and the three-dimensional nature of the clothing itself. However, although different in appearance, on a structural level, it functions in similar ways to the western fashion system.

Edo (1603–1868)

Culture and Society in Edo

Edo period culture has been enjoying a boom in interest since the 1980s, seen as somehow embodying Japaneseness in a distilled form. Gluck writes that it is: "not only a historical time, but a cultural space, a repository of traditions associated with a Japanese distinctiveness" (1998:263). Edo's fledgling capitalist economy and its culture of the people offers itself for comparison with today's Tokyo with its continuing growth and popularization of postmodern art forms and entertainments. Edo is conversely framed as both the antithesis of present postmodern Tokyo but also as its birthplace, where manga, mass culture, and consumerism were born. At the beginning of the period the new capital, Edo (present day Tokyo), was nothing but a swamp. By the end of the seventeenth century, it was the biggest metropolis on earth with a population of 1,200,000, when London had a population of 800,000 and Paris only 500,000. The population density was far higher than it is today, meaning that most of the ordinary people lived in slum-like urban sprawl. Japan boasted three large urban areas, Edo, Kyoto, and Osaka, and also two important trading ports, Sakai and Nagasaki.

After years of clan wars, the Edo period was a time of peace. Society was divided into four classes, excluding nobles, who were above the system, and various untouchable groups, such as nomadic people, actors, those who were unclean through working with blood or death and foreigners, who were below it. The four classes were the samurai, a military class; farmers, who grew the nation's food; craftsmen, who made all the necessary goods to sustain life; and traders, who supplied all the goods made by the farmers and craftsmen. There was virtually no social mobility between the classes. All the lords in their various fiefdoms around Japan were expected to travel to Edo and live there half the time, to report to the shogun. In this way, the government could monitor their activities while keeping most issues locally governed. It also meant that lords effectively had to keep two households, one in Edo and one in their fief. All the expenses involved in traveling with a huge number of retainers and servants ensured that they did not become too rich or powerful. This social system necessitated an extensive network of roads across Japan, all of which led to the capital.

Francks (2009) describes the Edo period as the period of the rise of the consumer. The growth of huge urban centers affected not only the building industry for new housing but also arts, crafts, and commerce. Workers flocked to the cities, and goods that were needed in the city were made outside and transported in. The great rise in trade and commerce benefited the lower classes. Conversely, the socially higher ranked samurai, who were effectively an unemployed military class, and the farmers, who were heavily taxed, did not fare so well. The cities' economies were largely feudal, meaning that exchange of goods was common and taxes and levies were paid in rice. Agriculture, technology, and education flourished but eventually there grew up an inverse relationship between social status and wealth.

Breward (2004:11) believes that the link between the building of new cities and clothing has been largely overlooked. He argues that sartorial behavior is an essential element of the new, urban environment, and he sees fashion as a motor for urban change and metropolitan identity. Maruyama (2008:15) argues that in order to understand the impact of the clothing at this period in history, it is important to remember how dark city people's lives were. In the urban sprawl, there was little room for greenery, and color is not a feature of Japanese interior domestic decoration. There was only sunlight by day and the moon and stars at night. Artificial light was both expensive and brought the danger of fire, so the city at night was a really dark place. In such an environment, it is logical that people were very excited by anything bright, and for most people the most colorful items were clothing. Bright, decorative clothing must have shone like the neon of Tokyo's nightspots today. Daily life was very dull, but such gorgeous garments could be seen at the theater or in the floating world (red light district). These locations became the sources of fashion leaders in the shape of the most popular *oiran,* the highest ranking courtesans, and also actors in the kabuki theater. Once working people had acquired some financial resources, they wanted to spend it on the theater, wining and dining, household goods, but especially on gorgeous, colorful, patterned clothing which they then displayed by promenading in the city.

Macro Changes in the Kimono

Between the Heian and the Edo period, there were several macro-level changes in the kimono dressing system. These represent evolution in dress shape but were too slow to be considered fashionable change. Generations of military governments had changed the roles of women and they could no longer be cocooned in seas of cloth. Women's garments were much more practical and simplified. The inner gown or *kosode* had emerged on top, and a white *kosode* with a red *hakama,* trouser skirt, was worn in the Kamakura period (1185–1335). This outfit can still be seen on shrine maidens today. These garments were worn underneath by the upper classes and on top by the lower, and this *kosode* can be considered to be the forerunner of contemporary kimono. By the Edo period, it was no longer white but highly decorated, and the *hakama* had been abandoned. The silhouette in the Edo period was completely different from the Heian one. The *kosode* was much slimmer and closer to the body, with several, but fewer layers. It has been suggested that the word kimono came into common usage in the Meiji period, to distinguish Japanese from western clothing, but according to Nagasaki, kimono and *kosode* were used interchangeably, and we find the word kimono (or keremon, a Portuguese equivalent) in the trading documents of the Edo period. In the Momoyama period (1573–1603), the most popular style of kimono decoration was *tsujigahana,* a sophisticated combination of tie-dyeing and ink-drawn flowers. It required a soft plain cloth and was thus a challenge to the thicker brocade-like garments worn previously. The obi developed from being a hidden tie, to being a fairly narrow brocade band that was visible on the outside of the garment. This development altered the location of the designs on garments, and many of them were made with *katasusomoyo,* shoulder and hem designs, which often had a plain, sometimes white, area in the center.

During the Edo period as figured grounds became more complex, *tsujigahana* fell out of style. The *kosode* would continue to develop on a macroscale, changing its shape to become longer and narrower. This change can be traced in the woodblock prints of the time, which show increasingly long and slender figures. The sleeves separated from the body on the inside seam until the shape emerged as similar to contemporary kimono. As the *kosode* kimono worked its way up from inner to outer wear, the obi continued to develop and became increasingly large and spectacular. The kimono can be seen as simplifying over time, whereas the obi conversely moved from function toward form, becoming ever more complex in the process. Starting out as a narrow, hidden tie made of cloth and about 160 cm long, it became a broad band of over 30 cm width, with a length of at least 3.6 m. At this point, it no longer functioned as a simple tie to keep the kimono closed, for it now necessitated its own accessories to keep it in place. While the obi has simplified a little since then, it is still considered by many to be a fairly cumbersome or debilitating part of the kimono outfit. However, it is an essential part of the kimono look, and a wearer is not dressed without an obi.

Edo: The Birthplace of Style

If the Heian period was considered a high point for the development of noble art forms, then the Edo period is considered a high point in the development of the culture of ordinary people. Maruyama (2008) describes Edo as the birthplace of Japanese style or mode, and also as the period when clothing became adornment. In the early Edo period patterns had generally been static and symmetrical. For the wealthy, small designs in brocades were common, and they were evenly spaced on the fabric, sometimes *katasusomoyo,* at the shoulders and hem and sometimes in *dangawari,* blocks. Throughout the Edo period, the pattern moved around the garment and changed in scale, content, and decorative technique. Favored fabrics also changed throughout the period. The changes were influenced by new technology, wealth, sumptuary laws, and social class. By relating fashion trends to such factors, they are revealed as anything but superficial, very systematic, and in an inseparable relationship to social life. According to Nagasaki (2006:14), it was hard to tell the difference between classes or gender from the garments at the beginning of the period, but as men were expected to be active in public social life, and their clothing must declare their status, it was less able to respond to trends. Women's clothing was more personal, representative of inside the house, and was therefore able to develop more freely. The fact that Japan did not have social mobility never stopped wealthy Japanese women from the lower merchant class dressing up once they had the financial resources to be able to do so. Neither did fashions always trickle down; there are also examples of other diffusion patterns.

Influence of Foreign Trade on Clothing Practices

Before Japan closed its doors almost completely in 1639, it conducted limited trade with a few nations, mainly through ships coming in via Kyushu. The most well-known relationship is the one with the Dutch East India company (VOC), but the Portuguese, Spanish, Thais, Chinese and for ten years from 1613–1623 the British East India Company also had a trading relationship with Japan. The British pulled out after failing to make a profit because of the increasing restrictions on their activities by the repressive Japanese government. Documentation survives in the form of a series of letters between London, the factory (warehouse) in Hirado in Kyushu, and the marketplaces of Edo, Miyako (Kyoto), Sakai, and Osakie (Osaka). The factor, Richard Cocks, also left a diary which details his lifestyle in Japan, and the trading relationship. This diary reveals what kind of cloth would or would not sell in Japan.

The British knew little about Japan, and they completely misjudged the market. They were expecting to be able to sell British wool, but they found that the Japanese were already basically self-sufficient in textiles, and that they had little use for the heavy woolen broadcloth that the British were eager to sell. It was used for long cloaks and armor casing, but as Japan was at peace, such items were hardly necessary. The British were also trading in Indian cotton chintz, which they added to their cargoes on their long journey across the world. Cotton was not grown in Japan, so it was a luxury fabric at the time. It was often used to make small items such as *sagemono,* hanging accessories, or tobacco pouches. It could also be patch-worked together to make larger items, such as kimono or undergarments. Only the richest could have afforded a *kosode* from such imported cotton. Figure 2.3 shows an elaborate garment made with patches of chintz in the design.

The traders noted that the Japanese demanded new and different chintzes every year and would not buy the same designs as they had brought the previous year. One trader, Ralph Coppendale, wrote that they are "a people desiring change," and that they already had better and cheaper linen and silk than that which the British could sell them. Richard Cocks's diary also confirms that the people loved change and the whims and fashions of the time, and he blamed this fluctuating nature of the market for the failure of the

Figure 2.3 Kosode: irises; painting, embroidery, and gold dust on fine satin damask ground and patchwork of sarasa (chintz); seventeenth to nineteenth centuries.

Source: Property of Bunka Gakuen Costume Museum.

Photo: Bunka Gakuen Costume Museum.

British enterprise. The British traders also observed that Japanese would buy Spanish cloth when it was expensive, but they would not touch it when the price came down, so they concluded that the Japanese love rare and expensive goods. They also noted that popular colors changed each season. Gradually, stamets (rust) and red went out of favor, and black and "sad hues" began to be popular. What was imported was purchased for its popularity rather than for necessity. It was very stylish and conspicuous to have imported Indian chintz. The trade in Indian cottons was almost certainly affected by the rise of the native cotton industry from around 1624, when domestically produced chintzes became available. These the British branded "fake."

Influence of Agricultural Development on Clothing Practices

There were sites of textile production all over Japan that were affected by developments in agriculture. Silk imports had come from China, but according to Maruyama (2007:56) in 1685 they were restricted, which provided impetus for the development of domestic silk industry. During the seventeenth and eighteenth centuries, more than eighty texts were written about silk farming, some of which were translated into other languages. New, hardy, and fast-growing silk worms were bred. This period laid the groundwork for Japan to become the world's leading producer and exporter of silk in the following era, and it was silk that funded Japan's early industrial revolution.

Until the Edo period, those who were not of noble or samurai birth wore various types of plant fibers: linen, *ramie* and *bashofu*, banana fibres. The cotton that was imported, however, was found to be stronger and softer than the native plant fibers, and easy to dye with indigo, which was readily available. Indigo was the favored dye for farming people not only for its availability and beautiful color but because it has insect-repelling properties. When the domestic cotton industry was established, cultivation spread in the Kinki and Kansai regions as cotton needs sunshine and plenty of water. Linen-like plant fibers were still grown around Japan and were the common wear for farming people. There were many different grades of linens, and the finest quality light weaves were popular with the samurai class. The finest was called *jofu* and was soft, light, and very cool in summer. Samurai women made cool unlined summer kimono called *katabira* from it, and fine linens were used for samurai *kamishimo,* a kind of *hakama* trouser skirt and vest.

Influence of Printing Development on the Diffusion of New Styles

Shibori, tie-dyeing, and *shishuu,* embroidery, were the most common techniques used in decorating *kosode,* or kimono at the beginning of the Edo period. Both of these techniques were extremely time-consuming and expensive. Figure 2.4 shows a typical silk kimono with embroidery, ink drawing and some stenciling on it. Note that characters are sometimes used as part of the design.

Successful members of the lower trading classes began to have the economic resources to start buying silk *kosode,* expanding its market. There was a need for a decorative technique that was faster and less costly to produce than tie-dyeing or embroidery. In the seventeenth century, this emerged in the form of a new dyeing technique that changed kimono style forever. It was developed by a fan designer and maker called Yuzensai, who probably came from Kanazawa. His personal life is surrounded in mystery, but he is known to have worked in Kyoto, and both cities claim the *yuzen* dyeing technique as their own. The technique involved a particularly fine rice resist paste, called *itchin nori*. With this paste, exceptionally thin lines could be drawn onto silk using a small tube, somewhat like the tubes that are used to ice cakes. When dry, the dyes were brushed on between the lines. This enabled kimono patterns to become painterly in a way that they had never been before. Although *yuzen* is still considered a time-consuming practice today,

Figure 2.4 Kimono: bamboo and letters; embroidery, brushed black ink, and stenciled imitation shibori (tie-dye) on figured satin silk; 1780–1800.

Source: Property of the Victoria and Albert Museum, London.

Photo: Victoria and Albert Museum, London.

compared with tie-dyed dots or embroidery, the new *yuzen* technique could not only decorate surfaces more freely and much faster than before, reducing cost, but it offered entirely new opportunities for individual artistic expression. *Yuzen* quickly became popular with the merchant classes, as they enjoyed the amazing variety of patterns that could be created using this new technique.

Around the same time as the emergence of *yuzen* dyeing, due to developments in the printing industry, woodblock-printed *hinagata bon,* kimono pattern books, began to circulate around urban areas. They were the equivalent of style or fashion magazines today and proliferated from about 1650. Milhaupt (2014) suggests that they fulfilled the joint roles of manuals for designers, consumer catalogs, and fashion plates. They were produced by designers, woodblock carvers, and woodblock printers under the direction of publishers and are evidence that the publishing and textile industries had a very strong relationship. Kimono shops would keep these books to lend to customers to help with the ordering of new kimono. They could also be considered as an early form of mail order catalog. The majority of Edo period books are black and white and show a spread back view of a kimono, with notes about colors written on the sides. Over time, they increased in size and some later ones are in color. Some were in sets of four or five books and contained anywhere between 20 and 200 designs. There were books aimed at different groups of society or different age groups. Townswomen were fascinated with creative patterns; so these books were some of the most popular of the day, and according to Maruyama (2008), the *kosode* functioned as a space for the public display of fascinating patterns (2008:19–20). Figure 2.5 shows pages from a typical hinagata bon, showing plants and water.

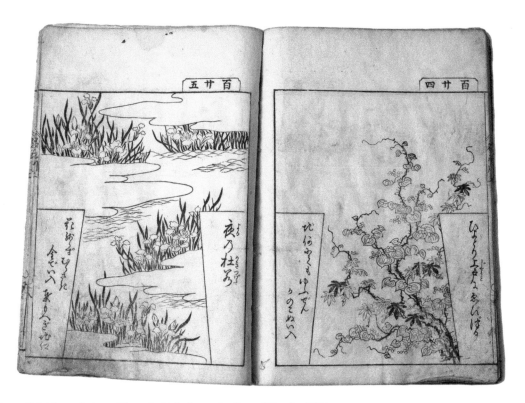

Figure 2.5 Hinagata bon: Hinagata Natorigawa by Tousei Kourin, 1734.
Source: Property of the Author.
Photo: Todd Fong.

Figure 2.6 Kimono: cranes and pines; yuzen with embroidery on Edo chirimen (crepe) silk; mid to late nineteenth century.

Source: Property of the Victoria and Albert Museum, London.

Photo: Victoria and Albert Museum, London.

According to Nevinson (1967), although some fashion plates and portraits existed before this, fashion plates did not circulate widely in Britain until the 1770s with *The Lady's Magazine* and circulated in England before France. *Hinagata bon* were circulating in Japan from the mid-seventeenth century, predating English circulation of fashion plates by over 100 years. Maruyama (2008) tells the tale of how three styles of *yuzen*-dyed kimono spread through Kyoto within about an eight-year period. First, the *yuzen* was confined to fan or circular areas on a plain ground; then such outlines were abandoned, and the *yuzen* covered the whole kimono with designs such as waterfalls and landscapes. Finally, the artists abandoned making the sketches with ink on paper first and began to draw large landscapes with ink directly onto white kimono. The speed of diffusion of these trends parallels contemporary fashion changes and was made possible by the circulation of *hinagata bon*. The kimono in figure 2.6 is a typical yuzen all-over design, with auspicious pines and cranes, embellished with embroidery.

The Trend for Cotton and for Stencil Dyeing

Stencil dyeing was used before the Edo period on leather and as decoration on items of armor. In the Edo period stencil dyeing became a popular way to decorate kimono for several reasons. The growth of the domestic cotton industry greatly reduced the price of cotton kimono, making them a very popular product, especially among townspeople. Stencil dyeing on cotton is easy. Another reason was the increasingly severe sumptuary laws placed on the trading class by the government, which are discussed later in this chapter. Several kinds of stencil dyeing were practiced. Domestically produced *Edo sarasa,* chintz, was much cheaper than that imported, so became popular. It could be made with wax or rice paste squeezed through a tube, or with stencils, or a combination of both. The stencil process however, was rather complex, involving the use of many stencils, one for each color.

A much simpler garment, the blue and white *yukata,* cotton bath robe, has an interesting history and became popular for at least two reasons. First because of the change in perceptions of cleanliness and bathing habits, and second because of the sumptuary laws. The *yukata* is thought to have developed from a *yukata bira,* which was a silk *hitoe,* single layered kimono which was worn by the upper classes in the bath. The bath was previously a kind of sauna, rather than a tub full of water. In around 1800, priests began to bathe in water, for reasons of purity. The samurai and noble classes followed suit. Silk was not suitable for getting into water, so people changed from using silk to wearing cotton or linen-like fabrics. Finally the custom of getting into water spread to the middle and lower classes too, and public bathhouses opened in Tokyo. It is thought that there were about five hundred of them in the late Edo period. The world of the *ukiyoe,* wood-block print, is a fantasy world, and most ordinary people would never have been able to afford the patterned and stenciled *yukata* seen in these beautiful prints. The three most common colors were shades of brown, gray and indigo. Poorer people would have bought used ones, too. However, once people started walking to the bath house, they began to desire stencil dyed *yukata* to wear. The *yukata* emerged from the bathhouse and was worn in high style by the Edo townspeople, who came to love the combination of blue and white stencil designs.

The original technique for dyeing *yukata* was called *nagaita chuugata.* A small stencil was pasted repeatedly onto a length of cloth stretched onto a six meter board. This process was repeated for another six meters, and then the cloth was turned over and pasted again on the other side matching the stencils on the two sides exactly. Shimizu Keizaburo, head of the Yukata Museum in Tokyo, whose grandfather Shimizu Kotaro was a designated living national treasure for his *nagaita chuugata* stencil dyeing, says that it takes twenty years to become accomplished at the technique. The very fine designs that became popular and demonstrated the skills of the artisan were made with two stencils, making the process more complex. The rise of the *yukata* as a fashion item at the end of Edo can be compared with the way that jeans, functional work wear dyed in indigo, moved from being the mark of a worker, to being a fashion item that spread

Figure 2.7 Nagaita chuugata: cotton yukata bolts by Living National Treasure Shimizu Kotaro (1897–1968).
Source: Property of the Yukata Museum, Yukataya Sankatsu.
Photo: Todd Fong.

through the masses in the US and then in Europe in the 1960s and 1970s. Two fine examples of Shimizu's work are shown in Figure 2.7.

Even more simple in appearance, but extremely impressive was *Edo komon,* small white dot stenciling. *Edo komon* was originally worn by samurai for their *kamishimo,* vest and trouser skirts. Each clan would use a distinguishing design, as they did with family crests. Appearing plain from a distance, it is only upon close approach can one can detect the pattern of fine white dots on the cloth. Thus *Edo komon* denies the amount of work that goes into making each piece. This understated fashion became popular toward the later part of the period. Although first confined to the samurai, by the late Edo period the individual clans became less important, and use spread down to the merchant class. It was then popularized by the merchant classes who made a large and sometimes playful repertory of designs, some of which can be seen in *ukiyoe* prints. The popularity of these designs then spread upwards among samurai women too. This is an early example of a trickle-up or bubble-up flow of fashion in Japan. As *Edo komon* increased in popularity, and it was simpler to make than *nagaita chuugata,* many of the craftsmen turned from the production of *nagaita chuugata* to the production of *Edo komon* instead. In the Meiji and Taisho periods, new and more economical methods of dyeing *yukata* were developed. *Kago zome* dyeing with a copper sheet cut into a stencil and shaped like a drum or basket, and *chuusen zome* where dye is dripped into the folded cloth and bleeds in a random pattern, became popular, hence the technique of *nagaita chuugata,* which is demanding in terms of both skill and time, has all but died out now.

Changes in Formality of Dyeing and Weaving

Maruyama (2008) writes that until the late Edo period woven *kasuri,* ikat designs had been seen as more prestigious than kimono made from white bolts that had had patterns dyed on them, as they are extremely exacting and time consuming to produce. Because of the samurai dyeing their *kamishimo* with small patterns, and the proliferation of newly developed dyeing techniques, *kasuri* gradually came to be seen as simple farming wear, and dyeing became more popular. To this day dyed kimono are seen as more formal than woven kimono in spite of the time consuming nature of weaving *kasuri*. As cultural sentiment about standards of beauty change, so do patterns and the techniques used to make them. Stripes, originally written with the same Chinese character as island, were seen as common clothing from southern islands, to be worn by common people. However, after silk was forbidden and cotton weaving and prints become popular, perceptions changed. At the beginning of the period, all the stripes seen on prints are horizontal. However, as the period goes on, people come to prefer a long and slender look. Thus vertical stripes come into vogue because they make one look long and slim. From the middle of the Edo period prints of beautiful women wearing stripes always show vertical not horizontal stripes. Stripes became so popular that there were books produced showing a huge variety of stripe designs, see Figure 2.8. Many designs had their own name according to the colors and width of stripes that would distinguish them from other stripes.

Figure 2.8 Shima cho (stripe book): mid to late nineteenth century.
Source: Property of the Author.
Photo: Todd Fong.

Sumptuary Laws and the Development of Iki

In the Edo period, the popularity of *yuzen* dyeing, and then later of stencil dyeing, was not entirely due to the economic situation. The military government was very repressive and interfering by today's standards. Visible displays of wealth and excessive expenditure on clothing were frowned upon by a government concerned that everyone knew their social place. The public display of gorgeous kimono by those who had become rich in the merchant class was considered by the ruling class to be a threat to the social system, and the government regularly issued edicts on the details of people's lifestyles, particularly clothing practices. Minnich (1963:209) writes about the increasingly severe sumptuary laws from 1683. Importation of gold thread and woolen cloth was forbidden, and gold brocade, embroidery and fine *kanako shibori,* fawn spot tie-dyeing were also outlawed. New orders came almost weekly, dictating how much could be spent on *kosode,* outlawing even purchasing of silk or the wearing of silk *kosode* already purchased. Samurai women were not restricted in their clothing practices, so they continued to use fine tie-dyeing and embroidery for decoration. The popularity of *yuzen* among the merchant class must partly be because of the laws forbidding fine tie-dyeing and embroidery to them. However, a silk kimono was still a luxury item that regular townspeople could not afford. Rich merchant class women also favored stenciling on silk, for example *Edo komon,* and then, when silk was forbidden to them, on the now cheaper, domestically produced cotton. Throughout the period, the designs on townswomen's clothing gradually became smaller and more detailed. From the huge dynamic asymmetrical designs seen at the beginning of the period, pattern becomes less and less bold, disappearing into fine dots, sinking to the lower part of the kimono, and eventually even disappearing onto the inside rather than the outside of the kimono. Figure 2.9 shows a formal kimono dyed on cotton not silk. It could have been used in a fisherman's household.

Interestingly, samurai women's clothing, which was not affected by the sumptuary laws, did not develop in the same way as the townswomen's did. Every samurai woman had a black satin *kosode* with small patterns embroidered all over it, and they continued to wear tie-dyed kimono too. Sometimes, samurai women wore two *kosode* in the *koshimaki*, hip-wrapping, style, which enabled one to show off two

Figure 2.9 Kimono: seabirds and waves; yuzen on cotton; eighteenth to nineteenth century.
Source: Property of Genka Mari.
Photo: Todd Fong.

garments at the same time. Their continued use of embroidery and fine tie-dyeing naturally distinguished them from the lower classes, so they were less interested in *yuzen* than were the townswomen. According to Nagasaki (2006), both the subject matter and its placing were also a little different. Samurai women favored landscapes and designs of famous places, Chinese influenced classical designs and scenes from *The Tale of Genji,* whereas townswomen were fascinated by the floral designs of the Korin school of painters. Figures 2.10 and 2.11 show the kimono and under drawing of a kimono made for an extremely wealthy merchant family, who followed the styles of the samurai class. Made for another branch of the family, figure 2.12 shows bamboo screens typical of the Tale of Genji inspired images.

Government interference in clothing practices is not unique to Japan. According to Hurlock (1965), it is common in most developed societies, but the Japanese laws were particularly severe. Ribeiro (1986:64) writes that in England such laws were said to protect the native textile industry, but in reality they were to protect the upper classes from the middle classes. Jones and Stallybrass (2007:188) say that sumptuary

Figure 2.10 Uchikake: floating fans; tie-dye and gold leaf imprinted on satin damask; nineteenth century. Once owned by the Minami-Mitsui Family.
Source: Property of Bunka Gakuen Costume Museum.
Photo: Bunka Gakuen Costume Museum.

Figure 2.11 Uchikake shita-e (design): floating fans; paper; (for kimono in Fig 2.10) nineteenth century. Once owned by the Kita-Mitsui Family.

Source: Property of Bunka Gakuen Costume Museum.

Photo: Bunka Gakuen Costume Museum.

laws are always difficult to police, and that in England they were "more honored in the breach than the observance." To obey the new laws was too boring and did not suit Edo citizens' fashionable tastes, but to ignore them was too dangerous. The Japanese could not give up their fashions, so they did neither. They adapted their fashion, making it oblique and subtle, and finally took it underground. As the laws did not cover the inner layers, it became stylish to wear highly decorated inner wear, and cover it up with simple stripes or plain linen or cotton outerwear. This is an example of the fact that Japanese fashion is not solely about the surface, but that it is three dimensional and caters to multiple audiences. Of course,

Figure 2.12 Uchikake: bamboo blinds with flowering plants and butterflies; tie-dye, embroidery, and gold dust on satin damask; nineteenth century. Once owned by the Minami-Mitsui Family.

Source: Property of Bunka Gakuen Costume Museum.

Photo: Bunka Gakuen Costume Museum.

hidden fashion has the potential of being very subversive, and it is a knowing and not innocent statement. The men's *haori* jacket lining in Figures 2.13 and 2.14 is such an example. It was probably made in the late Edo period when *yuzen* designs were sometimes incorporated into grounds of *Edo komon*. The front part of the jacket lining, which could be glimpsed when worn, depicts folding screens, and an observant viewer may notice that there are clothes thrown over the top of the screen, which would perhaps raise an eyebrow. However, it is only when the jacket is actually removed (which would only happen in a private setting) that one would be able to observe the two lovers on the lining, locked in a passionate embrace, in the style of the erotic *shunga* produced in the Edo period.

Figure 2.13 Front view of men's haori lining: folding screens hiding lovers; yuzen and Edo komon on chirimen (crepe) silk; mid to late nineteenth century.

Source: Property of the Author.

Photo: Todd Fong.

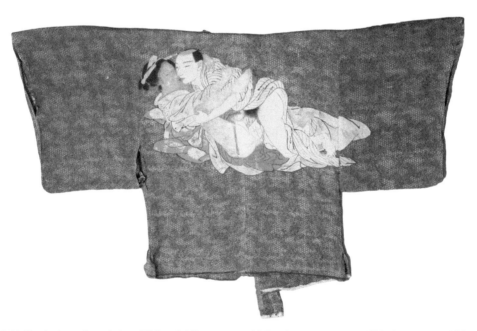

Figure 2.14 Back view of men's haori lining: folding screens hiding lovers; yuzen and Edo komon on chirimen (crepe) silk; mid to late nineteenth century.

Source: Property of the Author.

Photo: Todd Fong.

According to Minnich (1963:209) although the city was flooded with brightly colored *yuzen* and embroidered kimono in the Genroku era from 1688–1704, when the laws seemed to have been forgotten, in the Tempo era restoration of 1830–44 sobriety was so severely enforced that riots ensued in Kyoto among the silk producers. But the tide had turned and eventually more sober and simple aesthetics became internalized as the new standard of beauty, and understatement was the name of the game. This understated chic came to be called *iki*. The concept of *iki* has drawn the attention of many philosophers and thinkers and has been the subject of much discussion and even inspired books. *Iki* is usually translated as chic or stylish but is one of many Japanese words that has no equivalent in the English language. It embodies not only a style but an attitude. Kuki writes: "it boldly brackets everyday life, and engages in autonomous play in a manner disinterested and purposeless, as it breathes a neutral air, transcending all of life around" (2008:50). It is a consciousness rather than style and embodies chic, coquetry, dignity, grace, gallantry, a distain for money, and a resignation to the power of fate. It is sophisticated, fresh, and stylish. It also speaks of a perceived distance between a person and their material possessions, a sense of cool detachment. Perhaps Japan experienced postmodernity before it arrived in the West. To this day, to be called *iki* is a great compliment.

Explaining an Inward Looking Fashion

At first, a fashion that looks inward seems like a contradiction in terms. One of the aspects of fashion that has been discussed here is fashion as a way of presenting the self. Goffman expounded on self-presentation in *The Presentation of Self in Everyday Life* (1959). The Japanese *iki* fashion aesthetic appears to completely contradict such a communicative theory of fashion. Goffman assumes that clothing communicates through the surface, and in Japan, the surface and the presentation of the self are very important. This can be seen in the ubiquity of smart uniforms and formal clothing, in the love of branded bags and shoes, and the importance of complex makeup routines. In fact, not just in fashion but throughout the society attention is paid to all kinds of surfaces. Money is wrapped in envelopes and cloths; toilets are adorned in fluffy lid covers, seat covers, and toilet roll holder covers; and presents are professionally gift wrapped. In spite of such attention to the surface, the inner hidden layers of clothing are considered really important. This apparently paradoxical behavior did not start in the Edo period, even though it developed at that time because of the sumptuary laws. We find a precedent in the Heian noble women, for whom (although self-presentation was vital because it was essential to attract and to keep a male partner) the hidden layers carried significant meanings, marking the seasons through representations of plants. Not only were there many hidden layers of clothing, glimpsed only at the edges, but the women themselves were hidden, veiled behind screens, and living mainly in hidden, inner rooms. They could hardly have led a more hidden existence.

In order to try and understand the subtle concept of beauty, *iki,* better, a cultural psychological framework, as described by Shweder (2000:209) has been employed here. He suggests that rather than trying to demonstrate difference by comparing a phenomenon with a similar one in another culture (as in a cross-cultural approach), in a cultural psychological approach one would compare a phenomenon with other parallel phenomenon in the same culture, in order to demonstrate a principle at work. This approach reveals internal logic, which Shweder defines as rational actions, practices and persons, and rationality as the "intelligent pursuit of appropriate ends" (Shweder 2000:215). So in this case, the instances of wrapping of clothing and other goods, both physically and metaphorically, were considered, to determine if there are any underlying principles concerning wrapping in Japanese society. Anthropologist Hendry (1994) argues that wrapping is an organizational principle of Japanese life and is an important aspect of the presentation of self in everyday practices in Japanese society. It can even be applied to the use of language, such as women's language and forms of politeness. Hendry says:

> The principle of wrapping as a social phenomenon would appear to operate on many different levels, and in my view, an understanding of its importance in Japanese society can aid an understanding of many of the so called paradoxes pointed out by commentators on Japan. (Hendry 1994:30)

So one can argue that Japanese clothing, with its hidden layers and understated surfaces, has developed according to cultural principles which value wrapping and that is why fashion is not only concerned with outer presentation but hidden inner surfaces. The Heian examples were women in layers, hidden behind screens, the Edo period examples were hidden colorful silk under layers and inner layers. The silk was wrapped to hide it from the law. Thus the Japanese fashion system is not concerned only with the outer surface but also with inner wrapped surfaces which imply depth. The clothing can therefore cater to more than one audience, and there is more to it than that which appears on the surface. While inner issues are not a large part of western fashion, they are a very large part of Japanese fashion and are totally consistent with the Japanese principle of wrapping, which is in evidence in many aspects of societal behavior.

Summarizing Trends in the Edo Period

During the Edo period, all five aspects of fashion described in Chapter 1 are present. Advances in agriculture, dyeing, and printing technologies led to the availability of new fabrics and designs, and information about them was diffused through printed text. Printing developments led to pattern books being distributed about urban areas. Due to advances in textile production, cotton changed from being a luxury imported item to being an everyday domestic one in the seventeenth century. The cotton *yukata* then metamorphosed from being a lowly, functional bathrobe to being high fashion. *Yuzen,* with the help of the *hinagata bon,* pattern books, became the most popular way of patterning *kosode* for the merchant classes who were forbidden to wear fine tie-dyeing and embroidery.

The government's constant interference with sartorial behavior of the wealthy merchant classes actually spurred fashion change and new concepts of beauty. Repressive laws restricting the townspeople meant that eventually they could not enjoy embroidery, tie-dyeing nor even wear silk. While the samurai class was exempt from such restrictions, their clothing actually remained more conservative with small, embroidered patterns, designs of traditional songs or references to classical poetry, scenic views, Chinese-inspired designs, and Genji patterns. Townspeople were more innovative and favored plant designs particularly from the Ogata Korin school of painters, painted naturalistically in *yuzen,* designs from kabuki theater, and big dynamic designs. Designs became smaller throughout the period and settled near the hem line. They also, in some cases, disappear onto the inside of the kimono. People made necessity a virtue and came to enjoy stripes, cottons, and simple monotone stenciling, which they brought to high fashion. Even clothing that originated in bath wear or farming wear becomes a part of urban high fashion.

Fashion diffusion did not occur in a top-down direction, as lower-class people imitating their betters became prohibited by law. There was trickle across diffusion, as the classes were strictly separate, so a love of stenciling or stripes spread first through the merchant classes. Then there was a trickle-up pattern of fashion diffusion when the innovative stencils were seen by the samurai women. The townspeople also enjoyed inner, hidden luxury, turning fashion oblique and understated. They were the class that was leading the way toward the new subtle chic, and in doing so, to the new standards of beauty that continue to define Japanese aesthetics.

Sartorial display was seen as subversive and a social problem, but the lack of social mobility did not prevent fashion from developing. The findings contradict the theory that social mobility is necessary for fashion to develop. It was not social mobility but the inverse financial relationships between the upper and the merchant classes that led to the fashionable dressing up by the wealthiest merchants. "Looking the part" could be a reality for the wealthy when the sumptuary laws were not strictly enforced, but genuine social mobility was almost unheard of.

While it might be logical for us to assume that new technology in agriculture, textiles, or printing would generate new fashions, it is perhaps less obvious that socially repressive laws should do so. The development of *yuzen* dyeing, and then subsequently the outlawing of embroidery, tie-dyeing, and finally even of silk led to new concepts of beauty and fashion, which emphasized even more than before the importance of the inner layers over the outer, and understatement over direct statement. Japanese fashion continued to be strongly three dimensional and sophisticated, with trends found in the pattern, obi, and accessories, their placing and tying, and the way in which the kimono was worn. While the clothing system looks very different from the western system, it is similarly systematic, fulfilling all the same functions that a fashion system does. Not only this, but it would seem that widespread diffusion of fashion information in the form of pattern books happened in Japan at least 100 years prior to such diffusion happening in western Europe.

Bibliography

Breward, C. (2004) *Fashioning London*. Oxford: Berg.

Cocks, R. (2010) E.M. Thompson. Ed. *The Diary of Richard Cocks: Cape Merchant in the English Factory in Japan, 1615–1622 Vol.1*. Cambridge, New York, Melbourne: Cambridge University Press.

Dalby, L. (1993) *Kimono: Fashioning Culture*. New Haven, London: Yale University Press.

Flügel, J.C. (1930) *The Psychology of Clothes*. London: Hogarth.

Francks, P. (2009) *The Japanese Consumer: An Alternative Economic History of Modern Japan*. Cambridge, New York, Melbourne, Madrid, Cape Town, Singapore, San Paulo, Delhi: Cambridge University Press.

Gluck, C. (1998) "The Invention of Edo." In S. Vlastos. Ed. *Mirror of Modernity*. Berkeley, Los Angeles, London: University of California Press. pp. 262–84.

Goffman, E. (1959) *The Presentation of Self in Everyday Life*. New York: Random House.

Hendry, J. (1991) "Humidity, Hygiene, or Ritual Care: Some Thoughts on Wrapping as a Social Phenomenon." In BEN-ARI, Valentine Moeran. Eds. (1994) *Unwrapping Japan*. Honolulu: University of Hawaii Press. pp. 18–35. http://heritageofjapan.wordpress.com (Accessed April 28, 2014).

Hurlock, E. (1965) "Sumptuary Law." In E. Roach and J. Eicher. Eds. *Dress, Adornment and the Social Order*. New York, London, Sydney: John Wiley and Sons, Inc.

Jones, A.R. and P. Stallybrass. (2007) *Renaissance Clothing and the Materials of Memory*. Cambridge, New York: Cambridge University Press.

Kennedy, A. (1990) *Japanese Costume, History and Tradition*. New York, Paris: Adam Biro.

Kondo, T. (1985) *Yosoi no Onna Gokoro. The Heart of Women's Adornment*. Tokyo: Kodansha.

Kondo, T. (2002) *Fukusou de Tanoshimeru Genji Monogatari. Enjoying the Tale of Genji through the Clothing*. Tokyo: PHP Bunkou.

Kuki, S. trans. J. Clark. (2008) *Reflections of Japanese Taste—The Structure of Iki*. Sydney: Power Publications.

Milhaupt, T.S. (2014) *Kimono: A Modern History*. London: Reaktion Books.

Minnich, H. (1963) *Japanese Costume*. Rutland: Charles E. Tuttle.

Morris, I. (1969) *The World of the Shining Prince. Court Life in Ancient Japan*. Harmondsworth, Victoria: Penguin Books. p. 183.

Morris-Suzuki, T. (1994) *The Technological Transformation of Japan: From the Seventeenth to the 21st Century*. Cambridge: Cambridge University Press.

Munsterberg, H. (1996) *The Japanese Kimono*. Hong Kong, Oxford, New York: Oxford University Press.

Murayama, N. (2007) *Nihon Visual Seikatsu Shi: Edo no Kimono to I Seikatsu. Japan Visual Life History: Edo Kimono and Clothing* Life. Tokyo: Kadokawa Shoten.

Murayama, N. (2008) *Edo Mode no Tanjo. Edo, Birth of Style*. Tokyo: Kadokawa Shoten.

Murayama, N. (2010) *Nihon no Some Ori 5. Japanese Dyeing and Weaving 5*. Kyoto: Kyoto Shoin.

Nagasaki, I. (2006) *Kosode, The Origin of Modern Kimono Design*. Tokyo: Pie Books.

Nagasaki, I. (2009) *Kosode Hinagata. Kosode* Patterns. Kyoto: Seigensha.

Nagasaki, S. (1996) *Kasane No Irome. Coloured Layers*. Kyoto: Seeg Publishing.

Nevinson, J.L. (1967) *The Origin and Early History of the Fashion Plate*. Washington, DC: Smithsonian Press. e-release(2010). Gutenberg eBook (Accessed May 2014).

Ribeiro, A. (1986) *Dress and Morality*. London: Batsford.

Screech, T. (2002) *The Lens within the Heart: The Western Scientific Gaze and Popular Imagery in Later Edo Japan*. Honolulu: University of Hawaii Press.

Shikibu, M. Trans. A. Waley (1986) *The Tale of Genji*. Tokyo: Tuttle.

Shonagon, Sei. Trans. Morris, I. (1971 [1967]) *The Pillow Book of Sei Shonagon*. London: Penguin.

Shweder, R. (1991) *Thinking Through Cultures*. Cambridge, MA, London: Harvard University Press.

Shweder, R. (2000) "The Psychology of Practice and the Practice of Psychology." *Asian Journal of Social Psychology*. Vol. 3. pp. 207–22.

Steele, V. (1995) *The Corset: A Cultural History*. New Haven and London: Yale University Press.

Vlastos, S. (1990) *Peasant Protests and Uprisings in Tokugawa Japan*. Berkeley: University of California Press.

3 Mode Becomes Modern: Meiji to Twenty-First Century

The Meiji Mix (1868–1911)

Background to the Period: Industrial Development

The newly formed Meiji government, forced to open Japan's door to the West, was anxious to lead Japan into the future as cultivated and technically advanced, able to compete with western industrialized nations. The groundwork was laid in the peaceful and relatively isolated Edo period during which agriculture, industry, and economic infrastructure developed. Textiles, a light industry, was one of the first to modernize.

The Meiji period saw the building of the first silk and cotton reeling mills, of which government-owned Tomioka Silk Reeling Mill in Gunma, now a world heritage site, was the first. Japan's industrial revolution would have been impossible without the revenue from silk, and developments in sericulture continue today. From 1850 until the 1960s, silk was Japan's number one export, and Japan became the world's biggest exporter, accounting for 80 percent of the world's silk production in the 1920s. When other countries' silk worms became infected with pébrine disease, Japan was able to maintain the health of its silk worm population due to extensive research into advanced silk farming methods. According to Tsurumi (1990), the reeling and weaving factories employed a huge army of low-paid young women, who were part of the first wave of industrial workers in Japan.

While women in urban areas were taught to sew, all women in rural areas were expected to be able to weave. The three largest silk-producing prefectures were Gunma, Nagano, and Saitama. Chichibu town in Saitama has been a silk-producing center for over 2,000 years, and it boasted a cash economy in the Edo period, when Tokyo had a largely feudal economy, exchanging goods rather than cash. Shimatsu (2004) argues that Japan's industrial revolution has been told as the story of the introduction and triumph of western technology over backward feudalism. However, such rural mountain communities as Chichibu, which cultivated mulberry plants to feed the silk worms kept in almost every household, and where all households were involved in spinning, reeling, or weaving, demonstrated an industrialization process that was not western but Asian. Workers maintained some autonomy and power over their work spaces and were skillful laborers rather than cogs in a machine. The silk farmers and weavers negotiated with contractors from Edo, rather than working for bosses. According to Fukui (1984:97), to be a skilled weaver was more important for a woman than to be a good cook or house cleaner in such rural areas because weaving, although low status, poorly paid work, was an important contribution to the family economy. Although Chichibu once boomed as a silk-producing area, as of 2014 there are only ten families left raising silk worms in the city, and only three of these rely on it for a living. Shimatsu says that one reason for the world's demand for silk in the early- and mid-twentieth century was the West's insatiable desire for stockings, a new fashion item developed for newly revealed legs.

Meiji Styles: Understatement

The Meiji period saw several developments in the textile industry; the first silk and cotton reeling factories, the introduction of chemical dyes that would radically change colors and their fastness, and the introduction of western clothing. Aesthetics do not change suddenly, and according to Nagasaki (2008), the trending color for much of the Meiji period was gray. Design became so subtle and understated that it even disappeared onto the inside of the hem leaving the outside plain as in Figure 3.1.

Designs on formal kimono were usually symmetrical and confined to the front hem area, *susomoyo.* A short-lived trend in the late Meiji period was to have the design on the formal kimono on the right side, not the left, meaning that it was completely covered up when worn. Only on walking would a tiny flash of the design be visible. These fit in with the *iki* aesthetic described in Chapter 2. Such kimono usually feature *wakamatsu,* young pine trees and are *kasane,* two- or three-layered kimono, see Figure 3.2.

Figure 3.1 Muji (plain) kimono: design exclusively on the inside, satin silk; late nineteenth century.
Source: Property of the Author.
Photo: Todd Fong.

Figure 3.2 Formal black kasane (two-layered) kimono: wakamatsu (young pines); hidden inside, plain silk; early twentieth century.

Source: Property of the Author.

Photo: Todd Fong.

When new chemical dyes became available, they gradually began to make an impact on color schemes. Figure 3.3 shows a kimono incorporating new blue and pink dyes. Slowly people began to become accustomed to the new and bright colors that could be created with chemical dyes: brilliant purples, blues, pinks, and a red which was colorfast. Although there were some bright kimono in the Meiji period for formal wear, there would not be an explosion of color and design until the Taisho period.

The principle that clothing should not be too bright, particularly on informal occasions continued through the Meiji period and into the Taisho period too. The *haori* in Figure 3.4 is a typical women's everyday *haori,* of woven silk, but it has a beautifully bright yellow cotton *Edo sarasa* lining, hidden from view.

Institutionalizing Western Dress: Gendering the Nation

Meiji was an extraordinary period in the history of Japanese clothing. Previously, laws or edicts about sartorial behavior had been about maintaining social order within the nation. At this period, however, a self-conscious Japan emerges, specifically concerned with constructing or manipulating its image among

Figure 3.3 Crested kimono: susomoyo (hem design) showing the use of new chemical dyes, tsumugi silk; late nineteenth or early twentieth century.

Source: Property of the Author.

Photo: Todd Fong.

other nations. With hindsight, some of the sartorial behaviors that resulted from this self-consciousness seem quite ironic. In order to be taken seriously by western powers, Japan had to appear civilized, which meant going into trousers. Dalby (1993) describes this process with the Emperor leading the way by wearing a suit, followed by the armed forces and the instruments of law and state. Photographs and prints of the period show Japan's early diplomats and key figures in the new Meiji government almost exclusively wearing suits. Lisa Dalby says that the Emperor even went as far as declaring the kimono to be an effeminate garment in the Chinese style (1993:82).

Japan was gendering itself masculine by adopting western clothing styles which was an extraordinary move on two levels (Cliffe 2010). First, the group that is usually last to adopt new fashions, conservative elderly males, were forced into advocating the new western clothing and becoming its first wearers. Second, the new democratic government of an Asian nation was conducting its nation building business in foreign clothing. Slade says that, "Modernity was not the dominant tendency and it was not performed by traditionally avant-garde sections of the populace: the adoption of suits was a state-instituted fashion amongst the political and bureaucratic elite, normally a very sartorially conservative group" (2009:42). It was, of course, very expensive. The changes were not easy to implement, with neither the wool for uniforms and suits readily available in Japan nor the tailoring skills to produce the garments. The few tailors resided mostly in the ports of Yokohama and Kobe, and wool had to be imported from Europe. Gordon

Figure 3.4 Women's striped haori: silk with Edo sarasa cotton lining; late nineteenth or early twentieth century.
Source: Property of the Author.
Photo: Todd Fong.

writes, "Records exist for thirty-four tailor shops and just one dressmaker in Tokyo in 1880" (2012:18). Those gentlemen who could not afford a suit achieved an air of modernity and sophistication through the use of a hat, scarf, or a pair of western shoes. For several generations, the bureaucratic and business elite led a sartorial *nijuu seikatsu,* double life, with western clothing at work and Japanese clothing in the home. According to Gordon (2012), women, whose official roles in the period were to be good wives and wise mothers, and who therefore belonged to a domestic sphere, were touched by the changes about fifteen years later than were men.

The government built an event hall and ballroom, the *Rokumeikan,* Baying Deer Hall, for the purpose of entertaining foreign dignitaries with western music and dance. It was designed by British architect, Josiah Condor. Upper class women and *geisha* in Tokyo tried the dresses and corsets of Victorian Europe and wore them at *Rokumeikan* dance parties. According to Lisa Dalby, they were encouraged by Empress Haruko, who stated that western clothing as a two-part skirt and blouse was a natural descendent of the Japanese kimono and *hakama* (1993:81). However, Victorian costume with its S shape, tight neck, and bustle was repressive toward women. Slade describes such clothing as "a profound reaction against modernity...consequently immoderately ornamental, anatomically perfidious and formally arbitrary" (2009:41). It remained popular with the upper classes only for about ten years, after which women returned to their presumably more comfortable kimono. On a philosophical level, such modest and confining clothing as that of Victorian England was not out of keeping with the stated traditional role for women in Japan's new civil social structure.

Return of the Hakama

The biggest change for women at this time was probably the revival of the *hakama,* trouser skirt, which had been last worn in the Kamakura period, 400 years before. This was even worn by the Empress Haruko and her ladies in waiting. The *hakama* previously marked the end of inactive court life and the start of more active life as a samurai housewife. In the Meiji period, the *hakama* was sometimes accompanied by western shoes and accessories such as umbrellas or gloves, and it came to be associated with learning and cultivation. It was considered to be progressive and enlightened. Women were effectively going into trousers, though the female *hakama* at this period was probably a skirt and not a bifurcated garment. In the following Taisho period, *hakama* became firmly associated with education for women and was standard as the uniform for many girls' schools until the 1920s. In the beginning of the twenty-first century, the *hakama* gradually strengthened its symbolic role of representing education for women, and whereas thirty years ago almost all female students graduated from university wearing suits, now it is de rigueur for university graduation ceremonies. The strangely mixed and matched clothing of the Meiji period can be seen in prints by Umezo Kunitoshi, Adachi Ginkou, Utagawa Sadahige, and Hiroshige iii.

Meiji as a Turning Point

Women did not rush out to get dresses during the Meiji period. It would be more accurate to see it as the period when the groundwork was laid for a second fashion system to emerge alongside the already existing one. This took place through the gradual institutionalization of western clothing for men in the public sphere, the importation of new chemical dyes, the founding and development of spinning and weaving factories for cotton and silk, and the introduction of tailoring and machine sewing. Western clothing was becoming visible in Japan in the form of a bureaucratic class who distinguished themselves from workers by suits and uniforms. Dresses for women were much less visible, and the changes came more slowly. The adaptation of the kimono outfit was more important than the adoption of western dress at this period. In Chapter 2, the importance of the kimono's edges was discussed. The kimono dressing system is most permeable and open to change at its edges. For most women, changes occurred only at the edges of their kimono. Accessories—boots, parasols, scarves, hats, or gloves, could be added without compromising the kimonoed nature of the dress. It was even possible to wear a high-necked white blouse under a kimono, still maintaining the kimono look. Just as new colors were slowly being absorbed into the kimono system, so also were accessories. Aesthetically though, the tastes of the Meiji period were very much molded by the preceding Edo period, and fashion remained subtle, hidden, and understated.

Taisho Style (1912–26)

Industrialization, Marketing, and Consumption

Patterns of production, marketing strategies, and consumption changed radically in the Taisho period, and textiles were very big business. The effects of mass production were noticeable in many ways. Minnich records that, "In the years between the wars, there were over seventeen thousand looms operating in Nishijin, and the yearly production was valued at something like seventy million yen in 1924" (Minnich 1963:322). The textile industry, however, remained very different from the US or British models, and was, and still is, largely made up of small or medium sized enterprises, with the exception of a few large conglomerates. The resulting model is a flexible industry, responsive and able to cater to niche markets, rather than one that produces long lines very cheaply. This partly explains how the crafts-based kimono industry has managed to survive until today.

After the Great Kanto Earthquake in 1923, the dry goods and department stores that sold kimono reinvented themselves as new modernist enterprises, rebuilt in steel and concrete. They were a great democratizing force, radically changing consumption practices, as all classes of women could shop together. They set themselves up as cultural hubs, providing spaces for leisure, culture, and urban entertainment in the form of exhibitions, events, and spaces to eat and relax. Minami (1980:14) writes that Mitsukoshi department store set up its first trend-hunting committee as early as 1907, establishing itself as a fashion center for the newest kimono and collar designs. Kato (1980:47) says that women flocked there to buy the newest collars for their underwear. The collars were embroidered or dyed with a vocabulary of seasonal motifs, or designs relating to current events. After an Egyptian exhibition, Egyptian inspired kimono, and accessories became popular. The department stores were at the forefront of both producing and marketing trends. New items appeared, such as a *houmongi,* kimono for visiting wear, which was popularized by Mitsukoshi and has become a standard choice for formal occasions now. The stores also started selling kimono specially designed for children, so that mothers did not have to cut children's kimono from adult bolts. Figure 3.5 shows a Meiji period girl's *yuzen* kimono on the left and a variety of Taisho period *yuzen* kimono underneath it.

Figure 3.5 Selection of girls' kimono: Meiji period yuzen and Taisho period stencil yuzen on silk; late nineteenth to early twentieth centuries.

Source: Property of the Author.

Photo: Todd Fong.

Modernizing

Women's lives in the Taisho period were modernizing in many ways. Radio and magazines meant that they had more information available to them than previous generations. They could go to cinemas and cafés in the city and shop or browse in the new department stores. Many women started to work outside the home, or sewed inside the home, contributing to the family income. One item that was marketed to Japanese women as a symbol of modernity was the sewing machine. As Gordon's (2012) history of the sewing machine in Japan shows, the biggest limitation on the expansion of the Singer sewing machine in the Japanese market was the fact that women could not be persuaded to change from kimono to western dress, and machine sewing was firmly associated with western dress. Gordon writes, "Japanese users, despite efforts to convince them otherwise, had come to see western dress, western sewing, and the sewing machine as a tightly connected, and either mutually reinforcing or mutually constraining, bundle. Kimono, which were traditionally picked apart to be cleaned, could not be made on a sewing machine" (2012:53). Native fashion continued to fulfill the need of practicality and was aesthetically pleasing clothing for Japanese women. They bought sewing machines to sew western clothing for their children, rather than changing to wearing it themselves. The trend was not changing from Japanese to western dress, but rather to integrate new imported colors into kimono aesthetics, producing far brighter formal wear than had been popular before. The purples, pinks, and reds typical of the period are shown in the *dounuki,* inner kimono in Figure 3.6.

Figure 3.6 Purple dounuki (inner kimono from a pair): showing elaborate multicolored stencil dyeing in the center section on plain silk; early twentieth century.

Source: Property of the Author.

Photo: Todd Fong.

In comparison with the preceding Meiji period, when the mixing and matching of *youfuku*, western styles and *wafuku*, Japanese, was rampant, the Taisho period look was more clarified. The story of kimono has been told as being a straight transition from when western clothing arrived in Japan until today, with kimono standing as an antifashion, traditional, or old-fashioned garment. Slade has almost omitted the kimono in his *Japanese Fashion: A Cultural History* (2009), and Dalby writes of western clothing, *youfuku*, in the late 1920s:

Western dresses even began to take the lead in women's fashion. The lowered thirties hemline, the return of the belted waist, peplum blouses, T-strap shoes, and cloche hats all appeared in Tokyo almost as soon as they did on yofuku's home turf. Without stretching truth, yofuku by this time could claim urban Japan as part of its home territory. (1993:129)

This is almost certainly stretching the truth. It is impossible to write a history of Japanese fashion without taking into account that kimono remained standard apparel for the majority of women for the first half of the twentieth century. To ignore this is to distort the sartorial picture of Japan in this period. It is also probably fair to say that in rural areas, the takeover by western clothing was even slower than it was in urban areas, and that the takeover has in reality been slow and partial, never as simple or complete as it has been painted. *Youfuku,* western dress, was sold to Japanese on the grounds of modernity and practicality. However, being told that western clothing was more practical would not mean that one suddenly experienced one's own clothing as impractical. Kimono had been practical for Japanese for over a 1,000 years. Modernization largely meant westernization and perhaps practicality was the only vector on which *youfuku* could be framed as superior to kimono. But practicality, as all fashionistas know, is often the enemy of fashion.

Art Movements, Clothing Trends, and Moga

Japanese clothing was very much influenced by art movements from abroad. Japanese art products shown in Europe and the United States in the Meiji period (mid-nineteenth century) at great exhibitions had inspired the art nouveau and art deco movements which swept through Europe and the United States. Art nouveau with its floral patterns inspired by Edo period prints was reflected in all kinds of kimono, and Figure 3.7, a two-layered formal garment, probably for a wedding, is a good example. The salmon pink kimono in Figure 3.8 shows how roses, imported flowers, were incorporated with Japanese plants. Art nouveau and art deco were originally inspired by the art of eastern countries, but especially art deco with its emphasis on line, modernism, shape, and color was perfectly suited to the straight lines of the kimono, as kimono is all about surfaces rather than tailored shape. Jackson writes:

The evolution of art nouveau and art deco in Europe and America owed much to the inspiration provided by the arts of East Asia, and it was this cultural affinity that gave the styles such special resonance in Japan. The striking motifs on these kimono thus reflect both East and West. By wearing such garments, a Japanese woman was able to simultaneously embrace both the traditional and the modern. (Jackson 2005:31)

In western fashion, the S shape of Victorian clothing had given way to a kimono inspired straight line, and sometimes a large, kimono sleeve. Vionnet and other fashion designers were influenced by the kimono's simple lines. By the 1930s, the lines of clothing in the East and West were similar, and at this time, a few girls and young women began to wear western dresses, which was seen as daring and dangerous. In the

Figure 3.7 Formal black and white kasane (two-layered) kimono: hou (bird of paradise); yuzen on chirimen (crepe) silk; early twentieth century.
Source: Property of the Author.
Photo: Todd Fong.

popular imagination and the media the *moga,* modern girl, was framed as a progressive, promiscuous, and a playful consumer. She was the opposite of the good wife and wise mother that was seen as ideal by the Meiji government. She cut her hair and went to work in an office or café and was seen as less moral than her kimonoed sisters. According to Silverberg (2006), this figure was more of a media creation than a reality, and in his anthropological fieldwork, Kon observed that young women in western dress never walked alone, but in groups or with a partner to accompany them. While the reality was that there were few actual modern girls, the *moga* had a big profile in the media and was seen variously as a threat to social morals by an older generation, and an exciting and independent role model to follow by young females. It has even been suggested by Gordon that in reality modern girls could have been students of sewing schools, who were wearing their own creations.

Figure 3.8 Formal salmon pink kimono: peonies and roses; art nouveau influenced plant designs on chirimen (crepe) silk; 1920s.

Source: Property of the Author.

Photo: Todd Fong.

Studies of the Everyday

Kon Wajiro was the most important anthropologist of the early twentieth century in Japan. He studied his own "civilized society" by applying the anthropological techniques that were commonly used on tribes or other groups, because he realized that there were no such records of his own country - Japan. He thought that this kind of documentation was necessary for future comparative social research. Using observation and surveys, he recorded in finest detail people's lives, habits, and possessions. All this data, complete with illustrations, he recorded in a series of notebooks. The everyday clothing of the early twentieth century in Japan can be understood because of the legacy of Kon. He recorded what he saw in the street, such as twelve kinds of apron or sixteen different ways that girls wore their hair.

In one survey conducted in Ginza, Tokyo's fashion capital, between Kyobashi and Shinbashi, on four days in May 1925, he recorded whether people were wearing kimono or western clothing. Out of 1,180 people, he found that 67 percent of men wore western dress while only 1 percent of women did. Western dress was not yet fashionable for women, even in Ginza, though it was taking over the workplace for men. Kon himself was surprised at the results as the *moga* of the media, with their radical western dress, were almost nonexistent. Kon examined the types of kimono that were worn. Men's kimono were 5 percent plain, 50 percent striped, and 45 percent *kasuri,* ikat. All the men wore some kind of coat or jacket over their kimono. The women's kimono he divided into *fudangi,* home wear, or *machigi,* town wear. 90 percent of women wore town wear. No one wore plain kimono, 47 percent wore stripes, 45 percent wore *kasuri,* and 8 percent wore *yuzen* dyeing. Silk accounted for 68 percent of kimono, wool 16 percent, and cotton 16 percent. *Meisen,* cheaply produced silk kimono, accounted for 50.5 percent of all women's kimono. At this time, then, we can assume that *meisen* was largely striped rather than patterned, but that it was already considered to be town wear rather than home wear, and that it was far more popular than cotton or wool kimono. The production of *meisen* had made silk kimono available for the masses.

Kon also observed hairstyles at this time. He found that 31 percent had a traditional Japanese hairstyle, 27 percent had *sokuhatsu,* a soft bun considered to be between Japanese and western styles, and 42 percent of women had abandoned Japanese hairstyles for western ones. Slade states that adopting a western hairstyle was one of the easiest ways of gaining a modern western look, "Hairstyles provide the first way for the general population to flirt with western custom and modern aesthetics" (2009:126). Women were interested in getting a western look, but they were largely not interested, at this point, in abandoning their kimono.

Kon was surprised again when he went to Ginza and repeated his research on February 25, 1933. If the media was to be believed, then the change to western clothing was happening fast. In reality, he found that it was happening very slowly. He counted female pedestrians for forty minutes, 462 women and girls. 81 percent were in kimono and 19 percent were in western dress, but the figures were somewhat misleading. He divided the data into three groups, women, school girls, and preschool children. Then he found that 70 percent of preschoolers were in western dress, 50 percent of school girls and only 2.6 percent of adult women had adopted western clothing. In contrast with media hype, women seemed resistant to western dress, putting it on their children, but not wearing it themselves. This was the most fashionable place in Japan, so the figures strongly suggest that western clothing for women was not firmly established in the 1930s. According to Gordon, in spite of the depression and severe restrictions on buying sewing machines in installments, sales of domestic machines, "reached an all-time peak at 154,000 units in 1940" (2012:137). Gordon writes of sewing schools, "Photos from the 1920s showed virtually all students in kimono, with only the teachers in Western dress; by the mid-1930s roughly two-thirds of the students came to class or graduation wearing Western dress" (2012:130–131). He concludes that there was an increase in girls wanting to sew western dress for themselves. It was a confusing time for Japanese because they wanted a modern lifestyle, like the American middle-class lifestyle that they saw in Hollywood films, but such attractions embodied the values of the enemy, and were therefore under suspicion as not being morally good enough for the Japanese nation.

In the New Year of 1951, after the Pacific War during which women had been forced to reform their kimono into narrow sleeved garments, national dress or *monpe,* baggy work trousers, Kon returned to Ginza again. This time he found that 52 percent of women were in western clothing and only 48 percent were in kimono. In March of the same year, western dress accounted for 56 percent and kimono for 44 percent. From these figures, we can deduce that even the war (1941–45) had not persuaded all women to abandon kimono. It took until the 1950s for just half of Japanese women to be wearing western dress in the most fashionable area of Tokyo. Thus Kon's work demonstrates that western dress actually has a short history of just over half a century for the majority of Japanese women at the time of writing.

The Meisen Boom

According to Kon's findings, the biggest fashion movement in the 1920s and 1930s, at least in the Kanto area where it was produced, was the *meisen* boom. *Meisen* was high style and worn by almost half of women walking in the streets of Ginza. This cloth was originally used for making plain or striped homespun and soft furnishings such as cushions or futons. Japan's biggest export was silk, and *meisen* was made from the poor-quality silk which was rejected for export. It was originally marketed for its strength, rather than beauty, but according to Koizumi Kazuko in *Meisen no Kaisoka* (2004:102–103), this varied greatly with the price.

Meisen has the appearance of a very complex *kasuri,* ikat, and it was the only silk kimono whose production became semi-mechanized. It was much cheaper than other silk kimono and has been considered to be the jeans of the kimono world, easily marketed because of its price. The *kasuri* effect that is typical of *meisen* kimono was created using a new technology developed in Chichibu. (Also claimed by Isesaki). The technique was called *hogushiori. Kasuri* was made by tie-dyeing individual threads before weaving them together. When making *meisen,* all the warp threads were laid out and held in place with a few temporary weft threads. The warp threads were then stencil-dyed using *nassen,* a dye in resist paste technique. One stencil was used for each color, so they were dyed upto five times. Today, the process is performed using silk screens. Figure 3.9 shows a selection of *meisen* kimono and Fig 3.10 shows a bolt of *meisen* on a weaving loom.

Figure 3.9 Selection of meisen kimono: silk; early to mid-twentieth century.
Source: Property of the Author.
Photo: Todd Fong.

Figure 3.10 Meisen on loom: showing stencil-dyed warp threads.
Source: Property of Chichibu Meisen Kan.
Photo: Todd Fong.

After dyeing, the warps were transferred onto a weaving loom, and the cloth was woven up on hand or power looms. The technique of stencil dyeing at the thread stage enabled far more complex patterns to be created than before. Also a wider variety of colors could be used than are found in handmade *kasuri*. Weft threads could also be dyed using the hogushiori process. *Meisen* could be made for a fraction of the labor of *kasuri,* greatly reducing the price. This was very important as almost universally markets were falling due to the depression in the late 1920s. Of all types of kimono, only *meisen* experienced a domestic boom, because it answered the need for a colorful cheap kimono in hard economic times. It is estimated that at least 70 percent of all Japanese women owned at least one *meisen* kimono.

Yamauchi and Endo researched the *meisen* phenomenon and found that the boom was created by multiple actors, in response to the Great Depression. In 1910, *meisen* was serviceable home wear. The first step toward becoming fashion was when an influential leader, General Nogi, the president of the prestigious Gakushuin Girls' School, decided that in spite of their high-class backgrounds, school girls would wear a *meisen* kimono with a *hakama*, trouser skirt, rather than wearing colorful and expensive *yuzen,* to school. Many other schools followed Nogi's lead and a purple *yagasuri meisen,* arrow design kimono, and a brown *hakama* became standard girls' school uniform, at least in the Kanto region, until the mid-1920s. Having been accepted as school wear, it began to be acceptable to wear it in the city according to *Senshoku to Ryuko,* Dyeing and Trends magazine (1920:38–39, in Yamauchi and Endo).

The second step was clever marketing. Takashimaya Department Store was struggling in the recession and saw the need to expand their customer base at the lower end. They began to advertise *meisen* kimono on posters and in magazines which resulted in price wars between department stores and kimono shops. Department stores began to offer their own designs, and even a mail-order service. Although *meisen* was a Kanto area product, Mitsukoshi Department Store held a ten-day *meisen* fair at its Osaka branch in 1925. The department stores used a new and novel technique to market their kimono, a mannequin (Yamauchi and Endo 2010:16).

Meisen had only one rival at the cheap end of the market. This was wool muslin, an imported fabric. In order to fend off the threat from this import, producers, particularly in the town of Isesaki, began to pay much more attention to design. They produced complex and colorful art deco and art nouveau inspired designs using brilliant, new, chemical dyes. Figure 3.11 shows a selection of *meisen* designs that were bought and patented in Chichibu, and used for making kimono.

These garments seemed incredibly attractive because within living memory kimono had been almost universally dull: plain or striped. Along with luxury taxes on foreign goods, the rising price of wool, negative feelings about America and foreigners, and an award for being a good domestic product, *meisen* fended off the threat from imported wool. As *meisen* turned into a fashion item, the wording in magazines changed to emphasize it as decorative and fashionable, rather than strong and serviceable.

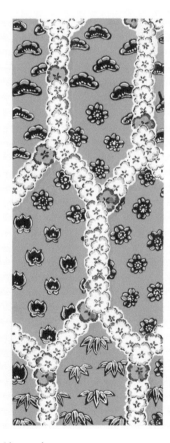

Figure 3.11 Selection of designs for making meisen.
Source: Property of Chichibu Meisen Kan.
Photo: Todd Fong.

The distribution system for kimono and bolts of kimono cloth is long and complex and is a part of the reason for their high prices. First the cloth goes from a craftsman or producer to a local middleman and then to a local distributor. From there it will go to a larger scale distributor before being sent to another location in Japan. It passes through many hands before arriving in a shop. Department stores, anxious to cut prices, tried to bypass the middlemen by trading directly with producers, creating their own lines and even opening subbranches near production sites. Inanishi from Osaka, the top *meisen* trader in 1925, trading 85,527 *hiki* (a Japanese measurement of about two kimono lengths or just over twenty meters of cloth) was aware of the dangers of the middlemen being bypassed by the stores and producers, so he was proactive in maintaining their importance. He started the magazine, *Senshoku to Ryuko, Dyeing and Trends*, "for the express purpose of stimulating new production and enhancing quality through the transmission of fashion information" (Yamauchi 2009:12). The magazine was to spread sound taste, give fashion information from home and abroad, and give a voice to department stores whose predictions for new designs and colors were in each issue, along with textile samples. Inanishi also started meetings where producers met with buyers, and also sales people from department stores who bought from the buyers, to discuss their market findings. Producers also met locally to discuss these market findings. From 1921, Inanishi planned annual textile fairs which were popular both with retailers and middlemen and allowed producers from different areas to showcase their work. Yamauchi says:

> By listening to the fashion information at the fair from chief buyers of department stores, producers could reduce the uncertainly and ambiguity of the distribution process, and department stores, as a result, could expect to disseminate their fashion ideas. (2009:16)

There were judges and prizes at Inanishi's fairs, and between 4,500 and 6,000 applicants wanted to show their work.

Yamauchi's research demonstrates how a fashion boom was created in a depression. *Meisen* went from domestic use to school uniform, from there to the street. This was due to the presence of a leader, clever advertising, strategic promotion, attention to design, and to the needs of the market. It became high fashion and was worn by well over half of women in the early twentieth century. Because *meisen* was not considered a valuable clothing item, production almost ceased when the Pacific War came, but since 2002, it has enjoyed a revival among antique kimono lovers. Several exhibitions of early twentieth-century kimono in major venues outside Japan have increased its cachet at home. In 1998, *Chichibu Meisen Kan,* Chichibu Meisen Hall, was established in order to preserve the legacy of the city, and also for remaining weavers to teach their skills to young people, in an attempt to preserve the technique. The *meisen* revival is perhaps because *meisen,* with its bold designs in bright colors, offers similar attractions to those it offered in the 1920s: durability, modern-looking designs, and exciting use of color on a cheap kimono, in a time of economic uncertainty.

Summary of Taisho Period Style

The biggest fashion trend of the early twentieth century was undoubtedly *meisen* kimono. Again, as with *yukata* in the Edo period, we see a lowly garment developing into an exciting fashion item. Many of Japan's trends emerge from low-status garments in the street. In 2014, short pleated skirts in imitation of Japanese school uniforms were found in popular clothing shops as school uniform style had become fashionable again. There is a strong parallel between this and the way that *meisen* emerged into the public sphere from its role as school uniform. Being worn by over 50 percent of urban women, it was unrivaled as a

Figure 3.12 Chichibu Meisen Kan Flyer.

Source: Property of Chichibu Meisen Kan.

Photo: Todd Fong.

fashion movement, *meisen* kimono were literally as ubiquitous as jeans became in western fashion. That it happened during an economic depression when markets were falling worldwide is particularly notable. The urban space, the street, coffee shop, and department store provided places for display of the radical and bold art nouveau and art deco designs, in bright chemical dyes, which contrasted with the dull kimono of modern memory. Women were eager to display their bright kimono, embroidered, dyed, or woven obi and their gorgeously embroidered collars, just as their predecessors had in the Edo period. While western clothing was being promoted as functional for a modern life, it did not provide the necessary spaces to make a display of such beautiful artistic designs nor did it offer women the chance to show their skills at manipulating their outfits through careful coordination of the various elements. The kimono outfit remained far more sophisticated as a fashion statement than did western clothing.

Early Showa (1927–45)

Background to the Period

The end of the nineteenth century and the first half of the twentieth was a long period of unrest for Japan. It captured Taiwan (previously Formosa) from China in 1895 and fought with China again in 1937. It was at war with Russia in 1904–05, and Korea was effectively under Japanese control from 1910 to 1945. Japan's expansion was justified by a very right wing government because the country lacked the necessary resources: iron, coal, and minerals, to continue its industrial development. Expansion was also an attempt to stop the outflow of control and resources in Asia by the West, in particular Britain, Holland, and France. The plan was to unite Asia under a "benevolent" Japan. So the 1930s were laced with discussions of war, at a time when Japan was trying to extend its influence throughout the Pacific region. It would go into the Philippines, Thailand, and Malaya (Malaysia) in 1941, the Dutch East Indies (Indonesia), Burma, and Singapore in 1942, and then full-scale world war followed with the United States being drawn into the battle. Both propaganda and censorship were a major part of people's lives, not only in the news but in films, literature, and textbooks. Boys were taught that it was more desirable to die an honorable death for one's country than be taken as a prisoner.

In spite of the undoubted hardships of the period, modernism meant that people had more conveniences than they had had in previous generations, and newspapers, radios, and electric light were a part of everyday life. While the nations' politics were serious, people wanted to play. They went to cafés, went to eat sushi and drink sake, watched films, went dancing, and listened to music. Women continued to sew in the home or workplace and spent considerably more time doing this than women in the United States or the UK. In the 1920s, sports organizations for women were started. In spite of it being a foreign sport, the popularity of baseball could not be halted, though the 1930s saw a strong rise in military arts, such as karate and aikido.

During the war years, the kimono was seen as unpatriotic because it used too much cloth. Women who wore it were in danger of having their sleeves slashed. Smaller sleeves could be made, but most women turned their kimono into *monpe,* baggy work pants, which has resulted in almost universal hatred of *monpe* among older Japanese women. Kimono were stored away until after the war and reemerged, if they had not been traded for food, during the hardest years.

Omoshiro Gara, Interesting Designs

Throughout the prewar period, the kimono continued to incorporate interesting and novel images, adding to the huge vocabulary of native Japanese and imported Chinese floral images that were already in use.

European flowers such as roses and tulips arrived in the Taisho period, and modern architecture, bridges, and technological items began to be seen. The men's *nagajuban,* under kimono in Figure 3.13 and Figure 3.14, shows an office scene with a typewriter and a view from an office building.

People were interested in the technologies of transportation: cars, planes, bicycles, motorbikes, and ships. Famous figures also appeared, and there was a fascination with lenses, and how they were used in film and other ways. The *juban,* underwear, in Figure 3.15 shows the making of the film *King Kong.* King Kong can be seen on the top of the Empire State Building, and the New York Skyline appears in the background. Also included are the camera and film crew, the name of the film and production company, and pieces of the film itself. It is a fascinating piece, revealing the desire for a world of film, and for New York. As the film was released in 1929, the garment was probably made between then and about 1935, after which Japan was heading toward war with the United States.

Figure 3.13 Men's nagajuban (underwear): modernist image of buildings and typewriter; silk; 1920s.
Source: Property of Bunka Gakuen Costume Museum.
Photo: Bunka Gakuen Costume Museum.

Figure 3.14 Men's nagajuban (underwear): modernist image of buildings and typewriter; silk; detail; 1920s.

Source: Property of Bunka Gakuen Costume Museum.

Photo: Bunka Gakuen Costume Museum.

Kon wrote in a 1937 essay that western fashion, which was about change in shape, had lost its way. The only new changes were in fabrics and in the addition of hats and scarves. Kimono, with its radical incorporation of the new, was more exciting (1973:170–171). He also said that women appropriated western fashion and kimono in different ways. Western clothing was appropriated through the book or catalog, and so women wore it according to the book. When buying kimono, however, women had a chance to enter into discussion with sales people, so were more likely to find something through which they could express themselves more easily (1973:168–169). Kon also observed that foreigners in Yokohama would like to see an unchanging traditional kimono, but that in reality it is always changing, which is a sign of youthfulness and health (1973:174).

Figure 3.15 Men's juban (underwear): The making of King Kong and the New York skyline; rayon. Early 1930s.
Source: Property of the Author.
Photo: Todd Fong.

The wave of propaganda and nationalism that swept through Japan in this turbulent period extended itself into all kinds of everyday objects, including clothing. Nationalism became fashionable, and there was no better way to express love for one's country than by wearing Japanese clothing, which offered a flat canvas, and multiple surfaces for decoration. The kimono was nearer to the heart than alien dresses and skirts. War textiles were not generated by the government but by the market. The majority of the more powerful images were seen in men's underwear in accordance with the *iki* aesthetic described in Chapter 2. Some *haori* jacket linings were special commissions which commemorated victories in battle, or famous figures, such as Figure 3.16, which shows Admiral Togo Heihachiro on the deck of the warship Mikasa in the 1905 war with Russia.

The majority of wartime textiles were poor-quality mass-produced items, mostly to inspire victory in battle. Some were extremely graphic. Figure 3.17 shows a patriotic song, warships, flags, binoculars, and bombs.

Like *meisen,* as poor-quality material items, wartime textiles were rejected as valueless until about 2000 but are now recognized as important historical records, largely thanks to the research, collection, and television exposure of Inui Yoshiko, and the exhibitions of propaganda textiles in the US *Wearing Propaganda* curated by Atkins (2005) and *Dreams of Empire* curated by Marcuson, Hall, and Jacobsen (2011). War designs also appeared on women and children's kimono, usually stylized, and on the outer surface as women and children were less constrained than men in the public sphere. On children's kimono war is sometimes enacted with children and toys. Figure 3.18 is a typical boy's kimono. Mt. Fuji came to represent the Japanese nation, and cherry blossoms represented the soldiers who fought and fell on the battlefield, their lives, like the cherry blossom, tragically short.

Such examples of fashionable inner wear can be seen to be the opposite of fast fashion, which can be made anywhere, and go anywhere. They are examples of a fashion which is specifically rooted to

Figure 3.16 Men's haori reversed to show the lining: Admiral Togo on the deck of the warship Mikasa; yuzen on silk; mid-twentieth century.

Source: Property of the Author.

Photo: Todd Fong.

Figure 3.17 Men's nagajuban (underwear): (a) war images including bombs, warships, flags, binoculars, and patriotic music; rayon; mid-twentieth century, (b) communication equipment and radio waves; wool; mid-twentieth century.

Source: Property of the Author.

Photo: Todd Fong.

a particular place and time. They were personal expressions but were mass produced for the market. They were new and relevant, and they demonstrated how the kimono system incorporated contemporary discourse. They also illustrated the importance of multiple audiences in Japanese fashion, because as male underwear, they would have only been seen in the act of undressing and not in the public sphere, and they therefore had the potential to be very subversive. These items embody deep meanings and an authenticity rare in clothing. Japan's modern history is literally written into its clothing, in a way that is unique among clothing systems.

Figure 3.18 Boy's kimono: boy soldier on horseback; rayon; mid-twentieth century.
Source: Property of the Author.
Photo: Todd Fong.

Summary of Early Twentieth-Century Fashions

Evidence from a variety of sources has been used to examine kimono in the early twentieth century. Department stores enabled democratization, and with their trend-hunting committees, magazines, and posters show that kimono were both available to many women and were in high fashion. Support for this viewpoint comes from the anthropological work of Kon, from Gordon's history of the sewing machine, and the study of trend creation by Yamauchi and Endo. Parallels can be drawn between the rise of *meisen,* a lowly fabric, and the rise of cotton, especially *yukata,* fashion in the Edo period when economic necessity and the law forbidding silk meant that a lowly cotton garment became fashion for the masses. There are also parallels to be drawn with the rise of jeans in western fashion. The textiles of the war period demonstrate how a culture of nationalist discourse became fashionable, and how it was incorporated in clothing. These textiles are an example of how kimono fashion is not fast but firmly rooted in a particular place and time, both reflecting and reproducing the political discourse of the period.

From Postwar Kimono to the End of an Era

Kon's work showed that at the beginning of the 1950s, half of the women walking in Ginza were wearing western clothing, which was on the increase as kimono wearing declined. Japanese women did not suddenly change from kimono to western dress, but even those who stayed in kimono brought up their children wearing western clothes. Thus kimono began to vanish from everyday life, and a postwar generation grew up without it. So the natural order of a mother teaching her daughter to dress was broken. Kimono gradually became confined to its role as formal wear for weddings, ceremonies and marking rites of passage, and to the world of Japanese culture and arts, such as the theater, the tea ceremony, and flower arranging. This had two negative effects. The manufacture of daily wear suffered, and second, as a result, kimono shops stopped stocking everyday kimono, as they could make more money by selling expensive formal garments. At this point, they began to stock only silk, while cottons or wools were sold at dry goods shops. This separation was another cause for a further move away from everyday kimono.

The postwar generation was the first generation not to have grown up wearing kimono in daily life, and the kimono dealers realized that if women could not dress, they would not buy kimono. Therefore, as a selling strategy, they began to establish lessons so that customers could learn how to wear the kimono they bought. These developed into the kimono *kitsuke gakuin,* dressing schools, which took it upon themselves to systematize the wearing of kimono. As kimono wearing became more rule governed, it also became less expressive. The form of kimono dressing seen in kimono magazines and promoted around Japan is the legacy of the kimono dressing schools and embodies modest and demure values. It is also rather serious, with white collar and *tabi,* socks, and can be considered to be a style descended from proper and modest samurai wives, rather than less self-effacing townswomen.

The kimono of the 1950s and 1960s can be described as self-conscious kimono. Wartime and postwar prohibitions on extravagance may have been lifted, but times could not have been easy, as almost every major city in Japan had been flattened during the last months of the war. The kimono look serviceable, and practicality was clearly in the mind of kimono producers and wearers. There were few kimono celebrating the traditional flowers and designs that are linked to specific seasons. Large stripes, checks, and abstract designs in black, white, and primary colors are notable, and many of the kimono of the period look as if they could have been produced from western dressmaking fabric. In fact, many of the kimono of this period resemble western clothes in a kimono shape. Perhaps minimizing the distance between the two clothing systems was a strategy to try and keep more women in kimono. Even the models stand in poses more typical of western fashion models than Japanese. Fashion writer and stylist Nakahara (1970) suggests that there was a huge gap between kimono wearing before and after the war. He says that postwar Japanese got out the kimono they had worn before the war put them into work trousers, looked at them, and wondered why those long sleeves, swooping necklines, and padded hems had ever seemed to be attractive. The zeitgeist drew kimono toward the western fashion aesthetic, and the white collar, close to the neck, resembles the white collar of a working man or woman; the patterns on kimono, the patterns on western dress, and the sleeves and hem are reduced to a less conspicuous form.

During the increasingly wealthy 1970s and 1980s, when women married to successful businessmen did not have to work, kimono wearing became increasingly associated with cultural training for the upper middle class and was jokingly referred to by non-Japanese in Japan as one of the "marital arts," along with tea ceremony, ikebana, and English conversation (as opposed to the martial arts, usually studied by men). Feminists, including non-Japanese, were critical of the kimono, and particularly of the obi. Goldstein-Gidoni, researching in a kimono dressing parlor, recounts stories of young girls being instructed to *gaman suru,* grin and bear it. "As if fulfilling their own role in training Japanese girls for proper female roles, the dressers, as experts of feminine knowledge, frequently remind the girls (at times quite severely) that they should know how to hold out and endure suffering" (1999).

According to Yano Research Institute, kimono sales peaked in 1985, which was the height of the bubble economy. This was not due to the popularity of the kimono at that time, but because a few extremely rich people, such as baseball coaches' wives or media superstars tried to spend as much as possible on the most expensive ceremonial wear. It was a period when companies were spending extravagantly on entertainment. Businessmen frequented the expensive bars of Ginza, and the hostesses spent recklessly on gorgeous kimono. It was also common for companies to take workers on trips to *onsen* hot springs, or to seaside towns, where *geisha* and entertainers in kimono would appear, entertain, and serve food and drink. At this time, kimono in the street had virtually disappeared, but those that were purchased were outrageously priced, and many women fell victim to the hard sales practices of kimono shops and were persuaded into taking out large loans for kimono that they would hardly ever wear. Yano's research explains the antiquated distribution system associated with a traditional craft industry, and how that has impeded the kimono as a fashion item. It also suggests that many of the kimono's problems appear to have been created by the industry itself. Yano Research interviewed women in the Kansai and Kanto areas and found that over 80 percent of women said that they liked kimono. However, most of them did not buy or wear them. The most three common reasons given for this situation were that they thought it was difficult to wear, expensive, and they had nowhere to wear it. These impressions are the results of the postwar trend for rule-governed kimono schools, the artificial inflation of prices, and the lack of everyday wear seen in kimono shops.

This was not, however, the end of the story. Just as in the Meiji period there was a backlash against the sudden proliferation of western dress, as the dreams associated with the boom economy of the late twentieth century melted away there was again a questioning of the takeover of all things western and the tyranny of fast fashion without regard for Japanese culture. The reevaluation began in the 1990s, with a worldwide boom in Asian chic. This was followed in Japan by a rise of interest in all things Japanese, which sowed the seeds of a kimono renaissance. Chart 3.1 shows the sales figures for kimono between 1993 and 2013, in 100 millions of yen. Were this to be in the number of kimono, there would be a very

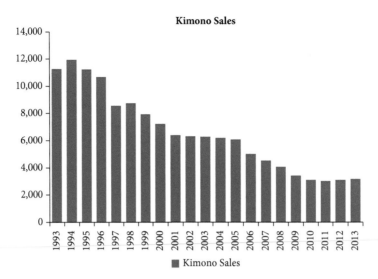

Kimono Sales

Chart 3.1 Kimono sales from 1993 to 2013 in 100 millions of yen. Constructed from Yano Research Institute Kimono Sangyo nenshi 2012–13.

different picture, as people are buying more kimono more cheaply than before. At the present time, the kimono industry is undergoing huge changes. Kimono wearers are rejecting the traditional channels for the purchase of kimono, but while kimono shops are facing hard times, others who have adopted new business models have found success.

A New Dawn: Twenty-First Century Fashion

The evidence of something new afoot began to be seen in the early 1990s, with micro trends appearing in the form of colored *tabi,* socks, embroidered and colored collars, and the opening of second-hand kimono outlets, of which there were few previously. The first major phenomenon was the *yukata* boom of the year 2000, which was also the year that the first kimono wearing group, *Kimono de Ginza,* started accepting women as well as men. The *yukata* boom spread from girls, who wanted to wear it for dates and summer firework displays, to their boyfriends. For many young men, this proved to be a way into the kimono world. New visually lavish magazines called *mooks,* magazine books, began to proliferate in the 2000s, and second-hand shops, online shops, blogging, kimono groups, and YouTube have made kimono easily accessible in the twenty-first century. Just as *yuzen,* domestic cotton, and *meisen* were new, reasonably priced alternatives to what had previously been available, polyester kimono and digital printing are changing the kimono scene again. Chapters 4–7 explore the making, marketing, and wearing of kimono in the twenty-first century.

Discussion of Japanese Fashion Trends

To return again to the five aspects of fashion outlined in Chapter 1, the economic fashion system was in place by the Edo period. This was evidenced in a lively textile market, trading, and importing at the beginning of the Edo period and developments in textile technology and printing which enabled diffusion of new fashions. In the nineteenth and early twentieth centuries, the importance of the economic system of fashion is indisputable, as textiles was one of the most important industries for Japan in the industrial revolution, and Japan's most important export was silk until the mid-twentieth century.

Another aspect of fashion is the importance of newness. This was in evidence in changes in the length of clothing in the Heian period, and in new ideas about coordination of colors, such as matching with the complexion of the wearer. Evidence that fast change caused psychological discomfort was seen in the reaction to lopsided clothing on courtiers or high clogs on young boys observed by Sei Shonagon. In the Edo period, it was demonstrated in the love for the new and exotic from abroad and the desire for original patterns and the new domestically produced cotton. Later, the desire for brightly colored *meisen* was also a desire for the colors and designs seen in European art on a silk kimono which was finally affordable. Subsequently, the new was realized in the form of images of technologies of war, entertainment, or transportation. Japanese history is literally drawn in the modernist textiles of the Taisho and Showa periods, particularly for men. How the new is continuing to be a part of kimono in the twenty-first century is demonstrated in Chapters 4–7.

A third aspect of fashion is form over function. Heian women could hardly walk in their many layers. Seeing layers at the edge of the sleeve draws attention to the hand, and at the hem, to the feet, and of course, the collar, and the back of the neck are an enduring focus of erotic attention in Japanese style. In the Edo period, the obi reached its most extreme size. The obi is now smaller and easier to tie but remains complex for special occasions. The kimono itself has become less complex over the years, by Taisho being worn in a single layer on informal occasions, but the designs on kimono suddenly became complex after years of dullness and plain or striped kimono. One feature of the kimono revival is accessorizing, which is basically a move toward complexity.

Group behavior was described early on by Sei Shonagon, who observed fashions for young boys, chamberlains, and fashion-conscious courtiers. In the Edo period, class was a dominating factor, with restrictions placed on merchant classes, forcing them to adapt their fashions which then resulted in the development of new tastes. Class continued to be very important until the Taisho period when there was a leveling between classes as new ways of consumerism and new channels of information flow began to cause a democratization of clothing practice. Trends were not only of middle class imitating their betters but were also born in the street and spread horizontally because the class boundaries were so strict. Sometimes these then moved up to affect the upper classes too. The 1920s' *moga* was a clearly defined but small group, and the schoolgirl look was another look worn by many groups in the 1920s. *Meisen* was unusual because of its wide reach, at least 50 percent of urban women, but it could be proposed that more conservative kimono would have dominated rural Japan.

Finally, the aspect of self-expression is a very important part of kimono. Dressing ahead of the season, making a contemporary statement, combining colors and patterns in interesting and classy ways, and of course being *iki* chic, learning to say much, by saying little, are important aspects of kimono style. At least since the Heian period, self-presentation in the form of good dressing has been important in Japan. This is no less true today than it was in the past, with the ubiquitous salary man and office lady suits filling the trains every morning, and the Lolitas and young fashionistas parading in the streets of today's fashion capitals of Harajuku and Shibuya. The kimono fashionistas are not being left out, and search through used and new kimono shops and websites looking for the kimono that is just right, and obi that match perfectly to make a unique and interesting statement. They also purchase or make a wide variety of accessories to complete the image they wish to create.

Trends in Japanese fashion can thus be established from early on, and the fashion system is both very different in appearance from the western one and systematic in the same way as the western one. The social system was different, so parading in gorgeous clothing served the function of imitating one's betters, but would never allow one to join their ranks. This display was considered subversive and was severely repressed during the Edo period. Interestingly, this led to new innovations and eventually the birth of new aesthetics, as people tried to find ways to get around these suppressive laws. This explains why we find more fashion coming out of the working or middle classes, rather than the more conservative upper classes.

In terms of macro development, western fashion is a history of change in shape and can therefore be traced through black and white illustrations or fashion plates. Macro development for the kimono system has also consisted of a change in shape from an unbelted triangle with little resemblance to the human form, to a tube-like shape that follows the lines of the body much more closely. The rise of the obi is also a very significant macro change. Micro fashions in the West have also been in changes in shape or silhouette, but in the kimono system they are not about that. Micro trends in kimono are about the color and patterns, the textiles, and the accessories, where the motifs are placed and technique used in the patterning.

Although the kimono dressing system appears very different from western dress, these five factors demonstrate that similar phenomena occur in each system. The Japanese system was not imported from the West; it is native and developed in spite of the lack of social mobility. There are several aspects of the Japanese fashion system that appear more highly developed or sophisticated than they are in the western system. One aspect is the kimono system's deep relationship with the natural world. While daisies and tulips can be worn at any time of year in the West, kimono is bonded to nature securely so that it is unthinkable to wear most flowers out of season. Seasons in Japan are represented by plum blossoms, cherry blossoms, wisteria, iris, pinks, bush clover, pampas grass, maples, chrysanthemums, bamboos, and camellias, among others. Some creatures are also seen at certain times of year: the Japanese nightingale in spring, the dragonfly at the end of summer, and rabbits playing under the moon at the autumn equinox.

Kimono does not only look outward to the natural world, but inward to its inner layers. Paradoxically, tailored and shaped western fashion tends to be almost entirely about the surface, and is therefore two dimensional, but kimono, which is flat and untailored, is actually multi-surfaced with many layers. It is therefore three dimensional and can cater to multiple audiences with its public and private faces. Not only does kimono reach outward to nature and inward to its own layers, it also has the potential to incorporate the past as well as the present. Evans (2003) suggests that fashion denies its past, which then comes back to haunt it, but kimono welcomes the past in the form of a huge repertoire of traditional Chinese and Japanese inspired designs that are continually rewritten in new and interesting ways. Because fashion change in kimono is about the designs and patterns, like a painted canvas, its flat surface is able to reflect art movements clearly and also to speak fluently about social and contemporary issues, in a way that perhaps western fashion only does through slogans on T-shirts.

Though fast fashion can be produced anywhere and go anywhere, kimono fashion is born in Japan and speaks to Japanese. It can be worn and read largely in Japan. One attribute this gives to kimono, that we cannot find in fast fashion, is interconnectedness. Kimono is literally passed on from one generation to another, but this is only one level of interconnectedness. It is deeply embedded in a specific culture, and therefore it offers the wearer authenticity, a highly desired quality in fashion today.

For the fashion-conscious Japanese, the kimono provides more challenge than western dress does. It demands the dressing skill and style sense of the wearer. Since the Edo period, the obi has become as important as the kimono itself. When a woman buys a dress, she largely buys a done deal. The outfit is complete and can be varied slightly with accessories. However, the kimono is much more versatile because it is not a complete outfit. Only when the wearer customizes the kimono with obi and accessories does the completed image emerge. One kimono can produce many different images according to the obi and accessories the wearer chooses to bring to it. This is how old kimono can continue to look fashionable, and why a 100-year old obi may still be worn. Wearers continually use kimono to create new and inspiring images through which they are able to express fashion sense, personal style, and a sense of Japanese identity.

Bibliography

Cliffe, S. (2010) "The Ironies of Japan Going into Trousers." *The International Journal of Costume Culture*. Vol. 13. No. 2. pp. 160–8.

Dalby, L. (1993) *Kimono: Fashioning Culture*. New Haven, London: Yale University Press.

Evans, C. (2003) *Fashion at the Edge*. New Haven, London: Yale University Press.

Fukui, S. (1984) *Momen Kouden. (Cotton by Word of Mouth)*. Tokyo: Housei Daigaku Shuupan Kyoku.

Goldstein-Gidoni, O. (1999) "Kimono and the Construction of Gendered and Cultural Identities." *Ethnology*. Vol. 38. No. 4. pp. 351–70.

Gordon, A. (2012) *Fabricating Consumers: The Sewing Machine in Modern Japan*. Berkeley, Los Angeles, London: University of California Press.

Himeoka, T. (2014) "The Gendering of Work and Workers in the Process of Modernizing the Textile Industry." In A. Germer, V. Mackie, and U. Wöhr. Eds. *Gender, Nation and State in Modern Japan*. London, New York: Routledge.

Inui, Y. (2007) *Kimono Gara ni Miru Sensou, Images of War; Kimono*. Tokyo: Tokyo Impact Publishing.

Inui, Y. Ed. (2008) *Sensou no aru Kurashi*. Tokyo: Suiseisha.

Jackson, A. (2000) *Japanese Textiles in the Victorian and Albert Museum*. London: V and A Publications.

Jackson, A. (2005) *Dynamic Lines and Syncopated Rhythms*. In A. Van Assche. *Fashioning Kimono*. Milan: 5 Continents Editions. pp. 30–7.

Kato, M. (1980) "Taisho no Haneri." In T. Kondo. Ed. *Taisho no Kimono*. Tokyo: Minzoku Ishou Bunka Fukyuu Kyoukai.

Koizumi, K. (2004) "Meisen No Kaisouka." In K. Fujii and T. Fujimori. Eds. *Meisen: Taisho Showa no Oshare Kimono*. Tokyo: Heibonsha. pp. 102–7.

Kon, W. (1972) *Fukusou no Kenkyuu. (Clothing Research Collection 8)*. Tokyo: Domesu.

Minami, H. (1980) "Taisho Bunka no Honshitsu." In T. Kondo. Ed. *Taisho no Kimono*. Tokyo: Minzoku Ishou Bunka Fukyuu Kyoukai.

Minnich, H. (1963) *Japanese Costume and the Makers of its Elegant Tradition*.

Nagasaki, I. (2008) *Kimono; Wa no Dezainu to Kokoro, Kimono; Japanese Design and Heart*. Tokyo: Tokyo Bijutsu. Co. Jp.

Nakahara, J. (1970) "Kitsuke no ima, mukashi. Dressing now and then. Onna no Heya." In J. Nakahara. Ed. (2005) *Kimono Dokuhon, Kimono Reader*. Tokyo: Heibonsha.

Shimatsu, Y. (2004) "In the Mountain's Shadow: Japan's Silk Reelers Blazed an Asian Path of Economic Development." *Journal of Mountain Science*. Vol. 1. No. 2. pp. 183–91.

Silverberg, M. (2006) *Erotic, Grotesque Nonsense*. Berkeley, Los Angeles, London: University of California Press.

Slade, T. (2008) *Japanese Fashion: A Cultural History*. Oxford, New York: Berg.

Tsurumi, E. (1990) *Factory Girls: Women in the Thread Mills of Meiji Japan*. New Jersey, Chichester: Princeton University Press.

Yamauchi, Y. (2009) *The Fashion Creation System in Japan, (1920–1930)*. HJBS Working Paper Series. No. 95. pp. 1–33.

Yamauchi, Y. (2014) "Why Was Meisen, Japan's Traditional Working Clothe, Accepted Well in the Market as Everyday Clothes and Stylish Garments between 1900 and 1930?" *Doshisha Shogaku*. Vol. 65. No. 5. pp. 767–81. http://ci.nii.ac.jp/naid/120005428259 (Accessed September 20, 2014).

Yamauchi, Y. and T. Endo. (2010) *Happen to Be Fashionable?: New Practice Creation Thought the Sequence of Multiple Actors*. http:hermes-er.lib.hit-u.ac.jp/rs/handle/10086/18566 (Accessed September 20, 2014).

Yano Keizai Kenkyuu Jo (2012) *Kimono Sangyou Nenshi. Kimono Industry Report 2012–2013*. Tokyo: Yano Keizai Kenkyu Jo.

4 In Press and Picture: Kimono Discourse

The Importance of Publishing

This chapter examines kimono in printed texts, both written and visual. This is important because printed text is largely responsible for the creation of trends and their diffusion among groups of consumers; thus it plays a key role in the fashion cycle. As Chapters 1–3 show, the written word is a key source for finding out about kimono in the past, as even when fabric or garments remain, these alone cannot enlighten us about their usage. Novels, trading documents, and pattern books are key sources for understanding the kimono of past times. From the Meiji period, there are numerous extant garments, but kimono books, pattern books, samplers, and advertising also enlighten us about kimono trends and the roles that kimono played in each period. Such texts also demonstrate how kimono knowledge was framed, and how kimono was taught.

New fashions appear in fashion texts and are also reported in newspaper articles. New texts appear with a fresh appraisal of kimono, and newspapers are also responsible for spreading news about kimono, which is sometimes about new fashion, and sometimes about the kimono industry. This news is not always rational or accurate and, at least in the English language press, sometimes appears to be in the business of reinforcing stereotypes, rather than reporting news. This chapter also reports some new approaches to publishing. These are in the shape of a new idea about documenting old kimono, and new approaches to producing images using computers and publishing them on the internet.

Meiji and Taisho Pattern Books

Pattern books provide excellent evidence for the kind of kimono in circulation at various points in time. In Chapter 2, there was an image of a page from a *hinagata bon* pattern book (Figure 2.5) and also an image of a *shima cho,* stripe book (Figure 2.8). In the Edo period, such books as these were very popular and were widely circulated in urban areas. They functioned as advertising, a way for dyers and weavers to show their works and also an early form of mail-order catalog for choosing kimono. The *hinagata bon* with one *yuzen* design over the whole kimono were produced less often toward the end of the Edo period, as aesthetics changed, and plain kimono, stripes, *nagaita chuugata,* and *Edo komon* increased in popularity. Dyers still produced such drawings as samples of their work and *shita-e,* underdrawings from which to work. Formal kimono in the period usually had *susomoyo,* a design on the bottom of the hem, and sometimes on the sleeve area, see Figure 4.1 which is an ink drawing from a series from a dyer's workshop.

Often, a separate pattern is seen on a padded hem. Kimono were still worn in layers on special occasions, which can be seen in the gorgeous woodblock print from a *hinagata bon,* in Figure 4.2.

Throughout the Meiji period, stripes and woven patterns continued to be popular, and below is a sample book for choosing *kasuri.* The samples in the book in Figure 4.3 are not actually woven but are painted onto black cloth.

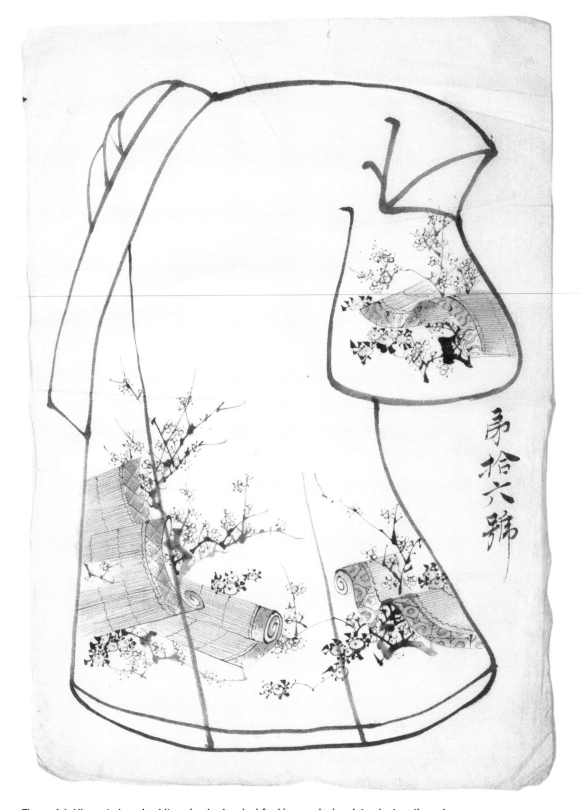

Figure 4.1 Hinagata bon: koshita-e (underdrawing) for kimono design; late nineteenth century.
Source: Property of the Author.
Photo: Todd Fong.

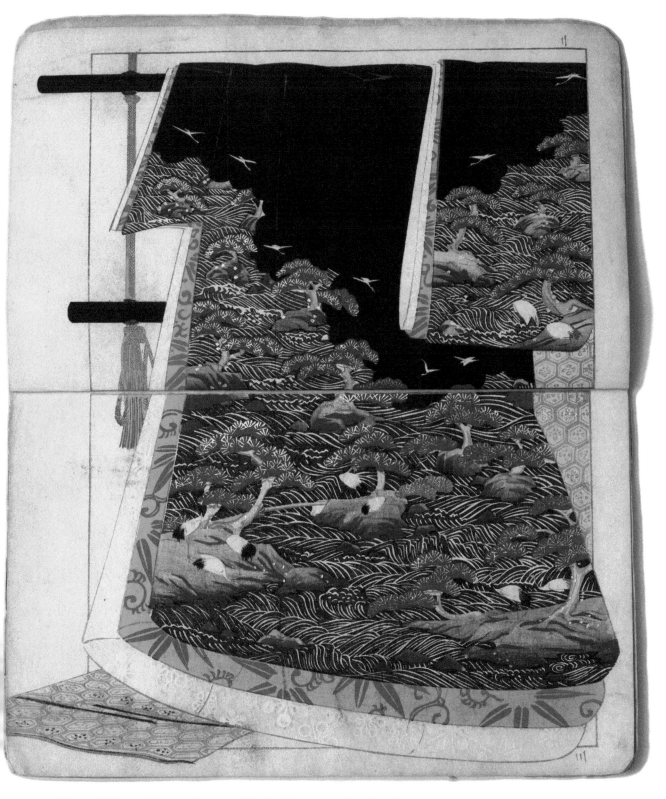

Figure 4.2 Hinagata bon: colored woodblock print; late nineteenth century.
Source: Property of the Author.
Photo: Todd Fong.

Figure 4.3 Kasuri cho: late nineteenth century.
Source: Property of the Author.
Photo: Todd Fong.

Figure 4.4 Stencil yuzen pattern book: 1920–1930s.
Source: Property of the Author.
Photo: Todd Fong.

Sometimes, dyers had books of samples of their work that they could show to customers. The one below shows typical Taisho period stencil-*yuzen* patterns. Dyers' pattern sample books continue to be produced by individuals and workshops, but it is possible that they will become obsolete, as increasingly archives of designs can be produced and stored in digital format. Preserving such documentation is an important project because of the information they provide about fashion circulation and about the craft techniques used in making garments.

The Kimono in Advertising

Edo Period

The word "*koukoku,*" advertisement, was not used until the Meiji period, but actually kimono were being advertised before then. Just as Edo people were sensitive to their *iki* style in clothing, they showed a similar discernment in other aspects of their lives. They disliked any message that was brazen, forceful, or vulgar. Because of this sensitivity, messages were "discretely wrapped." *Nishiki-e,* colored ukiyoe woodblock prints of actors, beautiful women, and famous scenes were very popular in the mid to late Edo period and were regularly used as vehicles for advertising. Posters of famous actors would have the name of a specific kimono shop, or a sign or crest in the background, or a brand name dyed on a jacket collar worn by the actor. It was subtle product placement. *Nishiki-e* showing beautiful women dressed in carefully patterned kimono of the latest styles walk in front of a kimono shop. Behind the figures, the crest of a kimono dealer can be seen in Figure 4.5.

Small posters that subtly advertised kimono sometimes included calendars on the picture, to make sure that the customer kept the poster up all year, and some were in the form of a game board, *e-sugoroku,* parchese, or ludo picture dice game where players make their counter travel around a board as shown in Figure 4.6.

Figure 4.5 Edo Suruga Echigoya Nishiki-e: colored woodblock print of Edo Suruga Echigoya.
Source: Property of Isetan Mitsubishi Holdings.
Photo: Advertising Museum, Tokyo.

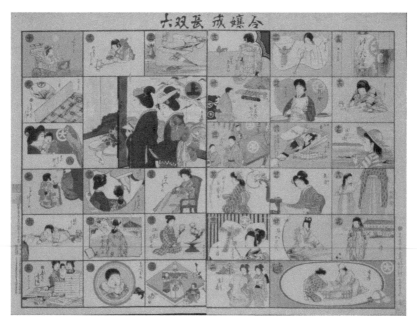

Figure 4.6 Rei Jou Seichou Sugoroku: growing-up dice game for proper young ladies.
Source: Property of Dai Maru Goufuku Ten.
Photo: Advertising Museum, Tokyo.

These items were given as presents by kimono dealers to valued customers, especially for New Year. By making the item useful with a calendar or game, the message was implanted in a casual and low-key way, and such gifts worked to improve the image of the company. Shops had elaborately carved wooden signboards outside, with products' and makers' names on them. All figures at this period were seen in kimono.

Meiji Period

In the Meiji period, *nishiki-e,* posters, and calendars were still used as forms of advertising. However, in some of the Meiji period images, western accessories and a few western outfits can be detected among the kimonoed figures, indicating that sophisticated people were experimenting with wearing western items. Messages still tended to be indirect, with signs, family crests, or flags inside the pictures. Often, one *nishiki-e* would advertise a whole range of products. A famous poster of the popular actor Ichikawa Danjuro Iraya by Toyohara Kunichika shows him standing in front of a wall, which has posters for more than ten different products on it. In addition to the *nishiki-e* woodblock prints, *e-bira,* picture flyers, came into common use. Many of these had generic designs, with standardized pictures, and a space for the details of the shop on one side. Others, however, were specially designed to sell a specific product. The wooden signboards of shops were sometimes painted as well as elaborately carved. The Meiji period saw the rise of letterpress technology and lithographic printing which led to mass production of newspapers and also enabled the easy production of color posters. These developments precede the start of advertising agencies.

Taisho Period

As Chapter 3 showed, after the rebuilding of Tokyo following the 1923 Great Kanto Earthquake, consumerism escalated. Japanese were buying into a modernist lifestyle. The department stores with their trend hunting committees set themselves up as the center of leisure, culture, entertainment, and new trends. They published their own magazines advertising their latest products, and they also advertised themselves with posters. Usually, these had pictures of kimonoed women on them. Sometimes, these figures hold models of the department stores, and sometimes the buildings appear in the background. As kimono remained standard women's wear throughout the period, it was naturally a normal image in advertising in the early twentieth century. Kimono-clad women were used to advertise a wide range of products as well as kimono itself. Drinks, household goods, books, and magazines were all advertised with women in kimono. If western clothing was high fashion, one would expect more images with western clothing, but at this period advertising shows that kimono, and especially *meisen* kimono, are in style.

Established in 1872, Shiseido was the first company to specialize in western-style beauty products and was famous for its well-conceived advertising campaigns. Its beauty products were advertised using images of both western dress and kimono, thus appealing to the widest possible audience. In the fascinating image Figure 4.7, the western dress is a throwback to a bygone era, and the kimono embodies the more contemporary art nouveau line. However, the kimono is relegated to the far edge of the picture, with the western dress taking up the majority of the space. The picture is ambiguous, with the placing and spacing leading us to believe that western dress is more important, but showing the kimono as high style in opposition to a clearly theatrical or ancient form of western attire.

Taisho advertising assumed that women wear kimono. Even when targeting an overseas market, the kimono was used. Images for the overseas market contrasted sharply with advertising for the home market, tending to be much more formal, sometimes with traditional hairstyles, and with *maiko* or *geisha* suggesting a kind of self-orientalization. The advertisement for Nippon Yusen Kaisha (NYK) shipping line in Figure 4.8 is for the overseas market and shows three girls wearing their best formal dress.

Contemporary Kimono Discourse

Academic texts represent a small amount of the vast and growing discourse on kimono. Books of essays on kimono are also popular, such as Kikuchi Ima's (2003) *Fudan no Kimono no Tanoshimikata, How to Enjoy Everyday Kimono*. Kikuchi is one of the most prolific writers and illustrators on kimono, has published more than twenty books and is contributing regularly to some of the mainstream kimono magazines. Her writing is aimed at young adults and those who want to wear kimono for everyday life, and accordingly she encourages the use of lower priced garments made of cotton, wool, etc. Self-help books form a large part of the market. These include how to sew kimono, how to wear it, how to live with it, how to coordinate it, and how to turn it into western clothes. In the English language collections, catalogs and glossy coffee table books are popular. Atkins (2005), Van Assche (2005), and Dees (2009) works are typical. Lavish and visual, they focus on a period of history previously underrepresented, the early twentieth century. Most earlier histories ended when western dress arrived at the conclusion of the nineteenth century. Okazaki brings us up to date with a 2015 photographic text that features both those who work in traditional modes and who exploit new technologies of production and art, crafts, western dress, and cos-play inspired by kimono. Since the 1990s, a wide range of new kimono publications has appeared, demonstrating increasing interest and development in the kimono world.

Figure 4.7 Poster for Shiseido makeup products.

Source: Property of Shiseido Art House.

Photo: Advertising Museum, Tokyo.

Figure 4.8 Poster for NYK. Shipping Line by Koiso Ryohei.

Source: Property of Koiso Art Club.

Photo: Advertising Museum, Tokyo.

Academic Texts

Historical costume, folk costume, and textile studies concentrate largely on the material properties of clothing. Folk costume studies document the clothing of ordinary, working people from farming and fishing communities. Often, they reveal textile production or patterning related to a particular geographical area, and they therefore have significance especially in anthropological studies. However, the label "folk costume" is problematic in the same way that the word "tradition" is. It tends to deny a dynamic evolving history and places emphasis on unchanging forms and repeated ancient customs, seeming to exist outside time. Signs of fashionable development are not to be expected in folk costume studies even though such clothing does slowly evolve. Fashion is rarely to be found in those studies which focus on textile techniques, such as those which explore *shibori* tie-dyeing, *roketsu zome* batik, or other decorative processes.

Investigations that take the kimono as the starting point for an examination of an aspect of social history have been referred to in the history chapters of this text. Nagasaki, Kondo, and Maruyama are considered to be contemporary experts of kimono and its social history. Below are outlined the contributions of researchers who are writing in the English language.

Minnich

Minnich wrote what remains the most thorough historical study of the kimono published in English in 1963. The research for *Japanese Clothing and the Makers of its Elegant Tradition* was conducted in conjunction with the Japanese kimono historian Nomura, whose kimono collection belongs to the Japanese National History Museum in Sakura, Chiba prefecture. It goes into great detail about many aspects of kimono history and development.

Dalby

Dalby's 1993 *Kimono* succeeded in enlightening the western reader about both the kimono's social history and its deeply signifying dressing system in an interesting way, perhaps for the first time. She documents the Heian period kimono in great detail and includes chapters on Edo fashions and the kimono system today. But Dalby made a statement about the kimono that was disputable even when it was published.

> Kimono was becoming more and more representative of tradition. From Taisho on, youfuku continued to change, according to fashion, while kimono froze into the set tableaux we see today. (Dalby 1993:129)

Dalby writes of kimono as fashion in the Edo period. However, assuming a smooth transition to western dress in the Taisho period, it becomes for her anti-fashion. Chapters 1–3 demonstrate that there is much evidence to show that kimono continued to be popular with the majority of women until around 1950 not only in the anthropological writings of Kon but also in the form of popular press such as posters, sewing, and style books. These provide additional evidence that points to the fact that kimono remained popular at least until the Second World War. Even though the kimono industry was still in severe decline when Dalby's book was published, the signs of revival were already there, at least in Tokyo. There was evidence of micro trends such as colored collars and *tabi* socks on sale, which demonstrated that kimono had not become traditional or frozen but was still evolving in fashionable ways. Perhaps because Dalby was immersed in the world of the *geisha*, which in the Edo period represented high fashion but now represents a surviving old tradition, or perhaps because she examined in detail the rules of the kimono dressing system from a kimono school, or perhaps because she was situated in Kyoto not Tokyo, she failed to notice the beginnings of a revival.

Goldstein-Gidoni

Another researcher who has perceived the kimono as a non-fashion item is Goldstein-Gidoni. Her research focuses on the kimono as used to denote Japaneseness in traditional weddings and to genderize young women in a kimono dressing salon. "… the kimono that is wrapped around the female body has become a national symbol of traditionality" (Goldstein-Gidoni 1999:352). She supports Dalby's argument that kimono is about tradition and not fashion. However, neither Dalby nor Goldstein-Gidoni were researching kimono in everyday, casual settings. Ceremonial clothing is usually conservative and conventional, not the place to look for fashion of the runway or street variety. Their findings are not representative of kimono in everyday life, just as historic books of *noh* theatrical costume are not indicative of what normal townspeople were wearing in the streets of Edo.

Assman

Assman's academic study (2008) made a comparison between the kimono-wearing group, *Kimono de Ginza,* and a conventional kimono school. This groundbreaking study explored how kimono was used as a tool for building relationships, consumerism, and play in *Kimono de Ginza,* which Assman calls a postmodern group. Assman compared this kimono group with the (so-called) traditional kimono school establishment, which is structured and hierarchical. She took a wardrobe studies approach, interviewing group members and students at a kimono school. The fieldwork was done in 2005–06, and since then many new groups have sprung up, meaning that the situation has changed since her work was published. Further work on the everyday, in line with wardrobe studies, is called for, and further investigation of kimono centered groups is necessary to draw any conclusions about them.

Slade

This is a text that must be discussed, though it is not a kimono text. Slade's *Japanese Fashion, a Cultural History* (2009) is important because it is an example of the western-centric bias that continues to trouble fashion theory. Slade explains fashion within Japan as a product, and even a producer of modernity. His history starts at the beginning of the Meiji period (1868) when western clothing was introduced to Japan for the first time, completely ignoring the possibility that Japan already had its own fashion system in place. Thus this text aligns itself with those who argue that fashion was imported from a western center, when the social and economic conditions were right. While a Japanese fashion history without kimono appears to be a bizarre exercise, the justification is that Slade sees kimono in the Meiji period as an invented tradition against which modernity was measured. Invented tradition, according to Hobsbawn and Ranger (1983), is when a traditional practice dies out and later a new tradition starts and appropriates the long history of the old, even if relatively disconnected. They give the example of the Scottish kilt, a fairly new invention, or various lace hats in France, reinvented for a tourist market. Slade writes:

> Modernity everywhere repeatedly clothes itself in reconstructions of the past, and Japan was no different, recreating a national costume and inventing traditions to authenticate this past and to authenticate the very idea of Japan itself. (2009:5)

Unlike the examples above, the kimono has been continuously in use. Slade does not explain why kimono, worn by everyone, all the time until the Meiji period, could suddenly become invented tradition. As Chapters 2 and 3 have demonstrated, kimono had been continuously evolving throughout its history. Slade found that western fashion theories did not account for western fashion in the Japanese case. Unlike in the West, enlightenment and modernity happened at the same time and were introduced from abroad. Everything became polarized as native or not, *Wa,* Japanese, or *You,* western. The reasons for changing into western clothing in the Meiji period were largely political and made the most conventional and conservative groups into leaders of the new, enlightened fashions (Cliffe, 2010). However, those changes remained in the upper classes, with many women later reverting to native dress. The majority of women were completely unaffected by such developments. Slade does briefly discuss the kimono in the Taisho period, observing that modernity was felt in kimono:

> By the Taisho period, the department stores started the marketing of trends in kimono designs, and what was once a symbol of tradition became part of the system of capitalism and the artificial creation of demand that is the modern fashion system. (2009:132)

Slade's statement is problematic in two ways. First, since the seventeenth century, Japanese dye houses had been generating superbly new and original designs and also developing new textile making techniques. Edo period kimono makers were already innovation experts. Not only that, but they were also adept at marketing, exploiting the new printing technology through the use of *hinagata bon,* an effective marketing tool that enabled fashion trends to spread like wildfire among townswomen. Neither technical innovation nor marketing were new in the world of kimono. Second, even if one agreed with Dalby and Goldstein-Gidoni's proposition that kimono is a symbol of tradition now in the twenty-first century, it is completely illogical to argue that in the early twentieth century, kimono was "once a symbol of tradition." Kimono, in its many varieties, was the only clothing that existed until western clothing arrived in 1868, and it was what almost everyone was wearing, men in private, and women in both public and private spheres at that period of time. It was kimono, rather than western clothing, that embodied new and modernist aesthetics with its art nouveau and art deco designs, and a fashionable *meisen* kimono was what every girl desired to wear at least until the 1930s, and possibly even later. The kimono embodied modernism and was not a symbol of tradition at all, but an embodiment of new and exciting designs, color schemes, and new textile developments.

Milhaupt

Milhaupt's contribution on the modernist period, published in 2014, is in her excellent understanding of the relationships between kimono and marketing, and also of the relationships between Japan and other countries when kimono were made for a non-Japanese market, an area also studied by Kramer. Although contemporary popular kimono literature is touched on, the text falls short of grasping the milieu of kimono since 1950.

Comparison of Two English-Language Kimono Guides

In addition to coffee table books, histories, and academic works, there have been two texts published for those non-Japanese who would aspire to wear kimono. They could be considered to be beginners' guides to kimono. A comparison was conducted between these two guides which were published twenty-nine years apart; *The Book of Kimono* by Yamanaka (1982) and *The New Kimono* by The Editors of *Nanaoh* (2011). This proved an excellent tool to examine how the framing of kimono knowledge has developed in the last thirty years. It provides strong evidence of new trends and values in kimono. Yamanaka is the head of a leading kimono *kitsuke gakuin,* dressing school, and this book was the standard tool for non-Japanese to learn about the kimono and dressing before the rise of the internet. A comparison of the chapter headings of *The Book of Kimono* and *The New Kimono* reveals significant differences in the two works, which evidence a major shift in the kinds of knowledge that are considered important for new kimono wearers.

In *The Book of Kimono,* Figure 4.9, understanding a large amount of meta-knowledge is considered essential for anyone to approach the wearing of kimono. This includes the history of kimono, dyeing and weaving types and techniques, formality rules, kimono etiquette, kimono care and cleaning, correct posture, and knowledge of men's and children's dressing techniques. The "curriculum" is designed to create the correct, competent, and informed kimono wearer. The dressing process is shown in a total of sixty-two separate illustrations, from underwear to finished outfit. It has been suggested that the purpose of this is actually not to help one wear kimono but to prove the impossibility of it, and therefore the superiority of the Japanese who are the only people who could possibly master such a complex process.

In contrast with the approach outlined above, in *The New Kimono*, Figure 4.10 stories from kimono-wearing women, advice about coordination and shopping are privileged. There is no section on history, specific dyeing and weaving techniques, dressing men or children, etiquette, nor anything about formal kimono or family crests. Abstract knowledge is replaced with stories of real women who wear kimono. Knowledge is framed as something that is passed on from kimono wearers to non-wearers in the form of women's stories or friendly advice.

The first book could be considered a grammarian's approach, and it accords with the kimono schools' vision of passing correct knowledge of kimono (their own system) to future generations, whereas the second text has shifted from a rule-governed approach to a more natural one where experienced women give inexperienced women advice. A Comparison of the contents of the two texts is shown in Chart 4.1.

Contemporary English-Language Newspaper Articles

Occasionally, English language newspapers, both inside and outside Japan, run articles about the kimono. Often these articles are marked by sensationalism. "Kimono Making in Japan is a Dying Art" from the *Daily Telegraph* in 2010, "Can Kate Save the Kimono?" from the *Guardian* in 2012, which is accompanied by a photo gallery of "The Decline and Fall of the Kimono," "Japan's Silk Farms Withering Away" from *Asia News Network* in 2015, and "Old Ways Prove Hard to Shed" from *The New York Times* in 2015. The accuracy of some of the journalism is to be questioned, and these articles paint negative and one-sided pictures of the kimono world. However, these articles draw attention to some of the genuine problems in the industry which Japan has to face, or it will certainly lose some of its textile craft heritage. "Old Ways Prove Hard to Shed" addresses the antiquated distribution system that is strangling the kimono industry. It highlights the case of *Oshima Tsumugi,* an expensive handcrafted woven cloth made on islands off the coast of Kyushu. A total of 20,000 craftsmen were involved in making *Oshima Tsumugi* a generation ago, but now only 500 people do so. The production process is complex requiring about thirty steps, and the work is divided up among individual specialists, so if one link in the chain disappears, production will stop. After production, the complex distribution web means that the kimono sell for high prices in Tokyo, but the weavers can hardly make a living, and those involved in the processes that prepare the threads for the weaving make even less money than the weavers. Even so, the islanders are bound into a network of obligations and feel that they are unable to break free from the system. "Japan's Silk Farms Withering Away" highlights the shrinking and graying of the silk industry, which is also an difficult problem. Grants to set up new businesses have largely failed to stop the demise of the industry as it is hardly possible to make a living from growing silk worms. The article says that in Gunma, the largest silk producing area, the number of farmers has dropped from 2,500 in 1960 to 26 in 2014. The average age of the farmers is about 75, and few have successors. Considering that in 1920s Japan was the world's number one exporter of silk and had 2.2 million silk farms, there is very little left.

Figure 4.9 Cover of *The Book of Kimono*.

Source: Kodansha International.

Photo: Todd Fong.

THE

NEW KIMONO

FROM VINTAGE STYLE TO EVERYDAY CHIC

THE EDITORS OF NANAO MAGAZINE

英文版 ニュー・キモノ
着物をもっと気軽に楽しみたい!

七緒 編

講談社インターナショナル

Figure 4.10 Cover of *The New Kimono*.
Source: Kodansha International.
Photo: Todd Fong.

Chart 4.1 Comparison of chapter headings for two English language kimono guides.

Yamanaka Norio *The Book of Kimono* (1982)	Editors of *Nanaoh* *The New Kimono: From Vintage Style to Everyday Chic* (2011)
1. A Brief History From Neolithic times to the present	1. Real Women and the New Kimono Everyday Kimono, How I Caught Kimono Fever, Vintage Summer Style, the World of Wool, New Year Dreams
2. The Kimono Dyeing and weaving, the parts of the kimono, standard size, formal kimono	2. Obi and Zori Choosing an obi, One kimono, Three Obi, Free and Easy—Your Very Own Nagoya obi, An Obi for Spring, My Favorite Zori
3. The Haori and Accessories Outer garments, undergarments, footwear, accessories	3. Coordinating Your Outfit Mom's Kimono Gets a Makeover, A Wool Kimono is Like a Pair of Jeans, Coordination Chic—Your Problems Solved, Spring Tsumugi
4. The Obi Obi development, kinds of obi, obi bows	4. Yukata and Dressing for Summer Yukata—The Summer Kimono, Yukata Tips, The Coolest Summer Accessories, Vintage Patterns for Summer Days, Beating the Heat—Tips and Tricks
5. Putting on Kimono and Obi Preparation, half-collar, tabi, undershirt and half- slip, body pads, full-length under-kimono, kimono, obi, proper kimono appearance	5. A Kimono Day out in Asakusa
6. Kimono for Men and Children Kimono for men, putting on kimono and haori, putting on the hakama, kimono for children	6. Putting on Kimono and Obi
Kimono Care Cleaning, folding	
Kimono Etiquette Posture and movement	
Appendix: The Family Crest	

Source: The Book of Kimono (1982) Yamanaka: Kodansha International The New Kimono (2011) Editors of *Nanaoh*: Kodansha International

"Can Kate Save the Kimono?" is a problematic article on many levels. It declares the kimono to be on the decline and says that only *geisha* and rich women can wear it. It cites *geisha* as being the largest market for kimono. While they each probably own many more kimono than average Japanese, this ignores the fact that the kimono market in Tokyo is much larger than the market in Kyoto due to their relative populations, and also that *geisha* wear one particular type of expensive kimono. The disappearance of *geisha* would have an effect on Kyoto-made *Kyoyuzen* kimono, but no effect whatsoever on the market for woven kimono, polyester kimono, *yukata,* or many other types of kimono. The article is a contemporary example of the worst kind of orientalism. The problems of the kimono world are compounded with *geisha* in a mixed up and misleading way. This article implies that if you wear kimono, you are a *geisha*. The writer completely ignores all the new things that are happening in the kimono world, the fact that the falling market has bottomed out, the democratization of kimono, and the innovative items that are flooding the market. Worst of all, the idea that Kate, Duchess of Cambridge, could be the person who (presumably with some kind of magic wand) saves the kimono is extremely insulting to all the Japanese people who have put so many years of labor and so much devotion and skill into the preservation and development of an extremely sophisticated garment that evidences the highest qualities of textile production. Orientalism is alive and well in western journalism.

Kimono Magazines

An excellent way to discover what is happening in the kimono world is to review the popular press. Women's magazines emerged in the late Meiji period, with *Fuzoku Gahou.* This was Japan's first visual magazine, including both illustrations and photographs. It ran for twenty-seven years, 1889–1916, and covered history, geography, war themes, and disasters as well as clothing and popular culture. After the Great Kanto Earthquake, *The Woman's Graph* was released. At one yen, it was an extremely expensive publication, and it was specifically aimed at wealthy women. It was a beautifully designed photographic magazine, and it ran from 1924 to 1928. The photographs often featured people from well-known families at leisure and revealed their homes and gardens as well as their clothing. The key themes of the magazine were culture and modernity, and it was designed to be a trendsetting magazine. Some of the cover images were created by the famous Japanese graphic artist and painter Yumeji Takehisa.

In the Showa period, popular writer, fashion designer, and feminist Uno Chiyo published *Style. Style* was the first magazine that was devoted to fashion. It was about eighty pages long, and the contents included short illustrated stories; pages on both Japanese and foreign films; interviews with well-known figures; advice on coordination; and new trends in seasonal clothing, hairstyles, skin care, and accessories. Each edition has several full-page photographic portraits of women, usually clad in kimono. They are stylish *geisha* from the Shinbashi or Kagurazaka areas of Tokyo, and popular actresses from *Shochiku* or *Nikkatsu* film studios. The early editions feature many full-length exotic-looking ball gowns, which decrease over time. New features arrive such as a double spread that visits the house of a well-known figure with photographs of their interior and garden and also a double spread discussing well-known couples. In both of these features, the women are mostly seen wearing kimono, and sometimes the men too. The image of a man content and relaxed at home is a man in kimono. Kimono is also seen in the advertisements in the pages of *Style. National's* iron and baby iron are advertised regularly with a woman in kimono, as are *Meiji* food products, *Pigeon* desserts, *Steel Man, Tonne* and other permanent waves, *Calpis* drinks, *Kinchoriki* insecticides, *Perman* soap, *My Skin* and *Kuraya* skin cream, *Misetto* cameras, *City* white skin paste, *Sankyo's* hair tonic, *Grande Beauty Parlour,* various other hair treatments, a face whitening tool, and traditional wigs. Also advertised with a woman in kimono is a product that claims to produce a western-looking double eyelid.

Today, there is a huge amount of literature published regularly about kimono in Japanese, including several glossy magazines with wide circulations. These largely feature expensive formal kimono photographed in exotic hotels, Japanese gardens, or other exquisite locations. *Utsukushii Kimono,* by Hearst Fujingahou, and *Kimono Salon,* by Kategahou, are the two major standard publications. They were both quarterlies, but now *Kimono Salon* comes out biannually.

Utsukushii Kimono

The magazine with the largest circulation is the quarterly, *Utsukushii Kimono, Beautiful Kimono,* which, according to its website, has a circulation of 110,000 as of 2014. This is a beautifully produced glossy, showcasing high-end craftsman-made formal kimono. This is considered to be the standard orthodox kimono magazine by kimono lovers, and on its website (http://www.hearst.co.jp/brands/kimono accessed 24/7/2014), it claims that 30 percent of its readers are in some way involved with kimono-related occupations. According to this website, a readers' survey showed that the average age of readers is 52.9 years old, 82.3 percent are married, 88 percent are in home owning families, 9.3 percent have a second home, and 21.1 percent own an imported car (a status symbol). Readers also report having money available for hobbies and consumerism, and 62.5 percent of readers report that they buy more than two kimono per year. These cost several thousand pounds. The women who read *Utsukushii Kimono* can therefore be described as coming from a relatively wealthy, middle-class background. The magazine was first published in 1953, and turned sixty in 2013, so developments in high-end kimono since the war can be traced through it. To commemorate its sixty years, it published a special fashion history of kimono from Showa to Heisei periods. As this is the orthodox and formal end of kimono wearing, it seemed like an unlikely vehicle for revealing fashion change. In reality, it showed fashion change very well. Using the special kimono history magazine, and several copies of *Utsukushii Kimono* from the 1970s and the 1990s for comparison, it is easy to perceive how kimono has changed over time.

For example, pictures showing kimono of the 1950s show the kimono of the period being very self-conscious and aware of western dress. Subtle shading or seasonal flower designs are notable for their absence and highly contrasting geometric designs, which can be worn at any time of year, are popular. There is a preponderance of black and white, red and yellow, and practicality is seen not only in the modern, wear anytime designs but also in the very short boyish hairstyles of the models in the photographs. Japan was under American occupation until 1952, and perhaps this could explain the western look of these kimono images. In the photographs, the models' poses are like western fashion models' poses, with the weight on the back leg and the front leg stepping out. These poses are unlike kimono poses at any other period in time. In the 1960s' photographs, the bob grows longer and larger, and a parallel can be seen with the beehive style that was worn with western clothing.

By the 1970s, a more feminine image is presented in *Utsukushii Kimono* with long hair tied up, and more traditional and seasonal designs returning to kimono. It is a more kimonoesque style than that of the 1950s. White, pastels, and bright colorful kimono are typical of this period, and natural makeup with peach or beige lipstick is popular. By this time, the cover model is kneeling down. Japan was becoming wealthier (heading toward the bubble of the 1980s), and there was a class of women, for whom *Utsukushii Kimono* is published, who were privileged enough not to have to work. Wearing kimono, doing tea ceremony and flower arranging became useful cultural assets when looking for a desirable husband.

In the images in the 1990s, the designs on the kimono became larger again. Collars were still white, but lipstick and nails were red. Accessorizing oneself was becoming more important. The models no longer looked at the camera but gazed away into space. The poses are more demure than those of the 1950s and are similar to contemporary kimono poses. A leather kimono coat, sign of conspicuous wealth, is included. The kneeling woman on the cover remained. This was still the bubble era, when wealthier women did not have to work. Finally, in 1999, the cover model stood up. While this may not have seemed significant at the time, it also happened to be the year that the first kimono-wearing group came into existence. The year 2000 marks the real start of kimono renaissance, and it is significant in hindsight that the cover model of the most established kimono magazine stood up. The kept woman of the bubble years was becoming an irrelevant image to women, as more women had to go out to work and contribute to the family economy. It was no longer an attractive image for working women who love kimono and who lead an active lifestyle.

Kimono Hime

For young women looking for a fashion magazine, however, *Utsukushii Kimono* is completely irrelevant. To them, it is a magazine for older women who are wealthy and cultured, and perhaps not concerned with fashion at all. It portrays a completely different world from theirs, one that they feel that they cannot take part in. Its very classiness creates a sense of alienation from kimono for ordinary young girls. The *mook,* magazine book, *Kimono Hime* by Shodensha, came out in the spring of 2002, with the purpose of putting kimono into the context of a fashion magazine. Rather than distance, the aim of the magazine is to create familiarity with kimono. It differs from *Utsukushii Kimono* in several important ways. While *Utsukushii Kimono* is on glossy paper, *Kimono Hime* is on more ordinary matt. The ages of the models are much younger than those in *Utsukushii Kimono.* Some of them are well-known fashion models or actresses. The kimono featured are antiques, used kimono, or kimono by popular new brands which make kimono of cotton, polyester or ready-to-wear kimono which are all more affordable than the high-quality couture items in *Utsukushii Kimono.* The kimono are often coordinated with shoes, handbags, ribbons, lace, or other items which would be thought of as accessories that go with western clothing rather than kimono. The whole look of the production is colorful and is about being cute and fashionable rather than being elegant and distinguished. *Kimono Hime* carries very little in the way of articles or advice. It is not about advising kimono wearers or teaching them rules. It is about enjoying kimono as a part of fashion. As it predominantly comprises photographs, it is not only bought by Japanese kimono fans but many non-Japanese too.

The first edition of *Kimono Hime* sold out almost immediately, and since then it has come out at least once a year. It was so radically different from the established magazines that it created quite a stir among kimono wearers. Since its inception, several other books and magazines have been published with similar styling and kimono in them, but *Kimono Hime* continues to be one of the most popular kimono publications on the market. By making kimono into fun and colorful fashion for young people, it has succeeded in reaching a younger generation. It has also considerably influenced the way that kimono is worn in the streets. Rather than sticking to the rules, young people can be seen wearing kimono with sandals or boots, caps or hats, belts on their obi, and carrying their usual handbags. In this way, it has encouraged creativity among young kimono wearers.

Nanaoh

Another popular *mook* is *Nanaoh.* The meaning of *Nanaoh* is many kinds of thread, and the name was chosen because kimono is a joining of many threads, and the joining of many cultures and ideas, like threads, together. It is also a girl's name, so it has a deeply personal aspect about it. It is not only a concept but a girl and her kimono life. In addition, the magazine's subtitle is "A life starting with kimono." This was the concept that drove the editor, Suzuki Yasuko, when she founded the magazine at the end of 2004. Unlike *Utsukushii Kimono, Nanaoh* is not a glossy but a matt magazine, and it features casual kimono in ordinary locations, urban or rural, often in slightly nostalgic settings. The readership is also younger than that of *Utsukushii Kimono,* with thirties to forties being the majority. *Nanaoh* has four regular seasonal editions and occasional special themed editions. At the present time, the circulation is about 30,000 copies. It contains about 128 pages and includes regular features on recipes, walking in the town, art, and film in addition to its kimono content. Figure 4.11 shows the spring 2015 cover of Nanaoh.

大人の「髪形」入門
「柄遊び」の世界へ
木綿着物で、花より団子?
着物バッグ3カ条

七緒 nanaoh
着物から
はじまる暮らし

vol. **41**
spring
2015
プレジデント
ムック

創刊10周年
特別企画
『七緒の
和トセトラ』
イベントのご案内

特集

「柄遊び」のトビラ

動物柄が好きなもので——ふじわらかずえ
「ときめき柄」と帯で再会?——小川糸 ほか

「着物バッグ」私の3カ条

特集
がんばりすぎず、でも、きれい

着物と、髪形。

提案 切らずにボブ
提案 大人アップ
提案 上品ショート ほか

連載
中川ちえ 文様のふしぎ
つるやももこ 手仕事ラッピン
和食部「ふきのとう」
book 又吉直樹
cinema 浅生ハルミン（ピース）
art 橋本麻里

Figure 4.11 Cover of *Nanaoh* magazine, Vol. 41. Spring 2015.
Source: Property of President Inc.
Photo: President.

Suzuki was working on a magazine concerned with food in 2004, and through looking at various dishes had become interested in the tea ceremony. One day, at her practice, a woman wore a cute kimono which Suzuki really liked, so the woman took her to a used kimono shop, and they looked at many kimono together. This opened a new world for Suzuki. She had not realized that there were so many different colors and designs on kimono, and she was hooked straight away. When her company told her to make a *mook* on any one subject she liked, she thought that it would have to be kimono. It's theme was "starting kimono," and the idea was to place it between the formal and expensive, crafts-based *Utsukushii Kimono* and the fashion-based *Kimono Hime.*

In 2004, people were reevaluating Japanese culture. In the face of the increasing complexity of Japanese urban life, there was a longing for a lifestyle that was simpler—something from the Showa period that felt of home, of mother, of nature, and good home-cooked food. Suzuki wanted the magazine to fit the zeitgeist of the times. She was influenced by Muji, in that the style and designs were not overpowering but were an expression of something that was simple, easy to live with, and useful for people. The kimono in *Utuskushii Kimono* were not only expensive but were for those who admired gorgeous things. They were another world for Suzuki. The cute kimono of *Kimono Hime* expressed a strong fashion style sense that was also another world. There was a need for an ordinary kimono magazine, not about formal expensive kimono, nor just for fashion. Suzuki wanted to make *Nanaoh,* a magazine about ordinary kimono for ordinary people. She wanted it to be a resource for the kind of information that mothers once had, but no longer did. She sees it as almost an anthropological project, the pursuit of the ordinary kimono that one can easily wear and easily fits into an ordinary lifestyle without trying hard. The first issue had many patterned kimono in it, and some antiques too, but gradually the magazine has featured more plain and simple kimono. Perhaps this is because more and more western clothing is plain and not patterned.

Suzuki sees *Nanaoh* complimenting *Kimono Hime,* one providing fashion inspiration, and the other the important information about dressing, kimono care, coordination, and shopping. Suzuki feels that the mood of the times is changing, so she has started to make some creative changes to the production. A new larger format and an altered logo have been adopted. Also, for the first time she has done special on coordinating formal wear, which is a new venture, as *Nanaoh* has only featured informal wear. Suzuki also wants to work on more enjoyable coordination and styling. Until now, she feels that the mood of the Showa period of a simple nostalgia influenced the *kitsuke* and style of the magazine. Now she feels that Japanese are getting more interested in looking further back in history, to the Edo period. It was a period of exciting and creative dressing, innovation, and play. She herself is becoming interested in this history. It marks a shift for *Nanaoh,* and it will be exciting to see where and how the influence of the Edo period takes the magazine into the future.

arecole

There is a small monthly magazine called *arecole* on the market. The title of *arecole* is an adaption of the Japanese word *arekore* meaning this and that. The magazine's title has no capital letter, suggesting its informality, and, by chance, when the K was changed to a C, it looked like school in French. Producer and editor Hosono Miyako thinks this is a lucky coincidence as her aim is to teach about kimono "this and that" through the use of her magazine. Before publishing *arecole*, Hosono was copywriting for adverts. Many of her customers had kimono businesses, and she made the flyers that they sent out by direct mail to their customers when they had special events and sales. Hosono noticed that the flyers were almost all the same, and she thought it was necessary to send some kimono information with them, to encourage people to be interested in kimono. She wanted them to realize that kimono is fun and fashionable. So she started making a small magazine, which could be sent with the flyers, for customers to read and enjoy, containing useful kimono information. In figure 4.12 Hosono shows edition 112 of arecole.

Figure 4.12 Editor Hosono Miyako holding *arecole*.

Photo: Hosono Miyako.

Hosono has been producing *arecole* monthly since 2005. It stopped at one point when the publisher no longer wanted to publish it, but she went independent and since then has been producing it herself. She says that there are several differences between her magazine and other available kimono magazines. Her concept is that *arecole* starts from the wearer and contains information that they want and need. It is not about promoting or selling expensive kimono. Sometimes she includes used kimono, or cheap fabrics, which once caused a kimono business to stop ordering it. It is one of only two monthly magazines. Hosono aims to give a little information each time, so that people come back and look again at the next edition. Being monthly means that she can bring out information in a timely way, capturing what has just occurred, like a fashion magazine does, rather than show what was on sale three or even six months ago.

Initially, the circulation increased to 12,000 copies, but then dropped down to 5,000. It was especially bad during the period of the Great East Japan Earthquake disaster. However, after she took up self-publishing, and after the earthquake crisis was over, it has been steadily growing again, and it now stands at about 7,500 copies; 1,200 are individual subscribers, and the rest are kimono shops. It is not distributed through the normal channels. Kimono shops buy *arecole* in bulk and send it to regular customers. It is also available for sale in kimono shops, and it is possible to subscribe through the internet. Because it is distributed in this unique way, it is not possible for it to carry advertisements as it would then be seen to be promoting specific companies. This means that the pages are full of genuine content so even though the magazine is small, it has plenty of reading matter. Hosono believes that the small size of her magazine is a plus point. While other kimono magazines are glossier, they are also expensive and heavy. Hers is light, small (handbag-sized) and sells for 400 yen. She also believes that as she herself is a real kimono wearer, she does not need to hire stylists to work on the magazine, like other magazines do. She has her own concept, and she mostly does this work herself, but sometimes uses stylists to get a change in taste and feeling.

Kimono, she says, flies on two wings: one is fashion, and the other is culture. It does not fly without either one, but the fashion must come first. It is through fashionable and fun images that people will become interested in kimono, not through formal pictures. This is why casual is the core of her magazine, although formal wear is sometimes featured. There is a message in the magazine for kimono sellers as well as wearers. Sellers, she says, still believe there is a hierarchy with silk at the top and then linen, cotton, wool, in a vertical line, but for today's wearers, this line has little meaning. They do not necessarily value silk more than other fabrics. For some wearers, the design is more important than the cloth. Others choose according to the occasion, but wearers see a horizontal axis and not a vertical one. She wants her magazine to show the kimono sellers what the wearers are interested in.

Sons of kimono businesses used to go and work in other kimono businesses to build experience before coming back home to take over the family business. But now the number of businesses has dropped, so they are more likely to go and work in another industry before eventually returning to take over the family business. These men have not studied how to operate kimono businesses nor have they built up the necessary networks and connections to make successful kimono businesses. They have no experience to read the trends. Hosono has held study groups for such kimono business people. Some of them are surprised that the daily ordinary looking things in her magazine are popular with younger customers today. However, because of all the ceremonies Japan has, and the theater, weddings, and formal occasions, Hosono does not believe that formal wear will die out. The culture of kimono is really important, she says. You can learn all about Japanese culture through kimono. But kimono is returning to its original way of being, mostly casual, fashionable wear.

Kimono Stylists

fussa

Figure 4.13 *fussa* **discussing kimono.**
Photo: Nakajima Hiromi.

Nakayama Asako and Kikuchi Sae, featured in Figure 4.13, who met by chance when they were both learning kimono tailoring on a training scheme for reemployment, have made the styling duo, *fussa*. They both wanted to work with kimono because it is work one can do all one's life, and both of them thought that it would be an advantage to have tailoring skills. The real purpose of the course was to train people to go into *wasai jo,* tailoring businesses, but the reality is that such places provide low pay and hard conditions, and people give up the work quickly. After training for one year, both women went into kimono businesses connected with used as well as new kimono because they liked antique kimono.

They would meet after work to talk, and in 2002 the *mook Kimono Michi* (which became *Kimono Hime*) was published, and they got together to discuss it. They had never seen a magazine devoted entirely to antiques before, and they were really excited about it. They thought the dressing was unrealistic with sleeves and hems popping out at the edges, but they were fascinated. They decided they would like to make a more realistic version of this type of book, and then they had a chance with someone that they knew in publishing. They decided to call themselves *fussa,* which means a bunch, like grapes, because they could do many things, tailor, dress, styling, etc. They published their first book, *Kimono no Tabi, A Kimono Trip,* in 2003. This book was successful and created a demand for their work as stylists. This was a new profession at the time. Kimono magazines used a dresser, and perhaps a tailor, but a kimono stylist was something new. Both women left their jobs to pursue this work full-time. *fussa* had skills in dressing, styling, and tailoring so they could be useful on photo shoots. They began to get work for fashion magazines with kimono specials, and they did kimono styling for a kimono club fashion show at Waseda University.

When *Nanaoh* started out in 2004, they were interested in the new magazine and curious about the plain, striped, and checked kimono that were featured in its pages. They went to see the editor, Suzuki, and asked her about the concepts behind it. They started to get their work in *Kimono Hime* in 2005. They now also regularly work for *Nanaoh,* recently working on covers as well as various pages. They feel that their job is to bring some more color and excitement into the magazine, but they tone down their look for *Nanaoh's* readers.

Their second chance to make a book came in 2004 with the publisher *Ondori,* now defunct, which specialized mainly in home sewing books. This book, *Kimono Techo (Kimono Handbook)* was like a manual or textbook for those who wanted to start wearing kimono. The design was simple and the text straightforward, but they were able to use many antique kimono in the photographs. They worked for magazines, for advertising and commercials, and were often called to dress for TV programs. In 2008, they made another book, *Okiniiri Kimono Junikagetsu, Kimono we like for twelve months of the year.* This was published as part of a series about Japanese culture and the months of the year. They found this book their most satisfying production. They were free to find any kimono they wanted to represent each month and introduced some small Japanese items and techniques for sewing kimono. They were able to control the design and photographic aspects of the book as well as the styling of the kimono.

fussa were given some opportunities to create new products too. They made a series of *yukata* in a collaboration with a kimono maker, and then Kyoto Marubeni asked them to make a series of bags and *zori*. These went with Kyoto Marubeni's *furisode* collection and were cute and colorful to appeal to young girls. However, after the Great East Japan Earthquake and Tsunami disaster, their work suddenly decreased. Many events were canceled, and magazines went out of production. The recovery has been slow, and there is still less magazine work than before. Many fashion magazines that used to have a kimono special at New Year and a *yukata* special in the summer, now only have the *yukata* one. Fewer people are buying magazines. They look for their ideas and inspirations online and buy through the internet, which is often cheaper. *fussa* sometimes does a commercial that will be shown on TV, in a shop, on a website, and poster. This means that they spend about three whole days in the studio.

fussa believe that color and pattern are the life of the kimono, and they feel it is sad that kimono is losing its connection to the seasons. Plain, stripes, and checks are just like western fashion, and kimono is getting closer to western fashion. They want to continue to do cute styling that is realistic and wearable. They also make efforts to suggest new items when coordinating for magazines. They believe that kimono artisans are not good at selling the items they create and do not know how to market them to young women. Sometimes the makers are really old men, who know nothing about fashion. If *fussa* put the kimono and obi together with various accessories, this inspires some young people to order the whole package. Things that they have suggested have become items for sale in the following season, which makes them feel happy. They would like to start their own brand, publishing books and also making accessories and even kimono, but they need a sponsor in order to take that next step. *fussa* have made a big contribution to the kimono publishing scene and continue to inspire younger kimono wearers with their fresh and colorful coordination and goods.

New Directions in Publishing

So far I have discussed conventional forms of publishing that have been used for many generations. There are some people, however, who are experimenting with new forms of, or new angles in, publishing. Several of the wearers featured in Chapter 6 have their own blogs or web forums that are accessed by thousands of fans. Here I introduce three people who are making significant contributions in the area of publishing, one in Europe, one who stands between Europe and Japan, and one in Yamagata, Japan.

Linda Kentie

Linda Kentie was born in Amsterdam in 1983, and she works as a senior interface and graphic designer at a game company, designing interfaces, characters, and animation for games. In addition to games, she likes Japan, fashion, and art. This interest in Japan started in her childhood. Her mother bought her Japanese comics in Dutch, and there were many anime cartoons on Dutch television too. She started drawing her own manga from when she was fourteen, and when she was eighteen, she joined a *doujinshi,* amateur self-published magazines or manga, group. They wrote in English and Dutch. This fascination with Japan led her to an anime convention where she bought her first kimono in 2004. She did not actually think of wearing it properly though until her friend was getting married in 2008. She wanted to surprise her friend by giving her a kimono and dressing her in it. She found this to be a really satisfying experience, and since then she has been trying to learn as much as she can about *kitsuke.* In 2011, she decided to start a Kimono Jack club in Holland. This is one of the most active kimono groups, and it continues to grow. Each year there are visits from kimono groups from other countries: England, France, Czechoslovakia, and Japan. Linda appears in Figure 4.14.

Linda learnt much about kimono from the Immortal Geisha online forum, run by Naomi Hormozi (see Chapter 6). Many of the kimono fans there became friends, and they were all very inspired by the kimono *mook, Kimono Hime.* This was the inspiration for Linda to publish her own online magazine, together with Michelle Winberry. First she saw Michelle Winberry wearing kimono in a way that looked like Kimono Hime style and, as a surprise, she took her photo and photoshopped it, so that it looked like a page from *Kimono Hime*. They both thought it would be fun to send it to the editor of *Kimono Hime,* but she heard that publication had stopped, so they were disappointed. However, Linda, Michelle, and their friends began to talk about how sad it was that there was no more *Kimono Hime* and decided to make a tribute magazine to it. This was the beginning of making the magazine. At the end of 2012, they gathered a group of online kimono friends from around the world: Lyuba, Naomi, Carolien, Sekita, Kim, Mei-ing, Tülay, and Heidi. As everyone was in a different country, coordination of the project was very difficult, and it took two years for the completion of the first magazine, but *Go Hime* finally came out in spring of 2015. Michelle appears in Figure 4.15.

Linda and Michelle both work in the design industry, and they are responsible for most of the design in the magazine. They are happy that *Kimono Hime* is still in production as this *mook* is their inspiration. They are planning further editions of *Go Hime,* and they would like people to send in their photos and keep it interactive. They will publish guidelines and screen the entries. This will give other people a chance to show off their skills at coordination and styling. They have many new talented people working with them and hope that they will be able to get edition two out in less time than it took for volume one. If possible, they would like to make a new one each year, but it is difficult because they all live in different places. They have not really thought about publishers as it is a tribute magazine to *Kimono Hime,* but they would consider an offer if it happened to come along. For now they love making it, and it is a labor of love and not about making money. Figure 4.16 shows the cover of Go Hime.

Figure 4.14 Linda Kentie.
Photo: Alex Kentie.

Figure 4.15 Michelle Winberry.

Photo: Robert Winberry.

Figure 4.16 Cover of *Go Hime*.
Photo: Linda Kentie.

Figure 4.17 Girl wearing meisen.
Photo: Magdalen Méan.

Figure 4.18 Girl drinking sake.
Photo: Magdalen Méan.

Figure 4.19 Girl with a book.

Photo: Magdalen Méan.

Magdalen Méan's photographs of models in kimono, see Figures 4.17, 4.18 and 4.19, are quite different from other kimono photographs. They seem to create a living space for kimono, where it is still worn. What started out as an exercise in documenting a collection has turned into the making of her art, a photographic record leading toward the eventual publication of a beautiful book that will bring alive early-twentieth-century Japanese fashion in a unique way, with a quite different approach to that which other kimono texts have taken.

A resident of Japan for sixteen years before relocating to Switzerland in 2015, Magdalen worked in some very interesting positions. Her latest one was teaching drawing and design at a school for *Hakata* weaving for eight years. *Hakata* weaving is usually used to make obi. She had this position because she was previously teaching design in a fashion school, had previously won two design awards in Switzerland, and because she had a large collection of kimono. The school needed someone with an international outlook, who could also understand kimono culture, and Magdalen was the perfect person for that job. Before this, she was doing fashion design freelance for two Japanese clothing companies, writing as a columnist for fashion magazines and holding exhibitions of her photographs. She also did a little buying and selling of old kimono and restoring of old kimono chests. Her time in Japan has been used mainly within fashion and textile-related businesses, and now she has over ten years of teaching experience too. During that time she has been growing her kimono collection, which she started when she was a student. Originally, she went to a shrine flea market in Kyoto and bought several boxes of kimono, and kept them with a friend. Unfortunately, the friend did not have enough space and put them on the balcony, where they got soaked in rain and were all lost. In spite of this setback, her collection is now very extensive, numbering well over 700 kimono.

Magdalen actually thinks that the first Japan influence was way back in her childhood, when her mother read her *Peter Pan.* It had illustrations by Arthur Rackham, an Edwardian illustrator whose strongly art nouveau world of young girls, fairies, trolls, ogres, and mystical creatures inhabit magical forests. Like most of the art work in Europe at that time, Rackham was strongly influenced by the work of Japanese *ukiyoe* artists. Magdalen is convinced that this art work led to her interest in Japan. She went on to study Japanology, linguistics, and art history in university, and with a mother in fashion and a father in film, considering the nature of the project Magdalen is undertaking, one wonders if it was not all in her genes. She liked designing and making clothes, and she made a line of western clothes incorporating Japanese fabrics. This seemed very original in the West at the time, and she received an award for her design work. She continued doing this and received a bursary from the Swiss Federal Office of Culture to continue her design work in Japan.

Eventually, however, Magdalen became dissatisfied with the work she was doing. Although she loved the fabrics, she hated to cut up kimono. If she cut up kimono and made clothes, they would be fashionable for only a few years, whereas if she kept them as kimono, then they could be worn for several generations. Magdalen began to strive for something more in the kimono itself, rather than just the quality of the fabrics and the patterns. As her collection grew, her friends told her she should document it. However, she did not want to put her kimono on stands and photograph them. This is how they are always shown in kimono texts. Magdalen finds that this decontextualizes the kimono and fails to show it as originally intended. This is because the kimono is never worn alone but with an obi, a collar, an *obi-age,* an *obi-jime, tabi,* and *zori,* footwear. The kimono is only one part of a carefully constructed composition.

Magdalen strives to put kimono into a meaningful context, not only by using models but also by placing them in meaningful space. She attempts to make a diorama, a microcosm representing the world outside, with its social and political meanings. She wants to show the changes in the early twentieth century, read through the language of the kimono. Although it started out as a way of documenting her collection, it has led to what was primarily a kimono collection becoming a collection of accessories and obi too, and also a collection of documentary photographs from which she derives inspiration. This has become her life work.

Then she needed to find locations. This has led her literally to go and knock on people's doors, asking if they would let her use their house as a location for a photo shoot. Of course, some people have slammed their doors in her face, but other people have listened, and some have given her space. She feels that taking photographs inside these old houses is important because she is concerned about the architectural environment. Japan does not do a good job of saving its historic architecture, and many lovely old houses just get torn down if there is nobody who wants to live in them or who can pay the expensive inheritance taxes on them. Magdalen feels that the wooden houses, with their tatami rooms, are an important part of the culture that led to the development of the kimono as a garment, and that having the houses in the photographs is important for understanding the garments, and well as meaning that the house will still exist, at least in photography.

As the work has progressed, Magdalen has become more and more concerned with issues of authenticity. She seeks to get just the right look for the time, and it concerns her if the clothing items are not of the same period, or if something out of place gets into a photograph. She finds a tension between this desire and the reality that what she is making is a reconstruction, and both her and all her team are inevitably influenced by their being creatures of the twentieth century. The progress of the work is very slow because she needs a whole team of people to make each photo shoot work. It is almost like filming a scene from a film. First, she has to secure the location for the day, and then get up to three models, up to three dressers, a hair dresser and makeup artist, lighting, and camera gear. She has to keep the whole crew fed for the day. The maximum number of scenes she can realistically shoot in one day is three or four. She does not necessarily select the finest items in her collection for the photo shoots, rather items that will go together to create something that looks authentic. To a certain extent people know about the artists who made kimono, but the story of the skills of the women who dressed in them and did all the coordination has not been documented, so it is important to her to highlight this. The Taisho and early Showa periods are fascinating for her, and also the 1950s, which she sees as tumultuous years presenting big changes for women. She thinks these changes are reflected in the bold and bright kimono of the time. She uses *bijin-ga,* Japanese paintings of beautiful women, as sources of inspiration and information, and her photographs can be seen as a photographic version of *bijin-ga.*

Magdalen does not wear kimono very much herself, twice a week at the most, but much less if she is working with furniture or something physical. She compares the renaissance in kimono, and in particular the interest in kimono from overseas, as similar to the interest that there was in the Victorian period when Japanese art works were taken abroad to be shown in great exhibitions. To be inspired by something is a great compliment, and everyone is inspired by things from other places or contexts. Magdalen's twenty-first-century version of *bijin-ga,* the beautifully and carefully reconstructed versions of earlier decades, is sure to inspire and enchant kimono lovers and Japanophiles from many different countries. They will extend the understanding of kimono through their styling and architectural context.

Akira Times

Japan has no beauty, but we need beauty. At the end of the nineteenth century, the whole world recognized the beauty of Japanese art. It became art nouveau and art deco. It was amazing! Now we have no beauty, so I have no choice but to make it.

Akira lives and works on his parents' fruit and vegetable farm in Yamagata prefecture, in the north of Japan. He left school at fifteen and stayed at home, feeling sick and depressed because he felt he didn't fit in modern Japan, a world with no beauty. He has always been interested in fashion, and whatever he wears is a statement. Dressed in black trousers, turquoise shirt, pink bow tie, stripy braces, and a straw hat together with a largely shaved head and a huge woolly beard, he cuts a stylish figure.

Akira says that people are looking for culture but they are looking in the wrong places. They are looking backward, trying to preserve things. But that is not how culture is born, and it will never make new culture. Fashion becomes culture over time, but culture does not make new fashion. The only reason for looking at old culture is to try and surpass it with something new. When Sid Vicious dressed up as a punk in the 1970s, it was new and was rock. Copying the same thing now is not. Rock is always rolling along on your own way, making your own fashions, and that becomes culture.

Akira dislikes Kyoto because it is appears to be only concerned with preserving old culture and making money from it. As this stance will never lead to any new culture being born, it has no attraction for him. He finds the Japanese desire for their own culture embarrassing. People cling to Kyoto because they have nothing of their own. He calls it Kyoto sickness and says that Kyoto is killing culture. You can never make culture by trying to save culture. He is fascinated by Mishima Yukio and his pure stance. Mishima believed that preserving culture is not culture, you are culture. Akira agrees with him. Why don't they try and make a new, more beautiful Kinkakuji? He wants to make his own Kinkakuji and burn it down. It is all about breaking taboos. Akira has one really valuable kimono that is considered a cultural treasure which he says he will wear till it falls apart.

Perhaps old temples and buildings are suitable in Kyoto, but Akira lives in Yamagata, north Japan, a world where boots and sneakers are the most appropriate footwear. The area where he lives has nothing, but it also has everything you need to survive: food, clean air, space, and water. Tokyo has everything, but if you don't have yourself, it is nothing. He believes it is because he is in Yamagata, on the periphery, and not in spite of it, that new ideas can come. He says it will take him at least another five years to achieve the level that he wants artistically, or perhaps it will take a lifetime. He will not be involved in selling his work because then he would not have time to make it. So many young artists waste time having shows and selling themselves instead of working to improve their art.

Akira also has no interest in the kimono wearing group movement. He thinks it's really uncool to meet just because you are wearing kimono. Do people get together because they are wearing western clothing? Wearing kimono does not make you Japanese, just as wearing western clothing does not make you western. He doesn't feel that he has anything in common with people just because they wear kimono. He thinks they are all about the surface, attracted to the concept of preserving culture. The person who wears kimono stylishly, he sees as a cultured Japanese, and that person will wear western clothing well, too. One has to keep one's own style. Trends will become old, but style will last forever. Japaneseness, *wa,* is a spiritual thing, it is not about the surface.

Akira believes he is already ahead of the kimono stylists. Everyone does the same *kitsuke* and the same coordination. It is all safe, and it has no edge (or poison as he puts it). We need a kimono hero. Akira laughs and says that he is just playing at being a hero. Usually, one can get hints from fashion magazines, but he believes he is already ahead of the magazines. You cannot make fashion unless you play really hard. There is nothing to inspire him in the contemporary scene, so he looks back, and he wants to be at the level of Klimpt, Mucha, and Yumeji. They are the artists he admires, and his style hero is the Frenchman, Serge Lutens. He was Shiseido's image creator in the 1980s and 1990s and worked with the Japanese model and actress Yamaguchi Sayoko. Akira's images appear in Figures 4.20, 4.21 and 4.22.

Figure 4.20 *Akira Times* montage.

Photo: Kimono Times.

Figure 4.21 Girl riding Miharu Goma, traditional wooden crafted horse, from Fukushima.
Photo: Kimono Times.

Figure 4.22 Sheila with banana telephone.

Photo: Kimono Times.

Akira first posted his own kimono image in 2011. He hoped that some professional designer/photographer in Tokyo would take up the challenge, but although his images attracted a lot of attention, no one did. So Akira continued to make *Yamagata Kimono Times*. People began to look for the real magazine, but there is only the cover that he makes and posts online. He liked the idea that the internet can bring into reality something that did not exist before. *Yamagata Kimono Times* is the main theme, but he produces images with other titles, such as *Yukata Times, Kakashi Times, Scare Crow Times,* a reference to his rural background, and *Yumeji Times,* a reference to the Japanese artist Yumeji who was a big influence on the Shiseido company. He collaborated with Ueda Mieko, a makeup artist who used to work for Shiseido, on the image for *Yumeji Times*. He has also done a collaboration with Mamechiyo, who produced a Mondrian style kimono for him. Through *Yamagata Kimono Times,* Akira wants to reveal true Japanese classical style beauty.

No money passes hands in Akira's production of images. The kimono, he says, is number 2. The most important thing is the person, so he picks his models carefully, and he has to feel a spiritual connection to them. Anyone can make a pretty photograph of a pretty girl, that is easy. Akira uses ordinary looking girls, not models. Some people cannot come 10 km across town to visit him, but someone will travel 1,000 km from Osaka, and the fervor of that stance is true beauty. Akira is entirely untaught, and says he hates study, but he undertakes every step of the whole process by himself. Each of these processes he has learnt entirely on his own. He uses only ordinary kimono in his images. Kimono got too great. It has to be ordinary or it can't change. Akira doesn't use many accessories or padding of the kimono. "I can use padding and make a pole," he says, laughing. He prefers to bring out soft, warm feminine lines. He says he is playing about with images from what he calls "the lost years" for kimono. The years after the war, when people stopped wearing it because it became too great. He wants people to rethink their stance about kimono. Akira publishes a blog, *Yamagata Kimono Times* and *No Kimono, No Life*. The concept behind *No Kimono, No Life* is contemporary fashion. The images in *Yamagata Kimono Times* and *No Kimono, No Life*, are split between those that are striving to express a kind of Japanese mode beauty and those that are pop and fun in character. Akira wants there to be more fun and craziness in culture, and this is reflected in the wooden horse image with the kimonoed rider. The wooden horse is a typical product of Tohoku area, but he has made it into a crazy, pop culture image.

As for the details of image creation, they remain Akira's secret. In the old days, there was a limit to how much you could find out about an artist. Now, because of the internet, it is hard to keep anything secret so there is no mystery or aura. He wants to keep the production of his works surrounded in mystery and romance. Japanese people still have the potential to make great beauty, and the kimono still has the potential to change. Things are moving fast because of the internet. He wonders whether his work is done. He says that, "life with an extra dress-code must be so exciting," but actually he is thinking about burning down Kinkakuji. Finally he laughs: "By the way, everything I have said is a lie. I am just a guy who loves women ….."

Publishing Past, Present, and Future

This chapter has discussed kimono discourse and has demonstrated how texts continue to change over time. The first kimono books were *hinagata bon,* showing kimono patterns and trends in the style of these paralleled changes in the garment. They grew in size, added color and different angles. When *yuzen* dyeing on silk kimono was forbidden for merchant class women, *shima cho,* books of stripe samples began to emerge. Meiji-period pattern books were larger and were composed of colored woodblock prints. By the Taisho period, stencil *yuzen* sample books showed the new chemical dyes that had been imported from Europe.

The chapter shows how kimono have been utilized in posters to advertise a range of everyday products since the Edo period. This continues today with kimono featured in posters advertising everything from McDonalds coffee to the latest flat screen televisions. It is especially seen in advertising for drinks, the domestic tourist industry, and health care products for the elderly. English-language newspaper articles have drawn attention to kimono industry problems, but the journalism is sensationalist and sometimes orientalizing, failing to research the whole picture, and writing in a stereotypical and uninformed way.

The three recent kimono magazines discussed here all contrast with the standard *Utsukushii Kimono* and are a challenge to its world, not only of high craftsmanship, but also of its exotic and gorgeous formality. They are aimed at younger readers, and *Kimono Hime* breaks the borders by suggesting new kimono fashion mixed with western items, while *Nanaoh* and *arecole* bring kimono into the everyday world. All three magazines were created by individual women who decided to use their knowledge of the publishing industry. They created magazines that they thought filled niches which were not being filled by magazines on sale at the beginning of the 2000s. The editors of these magazines are pioneers who have inspired thousands of others to bring kimono into their wardrobes and their daily lives. It is striking that these women were not kimono experts but people who knew the publishing industry well, and who all experienced a deep emotional response to their encounters with the kimono.

The fashion historian Breward (2003:11) has argued that there is a trend for more fashionable, "coffee table books," in which visuals and description replace discussion. This trend is apparent in kimono histories, some of which are based on iconic garments. While visual texts might lead to a bias toward iconic garments and thus be problematic in historical studies, photographs in contemporary studies make them more attractive and interesting for the consumer, though Breward argues that they trade visual appeal for scholarly discussion.

Another apparent trend is to highlight everyday dress. Previously overlooked kimono of the early twentieth century, particularly of cheap, *meisen* kimono, are the subject of several new texts and are examples of this trend. Within popular literature, there is a clearly defined move away from the formal, traditional, and expensive as revealed in glossy magazines, to the modern, casual, and cheap as revealed in matt magazines.

A third change is in the way that understanding of the kimono is framed. This change is from a theoretical and rule-governed approach, favored by kimono schools who would seek to police "correct" kimono wearing, to a more natural kind of knowledge, which is passed on from experienced people to inexperienced people in the form of anecdotes, advice, and stories. This is evidenced in the production of new magazines, such as *Nanaoh, arecole,* and also in the production of *The New Kimono,* which privileges personal knowledge and experience, whereas its predecessors privileged theoretical knowledge. Throughout the new literature, a younger and less wealthy target group is assumed. Contemporary popular publishing is bringing kimono back into daily life.

The importance of women in publishing is abundantly clear in this chapter. Women are finding new opportunities for work and are creating their own spaces and places within the kimono world. It did not take kimono experts to make new magazines that have heavily influenced the kimono world. It took women with experience in publishing. Kimono stylists have a huge influence and *fussa,* with their tailoring and styling skills helping to shape the images of kimono that are seen in magazines and commercial media. When thinking in terms of fashion, it is inconceivable that it should be left to elderly males to lead the way into the future. Artisans need the marketing and styling knowledge and skills of these women in order to create and to market their work.

Recent advances in publishing show commitment to the kimono as a fashion item rather than as a symbol of a traditional Japan. Linda and her friends have taken a new step in kimono publishing, generating new ideas from outside Japan. Because of their location, there is opportunity for them to incorporate many different influences, giving infinite possibilities for the continuation of the magazine. Rather than being historical or documentary as most English language texts have been, *Go Hime* is suggesting new ways of wearing kimono for new consumers across the world. The work of Magdalen is not repeating old formal photographs but is an attempt to reconstruct the wearing of everyday kimono at an earlier point in time. It is a challenge to those who document and photograph the kimono to do so in a way that gives a more accurate rendition of how the kimono would have been seen and used. Both Linda and Magdalen are drawing on past worlds to create something new. Both Magdalen's world and the world of Akira use ordinary kimono to create extraordinary worlds. They are both searching for authenticity, kimono as expressions of ordinary people, rather than a fake or formal front defined by a social role. Akira's message, however, is full of poison.

It is Akira who is calling for a break with the past, a radical revision of our values and thinking about kimono. There are no taboos for him. Akira wants to take a tiger's leap in the dark, to burn everything down and remake it. Akira says that to make new culture you have to play really hard. He plays on the cutting edge. Akira has perhaps understood better than anyone else how to go about making the future of kimono. It remains to see how far the industry itself and kimono wearers will understand and take up his challenge. It will certainly be necessary for something to die to create new culture, and it is a call for kimono wearers to rethink kimono wearing practice. Kimono wearers are increasing in number and are becoming younger. Ultimately, these magazines, even if they feature old or used kimono, are affecting kimono sales. It remains to be seen how kimono publishing will develop, whether it will become safe or remain on the frontline, but authenticity and fashion are certain to be central themes in the future.

Bibliography

Akira Times. http://akiratimes.exblog.jp/i7/ (Accessed July 22, 2015).

Asia News Network. http://www.asianewsnet.net/Japans-silk-farms-withering-away-66938.html (Accessed February 15, 2015).

Assman, S. (2008) "Between Tradition and Innovation: The Reinvention of the Kimono in Japanese Consumer Culture." *Fashion Theory*. Vol. 12. No. 3. pp. 359–76.

Atkins, J.M. (2005) *Wearing Propaganda*. New Haven, London: Yale University Press.

Breward, C. (2003) *Fashion*. Oxford, New York: Oxford University Press.

Cliffe, S. (2010) "The Ironies of Japan Going into Trousers." *The International Journal of Costume Culture*. Vol. 13. No. 2. pp. 160–8.

Daily Telegraph. (2010) http://www.telegraph.co.uk/news/worldnews/asia/japan/8082875/Kimono-making-in-Japan-is-a-dying-art.html (Accessed February 15, 2015).

Dalby, L. (1993) *Kimono*. New Haven, London: Yale University Press.

Dees, J. (2009) *Taisho Kimono, Speaking of Past and Present*. Milan: Skira Editore.

Editors of Nanaoh. (2011) *The New Kimono: From Vintage Style to Everyday Chic*. Tokyo, New York, London: Kodansha.

Fussa. (2003) *Kimono no Tabi*. Tokyo: Wailea Publishing Co.

Fussa. (2004) *Kimono Techo. Antique Kimono wo Jibun rashiku Kikonasu*. Tokyo: Ondori.

Fussa. (2008) *Okiniiri Kimono Juunikagetsu Kurashi no Saijiki*. Tokyo: Pie Books.

Guardian. http://www.theguardian.com/lifeandstyle/ 2012/oct/08/can-kate-save-kimono (Accessed February 15, 2015).

Guardian. http://www.theguardian.com/lifeandstyle/gallery/2012/oct/08/decline-and-fall-kimono-in-pictures (Accessed February 15, 2015).

Goldstein-Gidoni, O. (1999) "Kimono and the Construction of Gendered and Cultural Identities." *Ethnology*. Vol. 38. No. 4. pp. 351–70.

Goldstein-Gidoni, O. (2000) "The Production of Tradition and Culture in the Japanese Wedding Enterprise." *Ethnos*. Vol. 65. No. 1. pp. 33–55.

Goldstein-Gidoni, O. (2001a) "Hybridity and Distinctions in Japanese Contemporary Weddings." *Social Science Japan Journal*. Vol. 4. No. 1. pp. 21–38.

Goldstein-Gidoni, O. (2001b) "The Making and Marking of the 'Japanese' and the 'Western' in Japanese Contemporary Material Culture." *Journal of Material Culture*. Vol. 6. No. 1. pp. 67–90.

Goldstein-Gidoni, O. (2005) "The Production and Consumption of 'Japanese Culture' in the Global Culture Market." *Journal of Consumer Culture*. Vol. 5. No. 2. pp. 155–79.

Hobsbawm, E. and T. Ranger. Eds. (1983) *The Invention of Tradition*. Cambridge: Cambridge University Press.

Kikuchi, I. (2003) *Fudan no Kimono no Tanoshimikata. How to Enjoy Everyday Kimono*. Tokyo: Kawade Shobo Shinsha.

Milhaupt, T.S. (2014) *Kimono: A Modern History*. London: Reaktion Books.

Minnich, H. (1963) *Japanese Costume and the Makers of its Elegant Tradition*.

New York Times. http://www.nytimes.com/2015/02/10/world/old-ways-prove-hard-to-shed-even-as-crisis-hits-kimono-trade.html?smid=fb-share&_r=0 (Accessed February 15, 2015).

Okazaki, M. (2015) *Kimono Now*. http://www.hearst.co.jp/brands/kimono (Accessed July 24, 2014).

Slade, T. (2009) *Japanese Fashion, A Cultural History*. Oxford, New York: Berg.

Van Assche, A. (2005) *Fashioning Kimono*. Milan: 5 Continents Editions.

Yamanaka, N. (1982) *The Book of Kimono*. New York, London, Tokyo: Kodansha.

5 Making and Marketing

The Kimono Market

The market research data in the "Kimono Industry White Paper" revealed the strong downward trend in kimono sales after the economic bubble in the mid-1980s, see Chapter 3, Chart 3.1. The reasons were not only the increasingly poor state of the economy, but, as explained in that chapter, the unwieldy distribution system associated with a crafts-based industry and also the perceptions about kimono being expensive and difficult to wear that had been created by the industry itself. The effects of the kimono renaissance have slowly begun to have an impact on sales. The market as a whole has been on a slight rise since 2012. There are places where this is felt and others where the impact has not yet been felt. The second-hand market has been in existence since before the Edo period. During the boom years, it was rather frowned upon, and Buddhist ideas making the use of someone else's clothing taboo have had a negative effect on the used clothing market in Japan. However, used clothing of all sorts has become much more popular since the 1990s, making the second-hand market into an area of growth. Nakamura Shinichi, the head of Tansu-Ya, the largest chain of used kimono stores, has won awards for his new business model, which he himself says is not new at all. In my *Kimono World* YouTube video, *Kimono Shopping in Tokyo,* he discusses his business mission. He believes that there are millions of kimono and obi lying unused in people's *tansu,* cupboards, and he sees his role as bringing these back into circulation. Nagamochi-Ya, another recycle chain whose founder Ohashi Eiji was one of the first people to show Taisho period style kimono as polyester prêt-à-porter in the fashion shops in Tokyo, as part of his Bushoan Brand, has always wanted to sell kimono as fashion. These two chains are the biggest names in used kimono, but now there is also a plethora of individually owned second-hand kimono shops.

Another area of growth is the rental market, as increasingly graduates of universities have reverted back from wearing their recruit suits in the 1980s and 1990s, to wearing kimono and *hakama* for their graduations. The movement is also now spreading from universities to high schools, junior high schools, and even elementary schools. Even if it is not school policy, some students are choosing to graduate from school wearing kimono and *hakama*. The Japanese-style wedding market is also seeing an upturn. Women are shunning white wedding dresses for a formal kimono. Menswear is another growth area. As one of the interviews below shows, there has been a dearth of options for the kimono wearing male.

The interviewees here come from a wide variety of crafts and businesses and reveal the experiences of those who work within the kimono industry in their various occupations. They discuss how their businesses have been affected by the economy and the kimono renaissance. They point to some key factors which are important for survival in the kimono market today.

Figure 5.1 Silk for one kimono set, in thread form and in cocoon form.

Source: Property of Itoko Silk Gallery.

Photo: Itoko Silk Gallery.

Figure 5.2 Worker weaving silk cloth in the weaving house of Itoko Silk Company.

Photo: Itoko Silk Company. Ltd.

Figure 5.3 Silk bolts at Itoko Silk Gallery.
Photo: Itoko Silk Gallery.

Kitagawa Sachi is a third-generation businesswoman in Itoko Company Ltd., which sells white cloth. Involved with both the production and trading of white cloth, originally this interview was placed between those producing and selling kimono. However, the future of white silk cloth is so crucial to the kimono industry as we know it today, that it must go first of all the interviews. Without white silk cloth, crepes, and satin silks, the kimono world as we know it today would not exist. There would be no formal, semiformal, or informal dyed kimono, no *yuzen, Edo sarasa, Edo komon, muji* plain*, roketsu zome, shibori zome.* If there were no silk bolts then woven kimono and cotton, linen and polyester, very casual kimono would be the only types on the market. For this reason, the story of the white cloth merchant is highly significant for the future of all formal and semiformal kimono. Figure 5.1 shows silk for one kimono.

Kitagawa worked in a trading company importing fashion goods for three years before she decided to work in Itoko company, which her grandfather founded in 1931. Apart from two maternity breaks, she has worked for twenty years, and after her second child she effectively took over company management from her father. The company sells mainly to wholesalers and retailers, and also to some individuals. In 2014, they sold about one-tenth of the amount of silk that they sold twenty years before that, so their business has shrunk significantly. However, the figures since 2011 show a minimal rise. While the number of business players has been decreasing, the number of customers has also decreased. Kitagawa could not say whether the customers are older or younger than previously because some of the older kimono shops have been taken over by active younger people, who are in their thirties and forties and are eager to make a success of their businesses. Other customers are over seventy but are still hanging on to their kimono businesses. They have few customers in their fifties and sixties.

Itoko's founder decided to have the Itoko trademark put on the end of each kimono bolt, which is unusual. Usually, the *yuzen* dyer's name or the area name is on the cloth, but not the supplier of the white cloth. This has proved to be a good strategy, as people find the end of the bolts packed away with the kimono, and they see the name and look for the company. Customers pay more than they used to for a bolt, but buy it because Itoko brand is known as a reliable provider of high quality cloth.

Although in the Meiji period the silk industry was key in making Japan an industrialized nation, only about 1 percent of kimono are now made with Japanese silk. In 1901, there was an ordinance given that there were three types of silk cocoons which were not to be cross-bred but to be kept pure because of their special qualities. One of these was called Matsuoka Hime. Matsuoka Hime is soft with a beautiful luster and is produced in Yamagata, and recently in Fukushima too. When the samurai class lost their special social status in the Meiji reforms, they were instructed to learn trades like other workers. Many samurai gathered and cleared the ground to make a mulberry orchard for the silk worms to establish the Matsuoka Hime silk farm. Used to carrying swords, they had to get alongside farming people and wield farming tools. For Kitagawa, the farm has a significant history, and she feels deeply about the importance of the samurai working together with the farmers to establish the business. Great care has been taken over the years to maintain the fine quality of the silk worms. Not only are the worms farmed here, but the silk is reeled into thread in a factory and is woven into cloth at the same location. This is a unique venture with all the processes happening under the one brand name of Matsuoka Hime. Although the price of this cloth is high, the quality is assured, and Itoko asks the factory to produce new weaves each year. All Matsuoka Hime cloth is sold through Itoko, and a full 25 percent of Itoko's business is selling Matsuoka Hime cloth for Japanese kimono. The other 75 percent of their business is cloth made with imported silk, but all the cloth is woven in Japan, mostly in Tango and Nagahama. Factory weaving is shown in Figure 5.2. At the time of writing, there are only four silk reeling factories left operating in Japan. Two of them are larger factories, which produce reeled silk for export, and two are small scale and reel for domestic use. Matsuoka is one of these.

While Itoko is much smaller than it was in the past, the company believes that innovation is very important. They have twenty staff, four of whom are at a Tokyo office, and two of whom are *zuanka,* designers. They are not trained in graphic design, but in *Nihonga*, Japanese painting. Over the years, they have produced about 3,000 patterns for jacquard weaves, and every year they bring out between thirty and fifty new patterns. One designer is an older man, but the other is a younger woman. They exhibit the new designs in Kyoto and Tokyo in June each year. The company has a six-floor building in Kyoto, the heart of the kimono industry, which used to be occupied entirely by their business. Now they rent out several floors but maintain a small silk cloth museum in the building, as well as operating the company from one floor. There are several weaving businesses operating under their direction. Some of these have successors who will continue the work, but others are aging and have no foreseeable future. Because of this, they are developing new relationships with other younger groups of workers, who will be able to continue to work into the future. Itoko bolts from the silk museum are shown in Figure 2.3.

Itoko is expanding into producing new textiles for use in interiors, especially in the area of lighting. They have developed a kind of organza with jacquard woven lace-like patterns in it, and fused it to a material like washi paper. The fabric is wider than the 38 cm of kimono fabric and has many possible applications in interior design. In collaboration with another company, they have made a product with a layer of organza in glass which they call silk glass. Not only are they creating new products but they are also exploring new ways to market their goods. They deal with other kimono businesses now, but they have also a web presence; a page of their own and a shop on rakuten's network. Kitagawa believes that their web presence is very important for their future business. They are also members of Kyoto Textile Trade Association, the Japanese Silk Foundation, and Kyoto Chamber of Commerce and Industry.

Itoko is involved in the process of trying to persuade the government to allow Japanese domestic white silk cloth to be registered as a traditional craft. Because it is industrialized, therefore made in factories with electrically powered machines, it has not been considered a traditional craft until now, see figure 5.2. Kitagawa would argue that there is still much skill that goes into producing the cloth, from the pattern designs to the finished product, and as many Nishijin obi are also woven on power looms, there is really no reason why Japanese domestic silk cloth should not be registered as a traditional craft. Kitagawa does not believe that making white silk cloth will completely vanish from Japan, though it might all be made from imported silk in the future. The kimono is too important in Japanese ceremonies for it to disappear completely.

However, because of the falling population, she thinks it is possible that the market will continue to shrink. The future of Japanese domestic silk is not secure at the moment, though Itoko is doing its best through the use of branding strategies, to make known the name and quality of the domestic silk products that they sell.

Ishibashi Kouichi—Yunoshi-Ya Steamer

There are many kinds of hidden work involved in the production of a kimono. An unsung but essential part of the process without whom the kimono would not be realized is the *yunoshi-ya,* or steamer. Wherever there are dyers and weavers, there are also *yunoshi-ya.* Steaming fixes dyes and also returns the cloth to a perfectly straight even width, see figure 5.4. Depending on the kinds of technique the artists use, the steamer might be

Figure 5.4 Ishibashi Kouichi: *Yunoshi-ya.*
Photo: Todd Fong.

needed as many as four times in the production of one kimono. Steaming is needed at the beginning to ensure that the cloth is perfectly straight for dyeing, *shita yunoshi.* After this a design is drawn, or a pattern is dyed, other processes are carried out, and then it is steamed again to ensure the cloth is straight again. After the cloth becomes damp, it has a tendency to shrink, and so it must be steamed before the following process. When everything is finished and the cloth is washed, it will be steamed again before being sent to a dealer or tailor.

Ishibashi Kouichi became a *yunoshi-ya* because his father was dyeing grounds for kimono. In those days, all dyers had their own steaming machine. He has been working independently for about fifty-five years. In the early days, he would run the steamer all day. First, he would sew all the *tan mono,* kimono bolts, together into one extremely long strip of cloth. Then he would sit at the steamer and in one day he would steam between 200 and 300 *tan mono.* All he needed to do to survive was to steam the *tan mono.* These days, there are not enough *tan mono* to provide him with work so he only runs the machine for half a day. It is now necessary for Ishibashi to do all kinds of other kimono related jobs, in order to survive.

Ishibashi acts as a *shikai-ya,* a producer, for kimono. A customer can ask him to source cloth or have cloth dyed a specific color, or have the dye removed from an old kimono and get it re-dyed a new color. Someone may want a *mon,* crest, dyeing on their kimono. He sends out the work, then picks it up, and returns it to the customer. Sometimes, he has to think about how to mend a kimono with a hole in it. It can often be hidden by adding small patches of embroidery to the kimono. He also offers cleaning services: *arai hari,* which involves taking the kimono apart, washing it and sewing it back together, and *shimi nuki,* which is stain removal. He also offers a tailoring service. Some customers want their kimono made smaller to pass on to someone else. Ishibashi says that he needs to know about all the processes involved in making kimono, and turn his hand to anything that is required.

Ishibashi's customers are shops, middlemen, individual artists, and kimono wearers. *Yunoshi* has become more expensive than before because there are fewer customers and also because of spiraling fuel costs. He made a company web page a year ago, but he never looks at it. Customers come by word of mouth and they have relationships built on trust. He is not especially happy to have customers from far away. Occasionally, there is trouble, or someone doesn't pay. Then he can do nothing about it because he cannot go there. He prefers local customers whose faces he knows. There are four *yunoshi-ya* working in the Ochiai area of Shinjuku, and another five or six in Nihonbashi. Every other area of kimono production will also have *yunoshi-ya*. When dyers stop dyeing or a *yunoshi-ya* gives up his business, the maker of the steamers takes back the old machines. The parts are used again to repair other machines. These large and expensive machines last thirty to forty years, but some of the parts wear out with constant use. There is only one company left making the machines, so it is important to recycle the parts of the old ones. The *yunoshi-ya* will always be an essential link in the chain of the kimono-making process.

Tanabe Keiko—Edo Yuzen Dyer

Contemporary *yuzen* dyer, Tanabe Keiko, see Figure 5.5, who has been dyeing kimono since 1970, agreed to discuss how things have changed for dyers over the time of her career to date. She became an apprentice to a professional dyeing craftsman after she finished school, in 1969. Initially, she was assigned to more experienced apprentices for two months at a time, and her job was just to sit, watch, and learn from them. As a woman she did not live in, but traveled to and from her home. She was expected to arrive early to make tea and do preparation, help with shopping and housework, and she would leave late, after everything was cleaned up. After two years, her teacher wanted a successor, so he married her to his son, who was not continuing in the profession. So she worked under the name of the son, even though he was not actually dyeing kimono. She worked with her teacher only three years before he died in 1972.

Figure 5.5 Tanabe Keiko: *Yuzen* dyer.

Photo: Todd Fong.

Figure 5.6 Tanabe Keiko: *Yuzen* works.
Photo: Todd Fong.

During this time, she was working on his orders and also making her own kimono, for practice. She did not exhibit or sell under her own name. After her teacher's death, she received advice from a more experienced apprentice whom she followed, but not until the age of forty-seven on her divorce, she could finally begin afresh under her own name.

It is impossible to tell exactly how many *yuzen* dyers are actually working in Tokyo now, as there is no obligation to belong to any kind of professional organization, so many work completely independently. Some dyers also work part-time while holding down other jobs, as to survive by making *yuzen* alone is very difficult. Tanabe belongs to the *Tokyo To Kougei Senshoku Kyoudou Kumiai,* The Tokyo Traditional Dyers Mutual Association. This, the only professional association of *yuzen* dyers in Tokyo, was founded in 1962. She has been active in it since she started *yuzen* dyeing. First, she was an associate, and then after being recommended she became a full member thirty years ago. She is now active on their committee, which meets two or three times a month. There are about fifty-three members and associate members as of 2014, but when she started there were about three hundred and eighty members. The average age of the members is sixty-eight years old, and there are only about five members in their thirties and forties. There are ten women in the association, of whom Tanabe is the longest serving.

There are several other dyers associations in Tokyo, for example the *Shinjuku Senshoku Kyougi Kai,* Shinjuku Dyers Mutual Association, who are mainly dyers of *komon, sarasa, mon,* or plain dyeing. Shinjuku has been the center of Tokyo's dyeing industry since the Edo period. According to their website, in 2014, they have seventy two active dyeing workshops as members. There is also the *Tokyo To*

Senshoku Kougyou Kyoudou Kumiai, Tokyo Craft Dyers Mutual Association, whose website shows thirty four registered members, who are mainly *komon*, *sarasa,* and plain dyers. In addition to these associations, dyers can become *Nihon Dento Kougei Shi* or *Tokyo Dento Kougei Shi,* Registered Traditional Craftsmen of Japan or Registered Traditional Craftsmen of Tokyo. They must have been working in their chosen area for at least twenty years to be considered, and then there is a test to become a registered craftsman of Japan. To become a registered craftsman of Tokyo requires recommendation from a member. The responsibilities that go with being a registered traditional craftsman of Japan include being active in keeping the tradition alive. Tanabe goes as a volunteer to elementary schools to introduce the children to the *yuzen* dyeing process.

Although the antiquated distribution system is one of the reasons for the high price of the kimono, creating the long time lag between production and reaching the market, Tanabe tells me that it has changed considerably from the way it was in the past. She remembers as an apprentice that the first middleman would come to the studio and bring armfuls of white cloth which they would buy. The middleman would return and buy all the kimono and obi made with the cloth, then distribute it to other middlemen, and then it would go to market. She said they dealt with three middlemen from Kyoto, three from Tokyo, and also five or six shops, to whom they sold directly. This system has changed, at least in the Tokyo area. She goes to one of the very few dealers in white cloth and buys the cloth she wants to use. She now sells to one shop and her personal customers, whom she deals with directly. She also told me that another way of selling is to sell to a kimono dressing school. In this case, margins are taken by all the staff in between including the teacher of the student who is persuaded into buying the kimono. The markup on these kimono is very large, and so she does not favor this way of doing business.

Tanabe loves both bright colors and new and interesting motifs. She loves anything beautiful or magical, and she has made kimono and obi with fairies, princesses, glass slippers, ballet dancers, and even people's pets. She produces the designs using conventional techniques, but her world of beautiful and lovely characters has attracted attention. A few years ago these were not so popular, but now she even has orders from abroad. She is never short of customers and was the first woman in her union to receive the top award in their fifty-first annual dyeing exhibition. In the fifty-fourth dyeing exhibition in 2016, Tanabe and another female *yuzen* dyer took the two top awards, testifying to the high quality and originality of work that women are making in this field. Tanabe continues to exhibit regularly in solo and group exhibitions and also teaches workshops and student groups and participates in committee work. Her work is shown in Figure 5.6.

Nasu Sachio—Edo Yuzen Dyer

Nasu Sachio comes from Iwate prefecture in the north east of Japan. From his young teens when he learned about the Meiji period and the industrial revolution in school, he had problems with the idea of progress and what in Japan is generally considered to be a period of great enlightenment. He disliked modernity and progress, and decided that he wanted to make something with his hands. He practiced calligraphy and was skilled with a brush, so after finishing school he packed his bag and bought a one-way ticket to Tokyo where he became a live-in apprentice to a well-known and respected *yuzen* dyer, Arai Terutaro.

Apprenticeship means delivering goods, doing various errands, watching the older apprentices, and practicing calligraphy. He rarely had a chance to work on silk in the ten years he was there. He was the naughty apprentice who neither showed respect nor obeyed his master. Sleeping late and disappearing to go drinking were regular occurrences for him. His master went so far as to say, "I will not teach you. You have to steal the techniques!" Arai's wife, however, would always tell him how the master worried about him. His final graduating piece was a fine line drawing of a garden in Kyoto on calligraphy paper. After that he set out on his own.

Figure 5.7 Nasu Sachio: *Yuzen* dyer.
Photo: Todd Fong.

Figure 5.8 Nasu Sachio kimono: butterflies.
Photo: Todd Fong.

Nasu was successful and had contacts with many middlemen and kimono chains. He made kimono for wealthy *geisha,* for the wives of politicians, and even relations of the imperial family. Although he was living the high life, he found the relationships, politics, and the work pressure very stressful. Thirty years ago, he had a big show at the famous Hotel Okura, which was a great success. But Nasu became ill. He had to stop everything and was in hospital for many months, in danger of losing his eyesight and with serious lung problems. He decided to do a 180 degree turn in lifestyle. He felt the importance of nature for his life and work, and he decided to live as slowly and as naturally as he could. Nasu at work is shown in Figure 5.7.

Now he gets up when the sun does, and he waters the small plants around his one-room apartment. He has no apprentices, no family, and no obligations to anyone but himself. "My job," he says, "Is to make what only I can make." He wants to be like the Edo printmaker Sharaku, who died without anybody knowing anything about his life but left an incredible legacy in his famous woodblock prints. A few years ago, Nasu aimed to follow his master's work, but recently, he believes that he has gone beyond the achievements of his master. He speaks with a single-minded confidence about his mission. Now his teachers are the Edo-period masters of the Rimpa school, especially Sotatsu, Hoitsu, and Koetsu.

He believes that this unnatural, mechanized, and computerized world we live in needs the imperfect work of human hands. He is not concerned with customers and never deals with middlemen now after having some bad experiences with them. He does not even sell to any kimono shops. In 2006, he had a show at a large traditional house in Kamakura, inviting friends and some artists. Since then, he has not publically shown his work. He told me that he needs to sell two kimono a year to survive. He sells a few Japanese-style ink paintings, which pay for him to go drinking. He has just a few private customers but is considering having another show.

Perhaps only older women who have seen many kimono would appreciate his work. The subjects are traditional and sometimes relate to Buddhism, religion or classical themes. His work is painstaking and therefore expensive. The patterning is extremely delicate, and the colors are subtle, see Figure 5.8. He agrees that you would have to look at a great variety of *yuzen* before understanding why his is different, but he strongly believes that he is carrying on an important legacy from the Edo period. He says that there is a cycle, and that interest in his kimono will come around. Kimono is central in Japanese culture. There are no weddings, ceremonies, no noh or kabuki, no dance, and no *geisha* without kimono. If you study kimono, you can understand Japanese culture. His artist's name is *Saiki,* the color demon, but it could easily be the lone wolf. He is a member of no organizations, nor does he exhibit in any kind of group exhibition. He remains poor and lives a simple life but is totally dedicated to his singular vision. He has no concern with marketing, computers, his image, or anything that distracts him from the pursuit of his kimono quest.

Kobayashi Tomohisa—Hikizome-Ya Ground Dyer

Kobayashi Tomohisa, Figure 5.9, is a *hikizome-ya,* a ground dyer. This means that he dyes white cloth, usually crepe or satin. He does the kind of dyeing that is done with a *hake,* a large flat wide brush, rather than dyeing with a *fude,* which is more like an art paint brush and is used for *yuzen* dyeing and calligraphy. Working with *hake* and *fude* are two separate skills and are usually carried out by different people. The *hikizome-ya* dyes plain kimono, collars, and shaded kimono and also backgrounds for *yuzen* or other artists. He has been doing this, "dull work" for thirty-six years. He says it is very hard to learn the work. Formerly, he used to make many of the same item, but now there is less work, so he needs to make only a few of each item. As there is less work than before, it is hard for young people to take it up and increase their skills. Kobayashi has no apprentice. Kobayashi's workshop is shown in Figure 5.10.

Kobayashi has developed his own special dye *kakishibuzome,* made from fermented persimmon juice. Fermented persimmon juice is sometimes used as a finish on furniture or to preserve wood. It is both strong

Figure 5.9 Kobayashi Tomohisa: *Hikizome-ya.*
Photo: Kobayashi Tomohisa.

Figure 5.10 Kobayashi Tomohisa's workshop.
Photo: Kobayashi Tomohisa.

and natural. The process produces rich shades of brown. He says that finally he can make something new. After all these years working, he can make what he wants to make and so he is really enjoying it.

In about 2010, he began to realize that it was important to have a public face. Before that he was hidden away he realized that you do not exist if you do not have an online presence. At that time, he started a home page and blog and in around 2012, he started a Facebook page. He has also decided that it is really important to meet with customers, but as he is shy, it is difficult meeting them for the first time. He feels that Facebook really helps with this. When people say that they saw him on Facebook, it makes it easier for him to start a conversation so he puts up a post almost every day. He also comes to Tokyo two or three times a year to show his work at kimono fairs such as *Kimono Salone, Kimono Carnival,* etc. In spite of his shyness, he now enjoys interacting with his customers. He says it is great that they can tell him what they want, and he is delighted if they express thanks when he completes their orders. He told me that one woman actually cried when she saw the beautiful results of his work. This inspires him to continue his craft and strive for higher quality. He likes this way of working because sometimes it is his customers who generate new ideas, and he gets a great sense of satisfaction when he makes goods that he knows somebody really wants.

He still sells work through *tonya,* middlemen, but they always say to him, "When can you finish it? Can you make it faster? Can you make it cheaper?" So he gets much less satisfaction from this kind of work. They are always asking him for his special *kakishibuzome,* but he does not sell this through them. He only sells it to his special personal customers. As his other dyeing is also excellent, they still want his work, but really they want to get hold of his unique product.

Kobayashi is sure of his place in the market. His *kakishibuzome* is expensive, but he knows that it is worth the money, and he has customers for it. He says that other craftsmen are waiting for someone to do something for them, but he does not like to wait. He goes out and finds work. He has moved, gone online, created new products, and sold his brand. He says that others want more support from the Kyoto local government with which to supplement their incomes. The income for weavers is too low to support a family and so they are all old men who do it. He does not want to wait for someone to give him support. He can make his own living. He says that now his Facebook is more important than the *tonya.* After working since around 1980, his work is finally fun because there is variety, new challenge, and he meets many people.

Kitamura Kumiko—Futori Weaver

Kitamura Kumiko has been doing *futori,* which literally means thick weaving, for over twenty years. She studied design in college, but had no intention of becoming a weaver. She was more interested in *yuzen* or *katazome* dyeing, and had heard that she could learn *nassen* stencil dyeing, dyeing with color in resist paste, in the city of Chichibu. When she went to Chichibu, she found that they were not taking apprentices, but she was told about a Chichibu weaver, Ishizuka Kenichi, who was having a show in a Tokyo department store. Kitamura went to see the show and loved the beautiful warm and shiny silk cloth. She asked Ishizuka how long it would take to learn to make it, and was told it would take seven to ten years. She was excited by that prospect and decided immediately that she wanted to do it. She surprised Ishizuka by turning up as an apprentice. Ishizuka had another apprentice, but she only learnt how to make the thread, not the whole process. For the first five years of training, Kitamura worked without pay and did a part-time job in a Chichibu supermarket at night. Later, when she gained more experience and her teacher had passed away, she taught the teacher's daughter how to make the cloth, and now there are two weavers producing *futori.*

Futori is actually the forerunner of *meisen* weaving. Unlike other weavers in the area, Kitamura uses silk cocoons which are grown on a silk farm in Chichibu. Of the ten families still harvesting silk in Chichibu, this is the only one that uses naturally grown mulberry leaves, rather than food processed from them. The farmer

Figure 5.11 Kitamura Kumiko weaving with a back-strap loom.
Photo: Todd Fong.

is the sixth generation in his family farm, and the farm is the only one with a successor. The other farms are all run by aged farmers with no one to continue their work.

Kitamura's life rhythm is actually controlled by the silk worms. When they have made their cocoons the threads must be reeled off within about ten days, or the insects will eat a hole in them and break out, rendering the silk useless for making thread. In Chichibu, there are five silk worm cycles a year. Kitamura gets the first batch in early July; these are fast growing, and it is easy to make the threads from them. The summer ones also grow fast, and they are harvested in the middle of August. The early autumn ones are harvested in September, and they grow more slowly, and there are two batches harvested in October which grow slowly. The last ones produce much less silk. At each harvest, Kitamura must put the cocoons in water of over eighty degree centigrade and reel off all the thread, which is hot, hard work. Over the course of each year, she spends about half her time making thread and dyeing it. She can make six hundred grams of thread, which takes six kilograms of cocoons, in one day. Factory-made thread is automatically joined together, when each individual thread comes to the end, making it even in thickness all the way along. Kitamura's thread is thin at the beginning and ends and thicker in the middle. This gives a natural texture to the fabric that she weaves. Another special feature of the thread is that it is not twisted at all. Non-twisted threads lie close together, and she says that it makes strong cloth, which is important as *futori* was originally used for farming wear. This also gives the silk a beautiful lustrous finish, and it is very soft to the touch.

Kitamura not only utilizes local plant dyes such as chestnut, walnut, and maple but also buys some colors from a dealer, to increase the range of colors in her cloth. She grinds these herself. As *futori* was originally farming wear, it was usually brown or gray, so Kitamura has increased the range of colors. After making and dyeing threads, she weaves them into kimono which are plain, striped, and checked. She usually uses an *izaribata* back-strap loom, see Figure 5.11, on which she can weave about 60 cm a day if she works hard. This is about twice the time it takes to weave on a tall fixed loom; however, the customers say that the cloth woven on the back-strap loom feels lighter. This is in spite of the fact that Kitamura has weighed

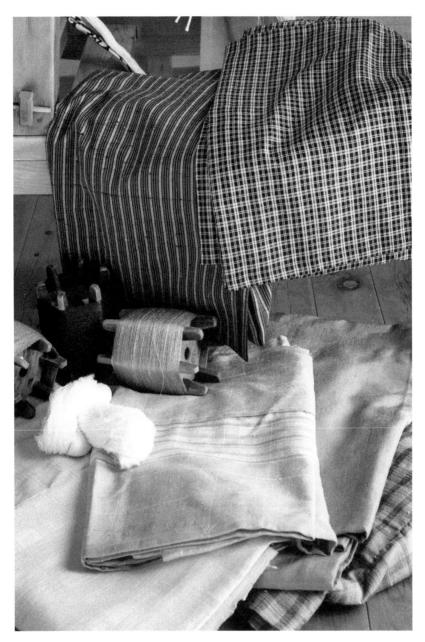

Figure 5.12 Kitamura Kumiko: *futori* **weaving.**
Photo: Todd Fong.

the weaving herself and found that they are actually heavier. Somehow they have a feeling of lightness and softness that cannot be obtained from more modern looms. Because she only spends half her year weaving, and the other half making threads, Kitamura can only make about six *tan,* kimono lengths, per year.

Kitamura does not have enough work to have an exhibition because each piece takes so long to make from start to finish. Her work is held by several kimono shops and also some goes to a *tonya* who puts it in the hands of major department stores in Tokyo. One kimono store, Nihonbashi Taniya, in Ginza arranges tours for their customers so that they can come to Chichibu to see how and where their kimono are made. Kitamura is happy to meet so many people through her work making kimono. Although she has no Web site, just a Facebook page, everything she makes is sold, so she has no need to promote herself. About five years ago, she started making shawls so that people who do not wear kimono can experience the loveliness of the silks that she creates. Asked what the key to her success was, she said that she thought there were two. First, she follows her teacher Ishizuka and weaves only thread that she has made and dyed herself. Her work is unique in that she controls the whole process. Second, the fact that both the warp and weft are woven with threads that are not twisted gives a special softness, shine, and warmth that is different from other silks. She also emphasizes that this fabric is very practical as it can be washed at home. The more it is used and washed, the softer it becomes and the more a part of the wearer. She tells her customers to "bring it up" she uses same phrase that we use for parents bringing up children. Perhaps it is similar to "wearing it in." In spite of the fact that it is an expensive handmade product, she has many customers who come back for more. A selection of her work is seen in Figure 5.12.

Suzuki Kiyoko—Hand-Loom Weaver

The experience of a lone weaver, like Kitamura, is very different from that of one in a weaving center, such as Oshima or Yuki where they make special types of *tsumugi*, raw silk. In the center, all the processes are divided up, and there are specialists in each process, but a lone weaver undertakes all the processes

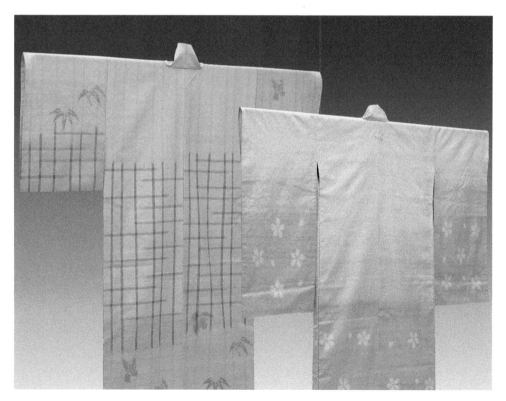

Figure 5.13 Suzuki Kiyoko E-gasuri kimono: take ni suzume (sparrows and bamboo)/sakura (cherry blossom); **tsumugi.**
Photo: Nishihara Katsumi.

Figure 5.14 Suzuki Kiyoko E-gasuri kimono: unami (April waves)/shokei (admiration); tsumugi.
Photo: Nishihara Katsumi.

herself. Suzuki Kiyoko is another independent weaver. She came to kimono weaving in a roundabout way. After graduating in English and working in an office, she was unfulfilled, but when she was twenty-seven years old, she encountered weaving and recognized that this was something that she would find worthwhile. So while continuing to work, she enrolled in the night school of Otsuka Textile School where she learned the principles of weaving. After that, she enrolled in the Bunka Gakuin Arts and Crafts Centre in Tokyo, where she learnt advanced techniques. Her teacher was a fiber artist, and Suzuki was weaving interior items such as mats and wall tapestries, but she felt there was a limit to how far she could take this. She continued to do office work, and at this time she thinks it was probably seeing her grandmother's beautiful old kimono in her chest that made her think that perhaps weaving kimono had more potential for her than making interior goods.

In 1983, through a friend's introduction, she left her house in Tokyo and went to apprentice herself to a weaver in Iida town in Nagano, where she wove *Iida tsumugi* from morning to night. The long, fine silk thread was difficult for her to handle after the wool and linen she was used to. A kimono length is over 12 meters, and it was almost unpaid work, but it was there that she learnt to handle the long silk threads.

After the year was up, Suzuki returned to Tokyo in 1985, and although her studio was small, she was full of ideas about what kimono she wanted to weave. Just as she was starting out, she went to an exhibition called *Kimono as Art—Modern Textile Works.* It was here that she first encountered the work of Shimura Fukumi, who is now a designated living national treasure. She was astonished by the beautiful colors of the kimono and went on to read her books. She says that this woman was a great influence on her work. This inspiration was important for her as she began her weaving career, and she remembers those as being happy days.

Suzuki doesn't use chemical dyes, not because of one way being better or worse, she just enjoys the processes involved with using natural dyes. Using plant dyes often starts from collecting the raw materials, then boiling them, and getting the colors out. She feels at this time she is working with nature, and she enjoys the sensations and the smells. She uses several different techniques. At first, she took a lot of orders for plain kimono from the people with whom she studied tea ceremony. Then she started to weave stripes, checks, and then *kasuri* and began to enter exhibitions. In 1987, when she held a show, one customer said that her kimono looked rather old-fashioned. She was not really sure what he meant by that, but it made her happy. She likes to use traditional designs such as *yagasuri*, arrow ikat, and *take ni suzume*, a sparrow in bamboo. Suzuki's weaving work can be seen in Figures 5.13 and 5.14.

She is often asked how long it takes to make a kimono. With any kind of traditional handcraft, the preparation takes much time. By the time she puts the threads onto the loom, 80 percent of the work is done. The threads are bought and prepared by removing the sericin. Then the dyeing takes at least a week. When making *e-gasuri* picture ikat, first she must make what is called a "seed thread." This is a thread that is used as a guide for tie-dyeing the weft threads for the *e-gasuri*. It is a single cotton thread that is threaded repeatedly onto a frame, which has pins on each side. This represents the wefts, and the design is marked onto this thread. This thread is then unwound, and the marked thread is used as a guide to tie-dye bunches of weft threads. This process is very complex. Sometimes she paints the colors onto the threads by hand. The threads must be tie-dyed and finally woven together so that the design appears on the cloth. It takes several times as long as weaving plain cloth or stripes. Even though it is really hard, she enjoys seeing the design appear in the cloth, and so she loves this technique.

When Suzuki lived near Kakegawa, an area known for weaving *kudzu*, Japanese arrowroot, she went to a lecture about making *kudzu* thread. She has been using *kudzu* in her work for over ten years now. The work is performed in the summer months. When she started using it, she found that it was very different from the image she had carried about it. The *kudzu* thread was delicate in comparison with other natural threads such as *shina*, wisteria fiber. It has luster and lightness. Depending on what fibers are used for the warps, different kinds of cloth can be made, but Suzuki uses silk for the warp and *kudzu* for the weft producing a light and shiny fabric for summer obi. There are only a few people left who weave *kudzu*, and it is only possible for her to produce about two or three obi a year, but she would like the craft to continue if possible.

Suzuki shows her work regularly at local art shows and in a craft gallery in Ginza. She has her own personal customers, too. She continues to enter her work for the show affiliated with the Japanese Art Crafts Association as much as possible, even though it sometimes feels like pressure. Regardless of whether she gets her work in or not, it forces her to continue to make efforts to improve the level of her weaving. As a fine art though, sales have been in a downturn for some years. The world is flooded with low-priced mass-produced goods. However, weaving done by hand and done on a machine is different. Natural dyes and chemical dyes are also different. Suzuki thinks that there are a few young professional women who appreciate this kind of labor-intensive work. As long as there are people left who appreciate these differences, she wants to continue her work.

Fujioka Hiroharu—Kumihimo, Obijime

Fujioka Hiroharu, seen at his loom in Figure 5.15, is a fourth-generation maker of *kumihimo*, which is the braiding technique used to make the decorative braids called *obi-jime*, that ties the obi in place. Unless one is wearing a summer *yukata* or half-width obi, these braids are an essential adorning element of the kimono outfit. They come in a wide variety of colors and styles, both round and flat, and some of them have very

Figure 5.15 Fujioka Hiroharu: *Kumihimo* **maker.**
Photo: Fujioka Kahori.

complex weaves. These braids can also carry an *obi-dome,* a brooch for kimono, which is held onto the braid by two metal loops on the back of the *obi-dome.* As the *obi-jime* is the central and prominent part of the kimono outfit, going across the front of the obi, the choice of this detail is very important.

Fujioka's Kumihimo Shop "Iga Kumihimo" is a family business in Iga city, Mie prefecture, far from Tokyo. Four family members are braiding, and also two other people who do it at their homes. There used to be another old lady doing it, but when she retired she was not replaced as there was not enough work. Fujioka suggests that the number of people who are willing to spend a lot of money for a high quality, small item

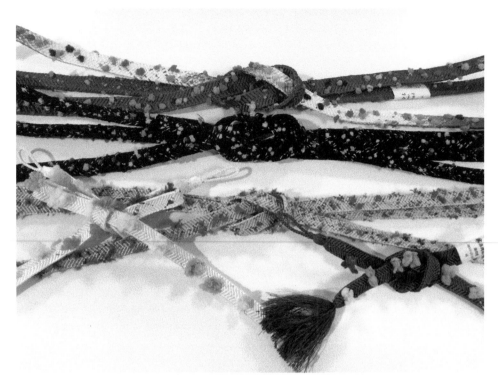

Figure 5.16 Iga Kumihimo: *Kumihimo* works.
Photo: Fujioka Kahori.

is small. Most people will settle for a used or a cheaply made *obi-jime,* rather than spending more money for higher quality. Fujioka's market has changed. Older women in their sixties or seventies used to buy his work, but now he thinks that they are very strict with themselves, and they have a limited budget over which they will not go. For this reason, the number of customers in this age group has dropped. However, he says that younger women, in their twenties or thirties, have little knowledge. If he takes time to talk with them and explain to them why his work is different from the ones that sell on the internet for a thousand yen, then they will listen and sometimes purchase his work. Customers in this age bracket have increased in number.

This younger market is a new market for Fujioka. He thinks hard about how he can be innovative when producing such a small item. It is quite a challenge, but in spring of 2013, Fujioka brought out a very original braid with a cat and footprint design on it. This has been selling very well, and there are many kimono lovers who also like cats, and this is a unique product for that market. In 2014, he started making braids that include a fine thread with fuzzy blobs on it. These end up as small colored blobs on a flat *obi-jime,* see Figure 5.16. They are unique and fun to look at. They appeal to those who are interested in a pop look. He thought young people would like them, but even older women have taken a liking to them. These fuzzy blob *obi-jime* are relatively expensive, but they have become a hit item, which has really surprised Fujioka.

The Fujioka family used to sell their items to a *tonya,* and they would never meet the customers or worry about where the items went. Now they do not work for a *tonya* but sell directly to customers through their shop in Iga city, and at kimono events. Ten years ago, Fujioka used to travel more, but now he rarely goes to department stores in countryside areas. He says that people do not wear kimono in outlying regions. In Tokyo and Osaka, the markets are large, and he goes to show their work at events in these locations. He feels that talking to the customers is very important. Sometimes they give him information about what is trending, or ideas for new products. He feels that the customers understand the market better than the craftspeople do. People who follow him on Twitter or Facebook will come to these events and buy his products. The majority of sales are through these events rather than through the shop, which is in a fairly remote location.

Fujioka told me that he was trying to make his family known on the internet. He said that if you are not on the internet, it is the same as if you did not exist. So he uses Twitter and has an Iga Kumihimo Facebook page. He also has a blog which is rarely updated and has uploaded several YouTube videos about how *kumihimo* are made. He does not yet have a Web site for online sales. If many people see something he puts online, his father will say that it is amazing, but his father really fails to understand the significance of having an online presence, so he is the only one of the family who makes an effort to use the internet for promoting the family's craftwork. He is very grateful to Facebook. He uses it as free publicity and as a noticeboard to give out information about events he will be participating in. He feels that this is a very important advertising tool for his family and a key to survival. He hopes that he can continue to promote the value of his handmade crafts and continue the business into the future, although it is hard to survive in the present market.

Jotaro Saito—Kimono Fashion Designer

Jotaro Saito is a third-generation *yuzen* dyer from Kyoto. He says that both his father and grandfather were innovators. It is the Saito family trademark. They are not afraid to try something new. Jotaro is unique in the kimono world because he is the only person who shows his work at Tokyo Collection, Tokyo Fashion Week. This means that he is the only kimono maker whose works are seen on the runways with Japanese designers who work making western style clothing, see Figure 5.17. Because of this, he has a unique place in the kimono world as an innovator and maker who has successfully challenged and entered the world of mode fashion. "But," he says, "They make a catalogue and I don't have a page, I don't appear in it." So he feels marginalized in the fashion world, even though he has found a space on the runway and has been showing there since 2002. Then he complains, "But I have no place to show my work in the kimono media either. My work does not belong in *Utsukushi Kimono, Kimono Salon* or *Nanaoh*. They are not about mode fashion." When asked why other designers have not made it and followed him into the fashion world as there are plenty of new brands, Jotaro suggests that they have not understood kimono as either mode or as traditional clothing. He says that one cannot throw everything away and make something completely new, and he thinks other designers are throwing away the good with the bad. Because something is easily made, or easy to use, or convenient does not necessarily mean it is good. The large sleeves of kimono may be inconvenient at times, but they create a certain purposefulness in movement, a care and an elegance that is very beautiful. If someone tells him that a tubular sleeve is better, he will not agree, even if it more convenient. Sewing on collars is also an inconvenience in wearing kimono, but the anticipation and the care put into sewing on the collar is part of the joy of wearing it.

Jotaro says that 2007–8 was the worst time for business. Nothing was selling, but he changed and stepped out with ideas that he had been thinking about for a long time. He made the change while other makers did not. Society has been changing, but kimono makers have stood still. When he asks a traditional craftsman to do something new, they say that it cannot be done. However, he believes it can be done, but has not been tried before. He believes that the makers must change, or die out, and perhaps, he suggests, it is necessary. Now he sees nothing but opportunity for those who can take up the challenge. It is not about rewriting a design from 300 years ago, nor must we stick to traditional thinking about color.

Red is no longer only for little girls, and gray and brown are no longer for old ladies. He wants to break down these old rules and thinking about color. Jotaro's color schemes are perhaps one of the main reasons that he has been able to show his work alongside that of other Japanese fashion designers. He works from

Figure 5.17 Jotaro Saito: 2015 Autumn/Winter Dark Fairy Tale Collection; women's kimono; crazy sarasa.
Photo: Jotaro Saito.

Figure 5.18 Jotaro Saito: 2015 Autumn/Winter Dark Fairy Tale Collection; men's jersey kimono.

Photo: Jotaro Saito.

a base of black, white, gray, and silver, and then he adds small amounts of color into the mix. This means that his work is easy to understand in the context of other famous Japanese fashion designers such as Yohji Yamamoto or Rei Kawakubo. His kimono resonate like smart and elegant suits, rather than being like traditional pink or cream flowery kimono. He credits his father as being the first person to design kimono and obi together. Before that, kimono were made in one place and the obi in another, and then they were put together, but his father had the idea of making a specific obi for a kimono to get a totally coordinated look. Often, these were of similar color as Japanese people are relatively short, and this makes the wearer look taller rather than cutting them in two.

Jotaro believes we are in a strange age where people who know nothing about kimono are the ones who spend a lot of money on a genuine handcrafted kimono for a wedding that is worn once by someone who suffers wearing it, and then is never used again. These kimono speak only of the role: bride's mother, bride's aunt, etc., rather than speaking of the personality of the individual. He doesn't want to make this kind of kimono. He wants to make a kimono that can be worn and worn and will eventually wear out. When he designs, he thinks of kimono as a long wraparound dress with a wide belt. However, his models do not wear shoes or western accessories, they have only the traditional accessories that go with kimono. He also sees some women who wear used or antique kimono who he feels have run away from western clothing, because they cannot wear it well. These women cannot wear kimono well either. He hopes that he can attract fashion-conscious women into wearing kimono.

Jotaro has put great effort into his materials. He says that he was the first person to bring denim into kimono, and he has developed all sorts of materials for his obi and kimono. Polyester kimono until now have done the same job as silk, but less well. The designs have imitated the designs on silk. He describes them as kimono for the poor. He dislikes this use of the material because polyester is a bad imitation of silk. Polyester kimono never have such clear bright colors as silk and nor do they hang as nicely. Saito believes they are ugly because they are trying to imitate silk. So, saying that it is half-way a joke, he has developed a kimono in a polyester jersey that references sportswear in its trimming, is stretchy, easy to wear, and easy to wash. He believes that this works well because he is asking polyester to do what polyester does well, and not what silk does. The kimono, shown in Figure 5.18, is popular among men.

In 2017 Jotaro relocated his Tokyo outlet from fashionable Roppongi to even more high-end Ginza, alongside top international fashion brands. This shop is very important for Jotaro. He sells some goods online, mainly small accessories, and denim kimono, but not his silk ranges which are one-offs and are fitted to the customers individually. Apart from this, he utilizes the regular selling routes of *tonya* and kimono shops for selling his work, though he would like to have an outlet in Kyoto, too.

Jotaro is doing well. In 2014, his profit was up by 10 percent from the previous year. Even though his kimono are not cheap, his customers' average age is in the early thirties. He has young craftsmen working in his company. Old craftsmen do one thing really well, but they can do only one thing. He uses young professionals who can adapt and do a variety of artistic work on the kimono. There is not enough work for those who can only do the same thing over and over again, so his workers need to be skilled in several areas. In an age where ink-jet printing is regularly sold as *yuzen* dyeing and accounts for 90 percent of the market in Kyoto, Saito stands out as an artist and designer who values his traditional heritage but wants to reprogram it to fit a fashion conscious world. His spring collection, "Go Beyond," in 2016, attracted a great deal of attention in both the Japanese and English language press.

Nakagawa Michina—Berry Koubou

Nakagawa Michina, featured in Figure 5.19, opened Berry Koubou, a small online shop selling kimono accessories, in 2004. She was using the knowhow she had gained in her job, as she had been head of web

Figure 5.19 Nakagawa Michina.
Photo: Berry Koubou.

Figure 5.20 Zori: Berry Koubou.
Photo: Berry Koubou.

design in her company. In 2009, she also opened a small shop in Nagoya, where she lives. Recently, she puts her work in a kimono outlet in Kichijoji, Tokyo, too, but she deals directly with the shop owner, as she once had a bad experience concerning money with a *tonya,* middleman, and she does not want to deal with them again. She mainly sells obi and *zori,* footwear, and also *obi-jime,* braids, and *han-eri,* collars. Her work is colorful, bright and incorporates many florals and stripes, though not necessarily Japanese traditional designs. Figure 5.20 shows a typical pair of zori.

Coming from a regular working background, she was neither connected to the kimono business world nor trained at an art school. Her strengths were her natural talent at design and the computer skills that she had mastered in her work. Although her work is aimed at a younger audience, she told me that her main customers were in the thirty-seven to forty age group, with a widespread audience both above and below this. She thinks the reason for this age group being central is the fact that younger customers think it is lovely but do not yet have the financial resources to buy what she makes. By their late thirties, they can afford to buy something.

As time goes on she has changed her approach, experimenting with an increasing range of textiles and also upgrading from cotton to silk. Thus the price of her goods has gone up over the years she has been in business. She says that her main business is on the internet. Having a shop is expensive since she has to pay rent and overheads. However, it is important to have a place where customers can come. Recently, she has shown at Kimono Salone, Kimono Carnival, and Meri Mero Marche kimono events in Tokyo. Sometimes, a group of small businesses like hers will have a temporary space at a department store, such as Takashimaya. These are important for her because they provide opportunities for meeting new customers, and the number of her fans increases. She gives out a lot of name cards. Particularly when selling *zori,* size is important, so she often sells the first pair face to face. After that, people know the size and can buy them on the internet. She believes that meeting her customers is very important. Nakagawa is not a member of any professional kimono guild or group, but she is an enthusiastic member of Aichi Prefecture Kimono Jack.

Nakagawa really understands the importance of the internet. She has her online shop and also a blog, Facebook, and Twitter, and she uses them all regularly. Her business is successful and is growing. She can support herself from her work. While she used to make the items herself, she now only makes samples and has the rest of the work completed by workshops or factories elsewhere. She sees the future of kimono as being bright. She thinks that the kimono will become cheaper because cotton, wool, and polyester kimono will replace expensive silk garments. Also kimono will be prêt-à-porter instead of made-to-measure and will be sold in S, M, L, and LL sizes. She has started to make goods for the men's market too, as she sees this as a potentially growing sector of the market. Nakagawa is really enjoying being a creator in the kimono world.

Shibasaki Rumi—Rumi Rock

Shibasaki stated,

> Kimono does not have trends in the way that other fashion does. It is not designed to be worn and then thrown away to make room for the next one. You cannot throw kimono away. Kimono have a history. They are given to people. They can be picked apart and re-sewn. Kimono are more natural because they are continually used. The job of the kimono keeps changing through its life. It influences people in different ways as it continues its history. The past is not thrown away. Kimono is a pattern culture and images are continually added. Finally a kimono can be turned into nappies.

The most important thing about kimono or *yukata* for Rumi Rock is the vocabulary of stories which brings interconnectedness. Because stories are loved by people of all generations and all cultures, there are unlimited stories that can be put onto them.

Shibasaki started out learning to sew clothes in fashion school, but she always liked kimono because she liked Edo-period dramas on television. When she graduated there was no one hiring designers, so she went into a company that was designing for kimono instead. The designs went to dealers in Tokyo and also to Kyoto. She worked there for three or four years. She had some prewar kimono at home, and she also went looking for kimono in the few used kimono shops that were around at the beginning of the 1980s. She couldn't really find what she wanted, and so in 1991, she bought herself a Mac computer, attached it to a digital cloth printer and she made her own polyester kimono. It was a graphic pattern, and it won a competition for using Adobe software. She made some *yukata* and won some other awards and then from about 1994, as the *yukata* boom took off, she began to get orders for *yukata* and *tenugui* small cotton towels. Her first order *yukata* was from a musician who wanted a design of the moon and a skull. Thus was born Rumi Rock, an edgy brand of cool *yukata*. Kaneko, her stencil cutter, had been working in traditional dyeing workshops but had stopped, and in 2004, Shibasaki asked him to cut stencils for her. So their collaboration began, and they started an online shop.

About half her designs are designs that customers have ordered, and the other half are ones that she has conceived herself. Though the designs appear very diverse, there are some themes that run through them. She likes stories, legend, and mystery. Some of these designs come from Edo-period culture, for example a design of Ryoma, which includes small details of pistols, boots, and a crest in it. She says that no one knows who he really was, perhaps he was just an arms dealer. A dark *yukata* with golden paper lanterns also has the feeling of the Edo period. Her Apollo *yukata* shows an astronaut in space and the moon. We don't really know whether he walked on the moon or not. Perhaps it was an elaborate hoax.

Figure 5.21 Super car *yukata*: Rumi Rock.

Photo: Ishikawa Mao.

Figure 5.22 Wolves *yukata*: **Rumi Rock.**

Photo: Ishikawa Mao.

The influence of popular culture, television, and film is strong. She has a design of women's mouths and eyes in the spotlight, reminiscent of a Hitchcock film.

She has taken an old design from Lyon with swirling plants and a rampant lion and put it on a *yukata*. She has used the magic mirror from Snow White, a mermaid from Hans Anderson, merry-go-round horses, keys, skulls, and various creatures such as crows, owls, wolves, and white swans. Sometimes there is a humorous element in her work, such as a rose made in barbed wire (which is a play on words as barbed wire is called rose wire in Japanese), and a design of hexagons with chemical symbols, which look scientific and new, but the hexagon is an ancient design for kimono, symbolizing the turtle. She wants people to relate to the stories. She says that you cannot hide in a *yukata*. It covers you from head to foot. She likes the garments to have an element of surprise in them, and for something unusual to happen when wearing them. She hopes they start conversations and hopes they are worn for a long time the garment in Figure 5.21 shows sports cars that used to be popular in Japan and Figure 5.22 a yukata with wolves.

Shibasaki likes to use old techniques, even if they are sometimes difficult or impossible to control perfectly. She has used the old and exacting *nagaita chuugata* technique, but mostly uses *chuusen zome,* a technique where the stenciled fabric is folded up, pressed together, and dye is dripped onto it. She likes the way the dyes soak into the cloth, which is somewhat uncontrollable. It has a spontaneous feel that cannot be obtained with a digital print, which she thinks is important. But today's people need designs for today, even if the techniques are old. Their experiences are different from people who lived in the Edo period. She produces a diverse range of obi, using many different fabrics. She says anything can be used for an obi.

Shibasaki takes orders for specific designs from people, which she thinks is unique in the *yukata* world. She listens to the customer's story and then creates the design for them. She also designs for western brands who want to have a *yukata* in their lineup. The cotton comes from Aichi and Shizuoka prefectures, and the dyeing is done in workshops in Tokyo or Osaka, so they are produced in Japan. She copyrights each design so that it can be used on other objects, and each design is exclusively owned. As of 2016, she had over 100 designs in her repertoire. In future, Shibasaki would like to design more patterns based on other countries' stories, and she would like to show her fabrics in Paris or London, and break into the international market.

Furifu

Furifu is the brand name of a range of kimono aimed at young people from its parent company, Mimatsu, a kimono company established in 1932 in Tokyo. The main store is in Kichijoji, West Tokyo. The original concept was to be able to assist in making special occasions beautiful. They now deal not only in kimono but also in formal dresses, accessories, and jewelry. In 2012, Mimatsu had thirty-six shops spread from Sendai to Nagoya.

Furifu was started in 1999. The concept was to make a brand for young people that was cute, a mixture of East and West, and was easy to wear. Originally, they decided to do this by selling a prêt-à-porter range of kimono made in Italian silk. They opened one shop in Shibuya. Although the silk was glossy, the colors were rather dull and designs conservative, added to which the prices were between 100,000 yen and 200,000 yen, meaning that the younger people they were trying to target were unable to buy them. A year later they decided to try making Furifu kimono in washable polyester. This had the effect of bringing the price down to between 40,000 and 50,000 yen, less than half the previous prices. They also began to use very bold bright colors. They wanted young women to feel that it was easy and you could wear it tomorrow. They also brought out a range of polyester obi to go with the kimono. Figure 5.23 features a polyester furisode.

Figure 5.23 Furisode by *furifu*.

Photo: Mimatsu.

Figure 5.24 Furifu Shibuya shop.
Photo: Mimatsu.

A few older, experienced kimono wearers commented negatively, because polyester was too hot and heavy, but people began to buy the kimono. They then brought out a range of *yukata* too, made of the new, silk-like polyester, Ceo alpha. The designs were deliberately influenced by western designs, and stripes and roses became popular. Furifu wanted to stand right between the West and East, and they not only stock kimono, obi, and kimono accessories but also a range of other kinds of accessories, bags and small items, fans, hair decorations, *zori* footwear, and western clothes made out of fabric with Japanese kimono-like designs on it.

The fact that Furifu kimono appear regularly in many kinds of media testifies to their popularity. They are in kimono magazines and books, and Furifu publish their own collections. Each *yukata* has an interesting and fanciful name to personalize it: Rainbow Party, Scorpion sign woman, etc. Furifu kimono have appeared in popular young women's fashion magazines such as *Sweet* and *Vivi*. They are often used in TV programs and in commercials. In 2015, Furifu had thirteen shops in the Kanto area. They have sold their garments on Yahoo and now on Rakuten online sites. Recently, their kimono are also available on Zozo Town, an online fashion shopping site. They want young Japanese girls to enjoy Japanese style, and they take customer relations seriously. In order to increase opportunities for wearing kimono, they hold Christmas parties and other events and provide a dressing service for women who buy their kimono. Their target market is the late twenties and early thirties, and their commitment to making kimono cute and attractive for young people has not changed. With thirteen shops opening since 1999, and regular media appearances, Furifu can be considered to be one of the leading brands popularizing kimono among young people.

Figure 5.25 Man in kimono and haori: Fujiki-Ya.
Photo: Fujimoto Daiichi.

Figure 5.26 Kidera Masaru in kimono: Fujiki-Ya.
Photo: Fujimoto Daiichi.

Kidera Masaru is in some ways a surprising entrant in the kimono business world, and he does not have any contact with the usual routes of doing kimono business. His first job after graduation was with a Japanese car company. He was interested in items made in Japan, but not really in cars. While he worked there he got a taste for wearing suits and decided that he wanted to work in the clothing business producing them. He went to a training school for a year and worked the weekends at a tailor's business. Then he got a job in a major Japanese clothing company, which was selling in Japan's top department stores. There he was in charge of having alterations done for made-to-measure suits. He dreamed of having his own business and eventually felt that he could grow no more where he was, so he gave up his job and went to Taiwan for two years, to learn Chinese. He thought it would be good to speak other languages with non-Japanese customers.

On returning from Taiwan, Kidera worked in a department store in Ginza. He is fond of the tea ceremony, and he wanted to wear a kimono for this. When he went to buy a used kimono, he found that they were all about 10 cm too short for him. Then he went to a big department store's kimono shop to look for one there. He was shocked when he found that even with a salary as a clothing worker, there was no way that he could afford to buy a kimono. It was far out of his price range. There was nothing but the cheap used one which was too short and the new silk one which was far too expensive. It was then that he had the idea of using his knowhow with suits and the apparel industry to produce affordable kimono for men. The idea of making kimono with suiting is not entirely new; some kimono shops also have rolls of such cloth tucked away on their shelves, but they are not familiar with suiting and cannot really advise about it. Kidera knows suiting, cutting, and selling and has been to see suit production sites in England, China, Italy, and other countries. He believed that he could use this experience to help him start a new kind of kimono shop for men. His idea centered on making reasonably priced kimono for men, using suiting and denim fabrics.

With his friend Fujimoto, who is the Fuji part of the name, who takes photographs and makes web pages, they started up online as Fujiki-Ya at the beginning of 2012. Fujiki-Ya has a web page, and Kidera also has a blog, Facebook, and Twitter. In the autumn of the same year, they started to sell in a small space inside a kimono rental business in Asakusa. They only opened at weekends, and the space was small, but customers were ordering denim and suiting kimono, such as in Figure 5.25. They also sold obi and yukata.

For promotional purposes, Fujimoto took a photograph of Kidera wearing a suiting kimono. In every other aspect of the photograph, he looks like a successful businessman. The background of the photograph is a glass-fronted high rise, and Kidera is seen reading an English language paper. He is also wearing his glasses, a watch, a white shirt, and a red tie, over which he wears a black kimono with an obi in the same red as the tie. Black, red, and white are the only colors in the outfit. The image was used in many places and was much talked about in kimono circles. It raised the question, "Why not?" Kidera expected a negative response from conservative-minded kimono business people, but it never happened. The image was powerful and by implication not only suggests a new way of wearing kimono but also the idea that successful people can wear kimono to the office. The image can be seen in Figure 5.26.

In autumn of 2014, two years after the initial opening in Asakusa, Fujiki-Ya moved into its own shop. It is located three minutes from Ueno station, making it very convenient to access from anywhere in Tokyo. Kidera believes the two years in Asakusa were very important though. He built up his customer base while he was there. Right from the start he had customers coming to his new shop. He has also started doing what he dreamed of years ago, making made-to-measure suits and shirts. His small shop has stocks and samples of kimono cloth, different colors, and weights of denim and swatches of suiting and shirting in various ranges. One can order a suit, line it in kimono fabric, or order a kimono outfit of denim or suiting. While before there were very limited options for men's kimono and buying one could be a high hurdle, Kidera has put kimono and suits side by side. Some kimono customers, having become used to made-to-measure, then come back and have him make them a suit. He also believes that it is important that it is a men's shop and he is a man, although it is quite possible to have a suit or kimono made for a woman there. It is easy for him to give advice man to man, and it makes measuring and fitting easier too. His strength is his knowledge of the apparel business and his ability to sell to customers.

He has introduced some new and playful items, colorful *tabi* with designs on the inside as well as the outside, and *haori-himo* handmade from beads. One can also order an obi that is in effect a wide belt made entirely of beads. Although it is expensive and handmade, he says it sells well. He says though, that he is not on the glitzy cat runway end of kimono fashion design. He is interested in more classical wear along the lines of men's suits. Not only has he been to see factories where things are made, he also is very careful to listen to his customers. Sometimes they stay and hang out with him after the shop is closed. He listens to their kimono stories about what they buy and their experiences. Sometimes he gets hints for new items this way.

Kidera has taken part in some large kimono exhibitions, which has brought him some attention in kimono magazines, but he would really like to be featured in a men's fashion magazine. He has had his kimono worn on television by a popular young boy band, from the *Johnnys* agency, which is great exposure for his work. In 2015 and 2016, he was on Nippon Hoso Kyokai (NHK) and other television channels discussing his business model of kimono for men, and his mixing of Japanese and western clothing on an equal basis. In April of 2016, he expanded his business space, taking over the upper floor of the building he rents and also took on some staff as he could no longer manage his expanding business alone. During 2016, his presence in the media became much larger, and he clothed not only several boy bands but had his dressing work featured in numerous fashion magazines and on television. Kidera is becoming the man that people go to for dressing men in the media, with media appointments of some sort every week.

Fujiki-Ya's stock has gradually been changing over time, with less space taken by used kimono and women's kimono retailored into men's, and more space taken by prêt-à-porter denim kimono in different colors and weights which make up the largest part of his sales. Kidera has found a perfect place in the market with little competition, and his popularity is increasing at a tremendous rate.

Morioka Masahiro—Kimono Tailor

Figure 5.27 Owariya Wasai Jo: Kimono Tailoring School.
Photo: Kobayashi Youichi.

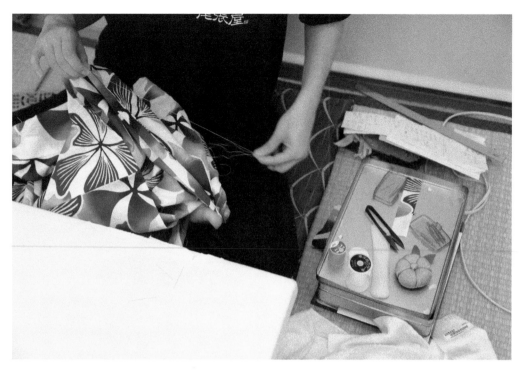

Figure 5.28 Sewing at Owariya Wasai Jo: Kimono Tailoring School.
Photo: Kobayashi Youichi.

Morioka Masahiro is a master tailor. As far as public opinion and union records show, his is the last remaining place in Tokyo that takes live-in apprentices to learn kimono tailoring. Four apprentices sit on the floor in a large tatami mat room, at long narrow low tables, see Figure 5.27. They sit cross-legged and work in silence. Another tailor works away marking up a bolt ready for sewing. The scene is calm and peaceful; the workers look down, concentrating on their own work. They are each working on something different, each in his or her own world. They do not fidget or wriggle, they do not discuss their work or chatter; it is a scene of serene industriousness as in Figure 5.28.

Morioka explained that the apprentices come from around Kanto. Some of them work as soon as they finish high school. They must study for five years to learn the trade. They spend the first month just sewing stitches to learn the way of holding the needle and cloth. Then they sew themselves underwear and then a *nagajuban* petticoat. After that, they start sewing various single layered kimono in different fabrics. At the end of the second year, they sew a lined kimono. The first year is the hardest, he explained. Recently, one apprentice gave up after three months. People say the work is too low paid, too hard, the rules are too strict, and the curfew is too early. For the first year, their legs ache until they become used to sitting in the cross-legged position. After five years they leave, go home, or marry, but he can still send them work.

Morioka is the fourth generation of tailors in his family. Originally, the family were *miya daiku,* carpenters specially trained in the art of building shrines and temples. However, his great grandfather had a bad leg and couldn't work as a carpenter, so he became a tailor instead. He came to Tokyo and started Kiku Owariya in 1883. The name became Owariya in 1923. Morioka was born to inherit the business, and he hated it and rebelled. Then when he got married, his wife's father asked him why he was so rebellious and what he wanted out of life. He thought about it and decided that he wanted to be useful. He felt Japan was not doing well, and he didn't want to see it go downhill, so he dedicated himself to learning the craft. In the 1920s, they had about a hundred apprentices, even in the 1960s there were about sixty. They did a lot of work for Shirokiya and some other department stores. Gradually, over the years, the number of department stores commissioning work has decreased. However, private work has increased little by little. Morioka's sister and his elder son are also tailoring. His wife runs the household and cooks for the family and apprentices.

Morioka has tailored for several famous actors and actresses. His work has been used on television and in commercials and he also does work for entertainers and musicians. He thinks of tailoring as a part of Japanese culture, connected with other arts and crafts. He is working on several projects. One is for a noh actor who has given him a 100 year old robe that he wants relined. Morioka told him that the life of silk was only a 100 years, but the actor begged him to try to replace the lining. It is a labor of love, and there is no one to teach him how to do it. He works on it in the evenings when his business of the day is over.

Another project that he wants to explore is the roots of today's kimono. He believes that the shape of women's kimono today is a shape that men have found the most pleasing, with extra cloth inserted from the bust and the collar ending at the hips, emphasizing these two areas. The part in between is held in by the tight and confining obi, which is much higher than the obi used to be. A curved sleeve is more practical than the rectangular sleeve worn today. The *kosode* was wider, and the collar was longer. The obi was worn lower and the sleeves of the garment were attached rather than swinging separately as they do today. There was no fold of extra cloth in the middle. Morioka believes that this garment should be easier to wear than the present kimono, and he is experimenting to develop a prototype. He thinks it will be difficult to persuade kimono wearers that there is no need for the fold of cloth in the middle, and also that they do not have to wear a Nagoya obi in *otaiko,* drum bow, style.

Morioka's workshop, being the last one operating in this way, has great historical significance and is open to visitors who want to learn about how kimono are sewn. They can experience it themselves, watch the tailors at work, and produce a small bag to take away. His desire is that through his work, he can somehow keep hope alive for the next generation, though the effects of the kimono revival cannot be said to have had much of an impact here. At the time of publication there is little work, so Morioka worries about whether or not the following generation can survive.

Shirataki Mikio—Shirataki Gofuku Ten

Gofuku Ten is an old name for a kimono shop, literally meaning clothing from Go, in China. Shirataki Mikio is the fifth-generation owner of Shirataki Gofuku Ten. He carries this old name with reason and pride rather than using the more modern and easy to understand, Kimono Ya. The shop was founded by his ancestor in 1853, the end of the Edo period. At that time, it was in Ueno, but soon, on marriage, it was moved to its present location in Akatsuka. Now it is a suburb of Tokyo, but at that time, Akatsuka was a small country inn town. It happened to be on the join between two major trunk roads, Kawagoe Kaido and Tokorozawa Kaido. This made it a convenient location for those who had visited Tokyo from the north and northwest to shop for souvenirs and goods to take back home to the country.

Shirataki Gofuku Ten is an impressive building with a large landscaped Japanese garden, but in those days it was even larger. It was a very successful *futomono sho,* a place selling not only clothing but every-day goods, such as futons and cushions. Crowds of people used to gather there to shop on their way back home, and it was said that there were so many people gathered there, that you would meet at least one thief, which is rare in Japan. It was a landmark and also had a central place in the life of the town. Sometimes, Shirataki Gofuku Ten was involved in making contacts through which marriages were arranged or land and property bought and sold. Even today, an old man or woman from the local area occasionally comes in and tells Shirataki that his father or grandfather arranged his or her marriage. When the Kanto

Figure 5.29 The spacious upper room at Shirataki-Ya Gofuku Ten: kimono shop.
Photo: Todd Fong.

earthquake struck in 1923, the shop was able to share water with the people of Akatsuka because it has a natural spring well in the garden. During the twentieth century, the shop changed from dealing in everyday fabrics and soft furnishings to dealing exclusively in silk kimono. The spacious upper sales floor can be seen in Figure 5.29.

When Shirataki took over the shop in 2003, he was over thirty. He stands in the garden in Figure 5.30. He had been working in architecture as a landscape architect, involved in city planning. When planning new buildings, his team would spend time researching the landscape and history of a place and make efforts to incorporate what they found into the new plans. However, he found that customers were largely not interested in such notions and did not take any notice, and he became disillusioned with the work. He is sure that Japan is on the way to making every city look the same, regardless of location, environment, or historical background. He realized that the difference between architecture and clothing was one of hard or soft, and that in principle both were creating the environment, so at that point, he decided return home to take over the family business. In the past, when a son was going to inherit such a family business, he was usually sent away to learn the trade in someone else's shop first. That way he would already understand the business when taking over. In Shirataki's case, he understood nothing, and when he thinks back, he is embarrassed about some of the advice he gave to customers. Though the staff did not direct him, he learnt from them and is sure that they were correcting his mistakes from behind the scenes. He also says that he learnt a lot from his customers. He feels indebted both to his ancestors and to the local people who have supported the company and he wants to continue all the relationships that have been carefully built up over the generations by his family.

It is this sense of relationships and the networks that have been created that seem to be the most important aspect of the work for Shirataki. He wants to provide a service for the local people, and increasingly for people who come from further away. He doesn't want to have to say "no," to any customer. He says that this distinguishes the Shirataki business from some other kimono shops. Other businesses might only sell a

Figure 5.30 Shirataki Mikio.
Photo: Todd Fong.

particular kind of kimono that is the flavor of the shop, or they might only be interested in selling new goods, whereas Shirataki wants to provide a service. In this way, he is like a Gofuku Ten and not a kimono shop. He specializes only in silk and only in order-made kimono, but he will provide any service he can connected with kimono, and he sells a complete range from extremely expensive handmade goods, to cheaper every-day wear. If someone comes to consult about how they can use their grandmother's old kimono, he wants to help. He does not want to turn them away even though other shops are often not willing to take on such unprofitable projects. If someone wants to buy a cotton kimono or needs advice about one or if someone wants a ready-made kimono, he will go out of his way to find the advice from an expert or obtain the ready-made kimono for the customer.

Times have not been easy for Gofuku Ten since the economic turndown of the late 1990s. The peak of sales was about 1990 for Shirataki, and then sales dropped steadily. Now they fluctuate, but have evened out. Shirataki says that everyone in a position like his must earn trust. As he is interested in continuing Japanese culture, and the business has large premises, he uses these in order to spread culture. Shirataki holds regular culture classes in kimono *kitsuke, sado, sencha,* and kimono tailoring. Once a year they also hold a week long culture festival. They invite young practicing professionals who perform *noh,* or *rakugo,* comic storytelling and have performances. These are reasonably priced, so people who would never go to see a major performance can enjoy the events. He hopes that people will find new aspects of culture that they can relate to, so he holds study groups where one can learn about different types of dyeing and weaving such as *yuki tsumugi, yuzen,* or *bingata*. Shirataki strongly believes that makers should be able to meet their customers. The customers are happy to know who made their kimono, and the makers get new ideas from the customers.

Lunco—Antique Kimono Salon

Lunco grew up with a love of making things. She knew she would never have a normal job; she just wanted to draw and use materials. She tried making all sorts of crafts, and she traveled around the world becoming interested in many different places. When she was thirty, she started blowing glass. She became absorbed in antique glass and would go out and look at it. One day, she was looking at glass at an antique market, and she noticed a big box of antique kimono fabrics and was stunned by the designs and patterns. She bought the whole box and took it home to make things with. Soon, the old kimono became more interesting to her than the glass that she was making. She liked kimono because her mother had always worn it, but it was the power of the designs and textiles that really fascinated her. She believes that as kimono are all one shape, it is the power of the designs and patterns that makes them great or not. She is amazed by the way that people brought the seasons and nature into the house by putting them on kimono.

Lunco has an antiques seller's license, but she does not belong to any organizations apart from that. She started selling in her own shop in about 2000, after borrowing space in other people's shops. She has used the present location for the past five years. She believes that when the first antique boom happened, it was a reaction to the stuffiness of the formal kimono world of *Utsukushii Kimono*. That kind of expensive kimono was associated with so many rules, and antique kimono could be worn more freely without thinking about rules. They were seen as both fun, and an alternative to the more expensive formal kimono world and also the world of western fashion, which fashionable women had grown tired of. The antique kimono was not only colorful but unique. In the first boom, in the early 1990s, she says that people did not worry about stains or even about size, they just enjoyed the designs and patterns on the kimono. Now they are much more fussy. They are sometimes too concerned with the rules and being bound by conventions on size, and people worry more about the stains too. All this she thinks is a pity. She wants the wearers to respond to the beauty of the kimono themselves and argues that if the sleeves are short or there are imperfections, it is part of the skill of the dresser herself, to make the garment look the best it can be. She says she is very free concerning how to wear the kimono, and also about conventions concerning age or even sex. Men like to come in and buy pretty cloth and her customers are all ages from their teens to their seventies. She describes herself as being a bit of a punk. The Lunco store can be seen in Figures 5.31 and 5.32.

Figure 5.31 Lunco antique kimono shop.
Photo: Todd Fong.

Figure 5.32 Lunco antique kimono shop.
Photo: Todd Fong.

She has occasionally been featured in kimono magazines: *arecole, Nanaoh,* and *Kimono Hime,* and she has also put on exhibitions for hotels and for department store events and also fashion shows in collaboration with musicians. She has published two books to inspire people with the beautiful fabrics, and she has a blog with fans from Okinawa to Hokkaido, but she does not sell online. When she does a special themed event in the shop, she makes beautiful flyers which are sent out to her customers. This is a big expense, but she hopes that the customers keep them to enjoy the patterns.

More than the business, Lunco just enjoys being surrounded by the kimono. They take away her stress and make her feel happy. She feels that they allow her to work with them. She does not have to try and persuade her customers about buying the kimono either. They are individualists who know what they like. As she is a positive and cheerful person who stocks a wide range of very beautiful Taisho and Showa pieces, her shop has many fans and a reputation for being a beautiful and elegant kimono salon.

Reflections on the Changing Market

The interviews show that business has changed in many ways even within one generation. One important aspect is that there is less work than before for most of the craftsmen, and this has affected both production and distribution. It has caused downsizing, one example of which is Itoko cloth company renting out spaces in their building, rather than using it all themselves. For the master tailor, this means supporting only four apprentices and not sixty. Another result of the lack of work is that it is no longer enough to be skilled at one thing. The *yunoshi-ya* once steamed cloth all day, but now he also acts as a *shikai-ya,* producer and advises about many aspects of kimono production. He has had to broaden his skills in order to survive. Jotaro Saito employs those who can turn their hand to several skills rather than employing older craftsmen who can perform only one skill well. Shirataki of the *gofuku ten,* kimono shop, cannot rest easily either. He is not only selling and advising about kimono but is also producing events and workshops. From Tanabe and Kobayashi, we learn that once it was enough to be a skilled dyer, because the middleman would bring the cloth to the *yuzen* craftsman and pick up the finished kimono. The craftsman did not have to worry about where they went. He or she was distant from the customer and concerned only with making the product. This system is breaking down and dyers now purchase their own cloth. They also largely market their own work or work with one *tonya* or one or two kimono shops. There is increasing evidence of women making their mark in the dyeing world, which was once almost exclusively a men's world.

Life has not changed very much for the lone hand-loom weavers. It is not easy for Suzuki to find a market for her work so she supplements her income with a part-time job. Kitamura has the advantage of being one of only two weavers making that particular product, *futori,* and it has a brand and rarity value, being a product of a specific place. She also has the backup of a kimono shop in the Saitama area, so she can sell all her work. Whether or not she can make a living wage from it is debatable. Both historically and in the present time, it appears to be difficult to make enough money to survive from hand-loom weaving. It is physically impossible to hand-weave more than a few centimeters a day, and the weaving is the last process in a long series of stages in the production of handmade woven kimono. Whether or not hand-loom weaving will survive seems in the balance at the present time, but the outlook is not good.

Downsizing has not only affected production but also information flow. Another change is that now even craftspeople are beginning to consider that they need a web page, a blog, or a Facebook page. They worry if they cannot have an online presence because they recognize the need to promote themselves. Just as in the Edo period new technology in printing enabled trends to spread across the city, today internet technology enables kimono information to circulate round the globe. One craftsman said that Facebook is more important than the *tonya*. He also said that without Facebook one does not exist. However, many older craftsmen, while being aware of the problems, and the increasing necessity of selling their own brand and promoting their own work, are unable to do so. Nasu is typical of the older generation of craftsmen who have not learned to use a computer or cannot use one to their advantage. He relies on his network of friends and acquaintances. Being a member of one of the craftsmen's associations gives some industry connections, and the right to participate in annual exhibitions, but joining involves a fee, and also the responsibility of committees, meetings, or volunteer work. Tanabe has been an active member of one such organization and has a wide network of business associates and personal friends and fans who support her artistic work.

In spite of many difficulties, there are some very positive aspects to these transformations. Kobayashi says that his work is much more satisfying than it used to be. He previously never saw his customers and had no idea who they were or what they wanted. He just stayed in his workshop all day every day. Now he goes to events and meets people, he explains his work to them, often he gets new ideas from them, and sometimes they ask him for a product they want. He updates his Facebook page regularly and although he is in Tango, an outlying area of Kyoto, he now has friends and fans from Tokyo and all over Japan. He gets great satisfaction from producing something that someone wants, particularly when he knows it will make them happy. The craftsmen are much closer to their market now than they were before. This is more interesting, it cuts out waste as producers can make what people want, but it comes with a responsibility that they did not have to carry before. In the past, they only made for the *tonya*, who took the decisions and carried the risk for them.

Jotaro Saito says that he sees only opportunity now and is critical of the kimono industry for its inability to move with the times. As far as he is concerned, the world is changed, and culture must change with it. He is innovative as his ancestors were, and he is enjoying great success in spite of the economic depression. He continues to experiment with new materials and new ways of doing things, while maintaining the integrity of the kimono. There is nothing gimmicky or compromising in his work, and his kimono models display perfect elegance on the runway.

The story of Furifu shows the importance of finding the right price range as well as capturing the right combination of kimono and cute in order to attract an audience. Their first attempt at attracting a new market failed because they were both expensive and too serious. Changing their approach to something more colorful and playful and switching from silk to polyester were decisions that helped them to hit the market they were aiming for. Both Furifu and Berry Koubou have found their target markets, and Nakagawa's story demonstrates that with appropriate use of networks, even someone with no experience in the kimono industry can be successful with the right product. There is still a problem in creating a popular kimono that is affordable for young people, as Nakagawa's story demonstrates. Kidera, coming from a background in men's suits, has found a niche in a field wide open. There was nothing for men between the cheap, used kimono and the expensive order-made one. His business model for Fujiki-Ya, putting the kimono and suit on equal footing, tailoring for the customers' needs, is an excellent and innovative model and is attracting increasing media attention.

New, cheaper models can strike terror into those working at the top end of the market. Thinking of historical parallels, the introduction of cheaper, bright, and relatively easy to produce *yuzen* would have struck horror into those making *shibori* or embroidery. Perhaps they thought that kimono, as they knew it, would vanish. *Yuzen* dyers today have the same fear, as digital print takes over. In the 1920s, hand-loom weavers may have experienced a similar feeling with the introduction of *meisen*. The reality is that although the market shares may have changed, embroidered kimono, *shibori* kimono, and handwoven kimono have all survived. Just as the haute couture end of the fashion market has shrunk with the economic downturn, it is inevitable that the luxury end of the kimono market will do so, too. However, the increasing number of options available and the undoubted success of new players in the market suggest a positive outlook. It is also inconceivable that a fashion item should be left in the hands of an aged male population, which is the last group to take up fashion trends. The input of a younger generation, especially women, is vital in attracting a new and younger market for kimono.

The study of Japanese economic history of the last 200 years by economic historian Francks (2009) focuses on consumerism. This has played an increasingly important role in Japan since the end of the Edo period. Gradually, starting from the city and moving to the country, throughout the twentieth century, Japanese people have bought goods to give them a more comfortable life. This has often meant buying western goods, promoted on the basis of being rational. These western goods extended from food and clothing, to electronic goods, cars, and western-style housing and furniture. Francks writes that in the 1970s and 1980s, Japan's boom years, Japanese consumers were faced with a choice of goods that surpassed anything they had known before. Being able to negotiate the range of both Japanese and western style products available in the marketplace, they became very discerning.

> Japanese consumers developed their taste for fashion, branding and product differentiation in a retail environment that could encompass both the extremes of niche marketing and the overwhelming, must-have fad. (Francks 2009:188)

Francks describes the Japanese consumer in the following terms:

> The Japanese consumer who shopped the world in the bubble years became renowned not just for their wads of dollars, but also for their sophisticated knowledge, their willingness to pay for the best quality or the most fashionable brand.... (Francks 2009:184)

Japanese people show a sophisticated understanding of the concepts of couture and branding, which is perhaps a legacy of their past experience with kimono, once all individually crafted pieces. Tobin writes in his introduction to *Re-Made in Japan,* that: "in a changing Japan, what people consume may be as important as what they produce in shaping a sense of self" (Tobin 1992:8). The Japanese shopper, a dedicated consumer, demands quality, attention to detail, style, and fashion and is concerned with value for money and appropriateness of the garment. This is as true of kimono consumers, as it is of any other shopper in Japan. A return to *wafuku* suggests that at least some consumers are reevaluating their native fashion system and are finding it suitable for their lifestyle.

In line with what Francks wrote about the Japanese consumer in general, value for money, convenience, and branding are key factors in today's kimono market. The success of new brands is dependent on the creation of an image which resonates for the target market and is placed at a price range which they can afford. Furifu, Berry Koubou, and others have managed to capture the heart of young female kimono wearers with romantic, dreamy, cute, and retro looks. Kidera's venture in putting kimono and suits together looks to have a promising future, but in general it appears that prêt-à-porter kimono will be the way of the future, at least for casual wear. This would be in line with movements in western fashion, such as the development of the prêt-à-porter suit.

This chapter shows kimono as part of the economic system of fashion. It reveals not only developments within the tradition bound kimono industry but also that it is possible to have a successful kimono business employing the logic of the fashion industry and remain outside the structure of the kimono industry. There is new innovation, a huge twenty-four-hour market on the internet, branding, and networking. Popularity is shifting from formal wear to cheaper, informal wear. Kimono is slowly becoming prêt-à-porter and is increasingly made on machines in polyester, cotton, or wool. Kimono is providing a way to be both Japanese and fashionable. Within this increasingly democratized market, there are still some craftspeople who continue to survive and even prosper using time-honored ways of production.

There are those who decry recent changes, seeing them as the devaluation of kimono. As kimono aligns itself nearer and nearer the western fashion system, it may lose something of the unique attractions of kimono. The kimono as an item inherited, worn for three generations may no longer be relevant, in the face of an emerging new market of everyday kimono in a low price range, for younger people. We can see striking similarities with the Taisho period. In an economic depression, mechanization made cheap silk kimono available for everyday wear. Today, used kimono, polyester and cotton kimono, and machine-made items make kimono more available than ever before. The increase in consumer options should be a wake-up call for the kimono industry which needs to streamline its unwieldy distribution system and become more in touch with the needs of the consumer in order to remain viable. Change is coming, but it is very slow, and for many areas of production, it may be happening too late. Chapter 6 examines the other half of the equation. Who is buying kimono and what do they look for? By listening to the voices of kimono wearers, perhaps a better balance can be obtained between those on the production side and kimono consumers.

Bibliography

Cliffe, S., J. Morris, and O. Boe. *Kimono Shopping in Tokyo*. https://www.youtube.com/watch?v=MpDmqORszJA (Accessed February 4, 2015).

Francks, P. (2009) *The Japanese Consumer*. Cambridge, New York, Melbourne: Cambridge University Press.

Shinjuku Senshoku Kyougi Kai, Shinjuku Dyers Mutual Association. http://tokyo-somemono.com/link/index.html (Accessed July 27, 2016).

Tobin, J. Ed. (1992) *Re-Made in Japan. Everyday Life and Consumer Taste in a Changing Society*. New Haven and London: Yale.

Tokyo to Sen Shoku Kougyou Kyoudou Kumiai, Tokyo Craft Dyers Mutual Association. http://www.tokyo-senshoku.com (Accessed July 27, 2016).

The Tokyo Traditional Dyers Mutual Association. http://www.tokyotegakiyuzen.or.jp (Accessed July 27, 2016).

6 Wearers and Wardrobes

Starting Kimono Wearing

The fashion system is realized in the creation of the fashion items, and in their diffusion to the public through media images. However, a fashion system does not exist without fashion leaders and followers. If there are no wearers, then there is no fashion. This chapter investigates kimono wearing practice through a wardrobe survey of kimono wearers, discussion of kimono groups, and also through interviews with kimono wearers inside and outside Japan. The real renaissance started toward the end of the 1990s, when there was a boom in the popularity of Japanese material goods and culture. This led to a reevaluation of kimono, and new kimono-related products began appearing in kimono shops. However, the new wave was only noticeable to those who were looking for it. The emergence of kimono wearing groups in the streets was significant in encouraging new kimono wearers, and then at the beginning of the 2000s, the publication of the new magazines that were described in Chapter 4 became important resources for inspiring and encouraging kimono wearing. There is also no doubt that the desire for new forms of Japanese culture from abroad has brought increasing attention to the kimono, but this has little effect on the domestic market.

Wardrobe Studies

Fashion research is more than often about the economy and production side of fashion. It is about marketing, production, famous designers, and collections. There is also much research about how people look, the cognitive end of the equation. There has been much less research done on the lived experience of clothing; what people choose to wear and why; what the intention of the wearer is; and the relationship between their clothing, their bodies, and identity. *Through the Wardrobe* (2001) by editors Guy, Green, and Banim is a collection of studies showing how women negotiate and "do" fashion through their clothes, within the fashion system, which is generally framed as patriarchal. Women may contest such control being unable to participate because of size, economics, or other reasons or through their own choice not to. Women are also active agents in constructing their own wardrobes with their own meanings; conforming to or subverting the system. They are able to reveal or conceal their true selves through their dressing practice. Shopping or collecting clothing is a part of the self-constructing project. Tseëlon, a pioneer in the field, argues that studying fashion is only just becoming respectable and has a history of marginalization because it is gendered area of research and is therefore often trivialized as being "just a women's issue" (2001).

Believing that there is much to be learned from the wearers as well as the producers of kimono, this chapter focuses on how people "do" kimono. Woodward (2007) describes wardrobes as embodying an aesthetic of the self, which develops and changes over time, throughout the wearer's life. Seen in these terms, the act of dressing is actually an act of constructing the self, from wardrobe items that are external to the self. The self is then performed through the wearing of clothes. As stated earlier, Miller (2010) described the importance of cutting a fine figure to Trinidadians, who, contrary to a western Cartesian self, see the true self as situated on the surface, in the dressing, makeup and in their performance.

There are many different ways of purchasing kimono, collecting, and storage and usage which are explored here. In addition to this, kimono wearers reveal many different reasons for their kimono wearing and attribute different meanings to it. Kimono can embody meaning as a part of a collection, as a memory or a nostalgic item or even as national dress. With these factors in mind, several different approaches are taken here, to inform about several aspects of the kimono wearing experience. Interviews were open ended, enabling the wearers to freely discuss their activities, their reasons for wearing and in some cases both memories of the past and plans for the future.

Kimono Wearing Groups

The years 1999 and 2000 are significant in the kimono renaissance because these are the years when kimono wearing in the street started to become popular. Starting with *Kimono de Ginza* in 1999, which began admitting women in 2000, kimono wearing groups have been emerging all over Japan and even overseas. Assman (2008), who sees today's kimono as an invented tradition, describes kimono wearing as a mine field, where not choosing the correct kimono according to age, gender, status, season, occasion, and taste will result in huge embarrassment and loss of face to the wearer. However, her study of *Kimono de Ginza,* which she called a postmodern group, found that many members were shunning silk for more casual cotton. She did not make the logical leap to see that it is not kimono wearing, but the *kitsuke schools* that are the invented tradition, and kimono wearing is continuing its own evolution in spite of the schools. New ways of understanding and doing kimono are emerging through casual kimono wearing groups and events. The *Kimono de Ginza* group and *Kimono Jack* group provided wardrobe surveys for this work, and overseas kimono wearers responded to an internet version of the same survey.

Kimono wearing groups meet on a regular basis, with the express purpose of enjoying wearing and discussing kimono together. The *Kimono Jack* movement (which comes from the concept of high-jacking a space with kimono wearers) has spread not only all around Japan, but also in the United States, UK, France, Spain, The Netherlands, Taiwan, Indonesia, and many other countries. Usually, the groups are informal, and unlike the kimono schools, nonhierarchical. They provide a safe environment for beginning kimono wearers, and a space where one can ask questions, learn from more experienced wearers, and enjoy learning about other people's outfits and coordination. In some senses, these groups are taking over the role of the kimono dressing schools.

Japanologist Harumi researched Japanese style tribes in postwar Japan (2012), and Kawamura has written about Lolita tribes in Harajuku, Tokyo (2006). There are some similarities between large groups of kimono wearers and such style tribes. First, they occupy the same spaces: Ginza, Harajuku, Roppongi, and Shibuya, though they are now moving into the provinces as well. These spaces were the upmarket areas where western goods and clothing were showcased to the Japanese people in the 1950s. By wearing stylish western clothing, young people set themselves against the hegemonic look of the day, which was kimono or plain and unflattering serviceable garments. Today, kimono wearers set themselves against the hegemony of western clothing by wearing Japanese dress. Second, the attention to appearance is similar. In the 1950s, when men were not supposed to pay attention to appearance, young men dressed in Ivy League style and were dandy. They were similar to the mod movement in British culture, in that they paid attention to tailoring and small details. Kimono wearers also pay attention to details and spend time on dressing and coordination. Third, both groups loiter and stand around occupying public space. Fourth, both groups require the gaze of the hegemonic majority. They are dressing to be seen.

There are also significant differences between the kimono wearing movement and postwar style tribes and Lolita's in Harajuku. Hebdige (1979) states that style tribes usually emerge from the working classes, and postwar tribes represented working people taking over upper-class environments. The kimono wearing movement is hard to define by class, but it is not predominantly working class. It comprises students, professionals, workers, and housewives. It cuts across gender, age, and class boundaries. Another important difference is that other tribes have appropriated the clothing of overseas culture, such as the borrowing of American styles or those of Victorian England, but kimono wearers are drawing on their own culture and history.

Kimono wearers have no intention of being subversive, and unlike the postwar tribes, they have not been moved out of these spaces, yet. However, when the groups become too large, they are warned by the police not to cause any blockage in the streets. *Kimono Jack* moves around different locations, announced on the internet, in order to avoid police harassment but have been guilty of causing blockages in the streets on Omote-Sando in Harajuku, when several hundred wearers gathered together. The police also warn kimono wearers to move away from a major crossing in Ginza and gather elsewhere to take a group photograph. In the Edo period, it was the display of inappropriate wealth that was a problem for the authorities, but now it is crowd control that is seen as a problem. It is ironic that the wearing of Japan's native garment should cause surveillance by the police.

If kimono wearers can be seen in any way as subversive, it is only in their rebellion against the anonymous and ephemeral fast fashion that is displayed all around them. They offer an alternative that is native, rooted in a specific location and can last for several generations.

Kimono Collections

According to Belk (1995), humans have made collections of items that they do not need since ancient times, but a rise in collecting can be seen as part of consumer culture. In Europe, the Medici family was famous for its collection of paintings, sculptures, gems, coins, and other artifacts. In Japan, it is likely that wealthy people in the Edo period collected large quantities of *kosode,* or kimono, beyond what they would actually need, because of their desire to parade in the streets showing off gorgeous new designs. One of the ways that governments tried to curb such behavior and maintain rigidity in social class was by enacting sumptuary laws, which sought to maintain the relationships between status and quality of clothing. These were usually unsuccessful but led to the generation of new styles, as discussed in Chapter 2.

It cannot be denied that many kimono wearers are also habitual kimono collectors, and some of them put considerable time, effort, and money into developing their collections. Where a wardrobe ends and a collection begins is not clear, but Belk describes some features of collecting as a distinct kind of consumption. It is consumption that is not for utilitarian purposes. The meaning of the items in the collection is more than their usefulness. Sometimes people collect sets of items, which are valued as a set. The collecting is purposeful and continuous, so collections are always improved, either by becoming larger or by becoming upgraded in quality. They are not subject to fashion change and retain value to the collector even though they are past models and no longer useful. According to Belk, the acquisitions often involve passion, and the collection is therefore given value by the owner, beyond what is rational. Belk gives the following definition of a collection.

Collecting is the process of actively, selectively, and passionately acquiring and possessing things removed from ordinary use and perceived as part of a set of non-identical objects or experiences. (1995:67)

In these terms, it is clear that some of the people here have kimono collections. An interesting fact about the kimono collections though is that kimono can be both an item in a collection and be in use as an item of clothing. This is because old items can be paired up with new ones, in order to create new images, bringing them back into fashion. The act of collecting is materialistic. Sometimes there is guilt in spending too much, or acquiring too much. The guilt experienced is justified by rationalizing the value of the collection. It is often considered to be "saving" items that would otherwise be lost or thrown away. It is given all kinds of justifications such as being for future generations, for education, or even for investment (though collectors are loath to part with their collections). The guilt is also offset by the pleasures involved in the shopping experience. This could be in commissioning new works from a favored artist, to the joys of planning a trip to Japan to go to shrine flea markets, or even the thrill of the online auction. Here are recorded the results of a small investigation conducted on kimono collections.

A study of fifty non-Japanese respondents was conducted through Survey Monkey, to find out about their kimono collections. This was compared with data from a similar Japanese wardrobe study conducted at *Kimono De Ginza* and *Kimono Jack* which also totaled fifty respondents. Only one-third of the non-Japanese respondents had actually been to Japan, meaning that Japan is still to a certain extent an imagined world for the majority of overseas kimono wearers. Most wearers became interested in kimono through other kinds of Japanese culture, and these were divided evenly between those who mentioned more traditional culture, such as antiques and art, and those who mentioned anime and cos-play. Several people mentioned *geisha* or *maiko* culture as an inspiration, and some said photographs or the film, *Memoirs of a Geisha.* Almost all the respondents were entirely dependent on the internet as a source of information about kimono, and seventeen of them said that *Immortal Geisha* was their main source of information. Only four respondents learned to wear kimono from a book alone, and in all cases the book was Yamanaka's *The Book of Kimono.* Before the internet made online resources available, this was the standard text to learn kimono dressing. The results showed an overwhelming preference for using the computer, and there are now numerous videos available on YouTube demonstrating the dressing process. It is far easier to follow a video than a series of drawings or photographs. Only sixteen wearers had worn kimono for over four years, and four wearers had worn it for more than eight years. Thirty-five respondents said that they wear kimono once a month or less, meaning that they are very occasional wearers, and it would be hard for them to develop their dressing skills since frequency of wearing is a condition of developing such skill.

Almost half the overseas respondents owned ten kimono or fewer, but one person had over two hundred. The respondents who have many kimono are those who love Japanese fashion and textiles. In these cases, they tend to be collectors of beautiful clothes. When asking about their wardrobes, it was apparent that most wearers have studied kimono to a certain extent as they were familiar with the names of different types of kimono. e-Bay, Shinei, Ryu Japan (now defunct), and Ichiroya were the most popular sources of kimono. While Yahoo Japan and Rakuten each have over 50,000 kimono on sale daily, they are not in the price range that most non-Japanese can purchase, and many of the stores do not ship abroad. This means that these kimono wearers are competing with each other to buy from the limited sources available to them. Most people wanted to wear their kimono for a special occasion, so they were meeting together in groups, such as Kimono Jacks, in order to do so.

The kimono collections of Japanese and non-Japanese kimono wearers were quite different. The whole Japanese group owned only eight *furisode,* whereas the non-Japanese group owned sixty-nine. No Japanese owned *hikizuri* or *uchikake,* dancing or wedding kimono, but several non-Japanese did. The non-Japanese group owned twenty-six *kurotomesode,* whereas the Japanese group owned nine. The Japanese group owned mainly *tsumugi* or *komon,* with a few *houmongi* or *tsukesage* for formal wear. In other words, their collections correspond to a functional western wardrobe mainly composed of casual wear. There were only nine *tsumugi* in the non-Japanese sample, meaning that woven wear, a staple of the Japanese wardrobe, is almost non-existent in non-Japanese kimono collections. Although kimono is no longer perceived as casual wear by the general public, Japanese kimono collections overwhelmingly comprise casual wear.

Non-Japanese and Japanese kimono wearers are starting from different points, the results of which are very different kimono collections. Several Japanese wearers mentioned that kimono was in their environment, or that their mothers, grandmothers, or aunts wore it. The majority of Japanese were taught by a real person, either a relative or a teacher in a kimono dressing school. Only one person in the non-Japanese sample had a living teacher. For most of the non-Japanese, the trigger for interest in kimono is photographs, pictures, or film. Non-Japanese enter from the outside, through the visual image. These collections are therefore very much influenced by the visual image. This leads us to question whether the visual images that one experiences outside Japan reveal the real Japan. One is more likely to take photographs in best dresses rather than casual wear, *maiko, geisha,* and actresses are more likely to be photographed than ordinary people, and formal kimono are brighter and more colorful than everyday wear.

Therefore it would seem that the images that reach people outside Japan continue to reproduce a Japan that is somehow more exotic than the real place. More than half of the collections of non-Japanese kimono wearers were formal or exotic wear such as *maiko*'s dancing kimono or *kurotomesode* which is used only for weddings. Conversely, casual kimono are vastly underrepresented in their collections. The Japanese kimono wearers have practical collections, and they do not tend to buy kimono they will not use, such as very formal garments. Japanese consider *tsumugi* as an important part of their kimono collection because of their use as everyday wear. These kimono, however, do not appear very bright or attractive in photographic images, and thus they are not being bought by non-Japanese kimono wearers. This suggests that if there is increasing interest in kimono from outside Japan, then there is a market for different kimono from the ones that sell most in Japan. At the present time, non-Japanese are not investing large amounts of money in tailored garments but are usually buying at the cheap and used end. However, the used formal kimono that are not very usable in Japan can find a new life with new meanings in different locations and contexts. As interest in Japanese manga, anime culture, and cos-playing continues to increase, it is reasonable to expect that the market for kimono overseas will also increase.

The other interesting fact about the investigation into non-Japanese kimono wearers was that the results demonstrated clearly that it is no longer necessary to go to kimono dressing school. There are some accomplished kimono wearers in other countries who have never set foot in Japan. They are not only accomplished dressers but are familiar with kimono vocabulary and have educated themselves in many areas concerned with the kimono. This shows the power of the internet both for education and the purchasing of kimono. Through YouTube, blogs, and web forums as well as shopping sites kimono wearing has begun to spread around the world. Just as the new department stores were a force for democratization in late Meiji and the Taisho periods, the internet is now performing the same function, bypassing official channels for the appropriation and education of kimono.

Interviews

This section comprises another type of wardrobe investigation. Rather than quantifying the numbers and types of kimono that wearers have in their collections, it is concerned with the reasons why people choose to wear kimono rather than the default western clothing. When someone digresses from the clothing norm in such a radical way, such an action is not taken without thought. Especially as it can be argued to be more expensive, inconvenient, or troublesome than western clothing, such a decision and practice must be seen as purposeful. The wearers interviewed here are relatively well known in kimono circles, at least in the Tokyo area. Either they work in places where they can be easily seen or they are involved in some kind of kimono work or kimono promotional activities or volunteer work. As such, they can be considered influential as style leaders. Some of them were willing to show parts of their collections in the photographs, and these images help to document their kimono, and how they store them.

Okumoto Akihisa—Kimono and a Camera

Okumoto is a professional fashion photographer and is around forty years old at the time of writing. When he was around thirty years old, he became aware that his grandmother, who had always sewn kimono, was getting confused and losing her health. He wanted something that his grandmother had made, so he asked her to sew him a *yukata*. When she had made it, he kept wearing it on and off throughout the summer. This was his introduction to wearing kimono. As he really liked the *yukata,* he then began to frequent the local kimono shops and second-hand kimono shops, looking for cheap kimono and *haori*.

As a person who is in touch with in fashion, he had always been interested in order-made and semi-made-to-order clothing, especially suits and jackets. Then he realized that kimono could be order-made clothing and so he had a kimono made for him. He now has his kimono order-made as they feel better than used ones he has bought. Before he even realized it, he was wearing kimono more often than western clothing. Western clothing began to feel tight somewhere, but in kimono he could relax. More important to him though was that because he is not tall and slim, he could never achieve the look he wanted with western dress. His ideal was to be very tall and slim, and the clothes that he liked did not look good on him because he is neither tall nor slim. He felt that with the kimono, his shape didn't matter, and the kimono was more forgiving, suiting his body type better.

Now he wears kimono almost every day, though not in the rain. He has not had any difficulty at work because of wearing kimono. He says that the only thing he thinks he could not do in kimono would be shooting in water. Apart from that he can go anywhere or do anything in it. He carries his gear in a large rucksack and wears sneakers or boots with his kimono. He has some used silk kimono, but mostly now he wears order-made cottons. He often wears women's antique *haori*. There are two reasons for this. First, he likes cute things and brightly colored designs, and second, he cannot carry his photographic gear in a men's

Figure 6.1 New Year card by Okumoto Akihisa.
Photo: Okumoto Akihisa.

Figure 6.2 Okumoto Akihisa and his kimono wardrobe.

Photo: Okumoto Akihisa.

haori, because the bottom of the sleeve is sewn to the body of the garment. Women's *hoari* have a slit under the sleeves, and the sleeves swing separately from the body under the arm. This enables him to carry his rucksack easily. Sometimes he asks for this slit to be made bigger, to accommodate his rucksack better.

His favorite shop is *Someori Kodama* from Miyazaki prefecture in Kyushu. This shop has sourced cottons from all over Japan, and Okumoto enjoys choosing from their selection when they come to Tokyo and have a sale. His personal style is an interesting mixture of East and West. Since childhood he has liked checks, so he has many checked kimono. Pink and red are his favorite colors. He usually wears a long sleeved T-shirt and sneakers or boots and only wears a *nagajuban* on formal occasions. He sometimes wears two kimono on top of one another, if it is cold. He also adds a *haori,* coat, or cape and sometimes even a down jacket to his kimono outfit. Although kimono keeps one warm, he finds it hot when he goes indoors, to a heated room. It is not easy to cool down if one gets too hot, so he prefers unlined cotton kimono. Using cottons, Okumoto says that made-to-order kimono are about 30,000 yen, which is not much different in price from high-quality western clothing. He almost never wears a *hakama,* which is historically more of a samurai and upper-class garment anyway. However, he wore one for his sister's wedding. Most of his own friends have more casual weddings, so he does not need to wear it. He is not strict about rules of appropriateness. For most weddings, he wears a lined pink silk *omeishi* kimono which has a nice shine to it. On top of it, he wears a black formal men's *haori*. He believes that this is the appropriate level of formality for the weddings he is involved with. No one has ever told him that kimono is inappropriate for his work. Often people ask him why he wears kimono. Sometimes he tells the story above, but at other times he just says, "Why not?" Most people respect him and say it is easy to remember him. A lot of people tell him they want to wear kimono, too. He would think twice now about wearing western clothing to work. Kimono has become his brand. People would be surprised to see him in other clothing. An Okumoto image can be seen in the New Year card, Figure 6.1 and his colorful wardrobe can be seen in Figure 6.2. Okumoto has about forty or fifty kimono. He keeps his everyday kimono on shelves and hangers and out of season ones in *furoshiki,* wrapping cloths. He has just one kimono chest in which he keeps his better items. Okumoto's vision for kimono is featured in his photographs in the final chapter of this book.

Lyuta Ito—A Tailor for Our Times

Ito Lyuta is about fifty years old at the time of writing and is a kimono tailor who has been wearing kimono on a daily basis since his late thirties. He previously worked as a writer, and while he was doing this work he experienced some serious pain in his lower back. One day, when he put on *yukata* and obi, he discovered that the back pain disappeared. He found that the obi corrected his posture and relieved his suffering. A while later he moved to the city of Kawagoe, which is nicknamed Ko-Edo, small Edo, for its traditional buildings. He found that in this environment he felt comfortable wearing kimono, and he started to wear it everyday. He learnt how to wear kimono through television, and he also asked questions on the Japanese social networking site, Mixi. He made some good friends here and found it a convenient way to communicate and learn about kimono. Lyuta wears everyday kimono in Figure 6.3.

His first kimono was a denim one, and then *Kawagoe Tozan,* a kind of cotton weaving made in Kawagoe. He also bought some *yukata* and some second-hand silk kimono. His formal kimono are mostly polyester, and he does not worry about comfort for formal wear because it is worn so little. It is impossible to tell that it is polyester just by looking at it. For Lyuta, everyday things are more important than formal ones. He has about fifteen cotton kimono and *yukata,* which he has tailored himself, and he has some winter woolens, too. He has a formal black kimono for mourning, but no suit. He hardly ever wears his silk kimono as he feels comfortable in cotton. Figure 6.4 shows Lyuta with his kimono wardrobe.

Figure 6.3 Lyuta Ito in his self-tailored kimono.
Photo: Lyuta Ito.

Lyuta began to think about what work he could do wearing kimono as he found he was comfortable in it and did not want to revert to wearing western suits. So he started to do tailoring, as he was interested in it, and he felt he was not too old to learn the techniques and make a successful living from it. He was already too old was to learn some other Japanese arts, such as becoming a professional Japanese musician. In addition, there is a shortage of male tailors. Many tailors do not actually wear kimono themselves, and as a man who wears kimono all the time he feels that he has some insider knowledge to offer, that women tailors or non kimono wearing tailors do not have. Although he started out wearing kimono to blend in with the traditional scenery of Kawagoe, Lyuta does not believe that the heart of kimono is about the patterns,

Figure 6.4 Lyuta Ito and his kimono wardrobe.

Photo: Lyuta Ito.

but about the structure. He is influenced by some well-known dressing experts. One of them explains that there are two important elements in kimono: The vertical principle (vertical lines that go with the standing human), which is balanced out with the horizontal principle embodied in the obi. For Lyuta, the most important parts of the kimono are the sleeves, which provide protection and comfort and the obi, which he has found has health benefits. He believes that the kimono improves posture, movement, and breathing. He also feels that it restores Japaneseness, a certain way of being and moving. After the structure of the kimono comes the cloth and finally the color and pattern.

People who come to order a kimono today are coming from a background of western style clothing. This means that they are used to wearing plain fabrics and are not generally accustomed to wearing a lot of pattern. Lyuta thinks that this influences their choice of kimono. Often they choose a gray or black plain kimono first and then move onto patterns when they have more experience. Older women also choose brighter colors such as pink, which used to be reserved for younger females. The lack of patterns, particularly seasonal references, make kimono more flexible and convenient and open up more possibilities for designers, which Lyuta sees as a positive thing. People can layer their kimono for winter, which is more flexible than lining kimono and wearing kimono underwear. He is interested in plain and in striped kimono rather than seasonal or traditional patterns.

Lyuta believes that wearing the kimono takes practice, and it takes a while before one can really feel comfortable in it. He believes that the argument that kimono is impractical for today's lifestyle is not true. Kimono was once worn by all Japanese, so how can it suddenly become impractical? One needs to practice to wear it well. He says that if one uses chopsticks once a month, one cannot get used to using them. If one wears kimono once a month, one cannot wear it well. It takes a little skill. It is not that there is something wrong with the chopsticks or the kimono, only that the user is unpracticed. He finds kimono comfortable, practical, and easy to wear in an urban and fairly international environment. There are people from many countries near where he lives in central Tokyo, and diversity makes it easier to wear something different from the mainstream.

Lyuta sews all his own kimono. He sometimes uses western dress fabric instead of kimono fabric. He freely mixes western clothing, sweaters, and polo-necked shirts with kimono and has also converted women's kimono into men's ones. Although he does not necessarily think that all Japanese should wear kimono, he thinks that it is a good lifestyle choice. He is concerned that Japanese have forgotten their roots, and their life is no longer natural. The kimono somehow makes Japanese think about living a simpler and more natural life than they do today. It is not easy, particularly for men, to choose to wear kimono, as they are still too expensive. He would welcome more cheaper kimono on the market. He believes that the balance between western dress and kimono is still not right. In the future, he would like to somehow integrate his skills in photography, music, kimono sewing, and styling, to teach people about a life in kimono.

Kento Itoh—Nomad with a Message

Figure 6.5 Kento Itoh standing on salt at Uyuni, Bolivia.
Photo: Kento Itoh.

Figure 6.6 Kento Itoh walking in the Sahara desert, Morocco.
Photo: Kento Itoh.

Kento Itoh is an extraordinary young man. Tall and slim, with a long pony tail and bearded face, he cuts a dashing figure in a denim kimono, a rustic looking *haori,* black *tabi* and *geta*. He carries a rather worn small canvas backpack. While this image turns heads, it is even more surprising to realize that the backpack contains almost everything he owns. His journey started when he was twenty-two, and he went to New Zealand for a year to study English. This gave him a taste for travel, and he spent the next two years in Australia, where he worked on a banana plantation and then took a diver's license and worked as a diving instructor, to save money. Around this time, his experiences abroad started to make him think about the earth and environmental problems, such as global warming. He also began to think about the relationship between place and culture, and what it meant to be Japanese. He decided in 2011 that he could express his Japanese identity through wearing kimono.

He returned to Japan for only one month before embarking on a year-long trip through the American continent from the north right down through South America. Following that, he traveled through Europe and the Middle East for another year and then spent 2014 making his way through Africa and Asia. This sounds like a rich person's privileged lifestyle, but Itoh is not rich. He performed many kinds of menial labor to save up to travel. He has slept outside, at friends' houses or occasionally at hostels or guest houses. Especially when he was an inexperienced traveler he got into some dangerous situations including being caught up in an uprising in Egypt with riots in the street and a bus set on fire. He experienced the pain of tear gas. He travels with his backpack, camera, and laptop, and a change of kimono.

Since 2012, Itoh has been wearing kimono everyday. He owns six kimono which were all gifted to him. Apart from his denim kimono which his friend designed, they are all used kimono. One is silk, one raw silk, and the others are cotton. He has two *yukata* and two *nagajuban* (which are too small for him). He was

Figure 6.7 Kento Itoh sitting in a cave in Antelope Canyon, Arizona, United States.
Photo: Kento Itoh.

given three pairs of *tabi* in 2012, and he is still wearing them, though they are beginning to get holes. He has three obi and two *jinbei* which he wears in the summer. He also has a few western clothes lying forgotten in his parents' house in Hokkaido. In spite of his minimal kimono wardrobe, his travels have attracted wide attention from kimono wearers on Facebook so that he has become a kimono icon. Probably he is the only really famous kimono icon with so few kimono. However, his reasons for wearing kimono are deep and serious. Not only does wearing kimono inform people that he is Japanese, but it also is an expression of the fact that he is born into Japanese culture. He believes that by respecting the environment and the culture that develops in each place, one can live more naturally and begin to solve some of the world's problems. His wearing kimono is a call to listen to our cultures. When he visits other people who devote their lives to maintaining traditional ways of being and doing, meeting them wearing kimono is his sign of respect.

When Itoh wears kimono he is watched. At first, this was difficult to get used to, but now he can enjoy it. One hurdle that men encounter when they begin to wear kimono is being in the gaze, when most men dress to blend in. For Itoh this is not a question of being a fashionable person. In his case, when he wears kimono abroad, he feels that he is representing Japan, and he must behave in an honorable way. If he behaves badly he will disgrace the kimono, his culture, and country too. When he is in Japan, he feels that his ancestors watch him, and he can communicate with his heritage more easily in kimono. The kimono has a calming effect for him. People also talk to him readily when he is wearing kimono, so this makes it easy to start conversation. He is spoken to more in foreign countries, but he says that he is watched more in Japan. Itoh has no job or home. Wherever he sleeps is home. Having returned to Japan, he has been continually asked by different organizations to come and talk about his travels, his ideas about culture and world peace. He thinks seriously about the future of Japan and in what direction it should be going. The drive for economic supremacy he believes is mistaken. Itoh has written a kindle book about his travels and what he learnt about culture through them, and his vision of Japan's contribution to the world in the future. This has proved extremely popular. He would like to design and produce a range of cheap, ordinary kimono for ordinary working people. When asked if there was anything (object) that he really wanted he laughed and replied, "a plane." Then he said, "a *hakama* and a little money to start my kimono business." His hope is that people will respect and learn from each other's cultures and get along peacefully together. Figures 6.5, 6.6 and 6.7 shows Itoh on his travels.

Nishiwaki Ryuji and Hisae—Cultural Event Planners

Mr. and Mrs. Nishiwaki are very active in promoting kimono wearing through the planning and producing of kimono based cultural events. The joint interview made for an interesting comparison as they had very different memories concerning their histories with kimono. Mr. Nishiwaki's grandparents were about ten years older than his wife's, and they had a couture clothing business in Tokyo. While his main childhood memories are of a fairly wealthy, stylish grandmother in the late Taisho period, Mrs. Nishiwaki comes from a farming family in the Fukushima area, and her memories are of a mother who struggled to keep her family fed in the lean postwar years.

Mrs. Nishiwaki's hard-working mother was always in the fields or kitchen. She was constantly reminding the children that times were hard so not to waste anything. She was almost always in work wear and dirty from the farm but would occasionally put on a kimono to take her daughter into town. On those days, her mother was transformed, a really beautiful image for Mrs. Nishiwaki. Looking back, she says that her mother probably wore a very ordinary kimono, but in her memory it is a beautiful image. Mrs. Nishiwaki has a curious photograph which says seven, five, three, aged four. She couldn't understand the meaning until her mother told her that her next door neighbor was celebrating seven, five, three, and Mrs. Nishiwaki had begged to wear a kimono too, so they dressed her up in one, even though she was not the appropriate age to celebrate the ceremony.

Her summer vacations were spent playing outside. During the morning the children did homework, in the afternoon they would run around, play ballgames, and explore. After dinner, they would take a bath and then put on *yukata*. The girls would then get together to watch fireflies or play with small fireworks. She remembers that one could watch the girls growing up through the *yukata*. When they were new they had large tucks sewn into the shoulders and waist, and as arms and legs grew longer their mothers would let the tucks out bit by bit. Every couple of years someone who had grown out of theirs would get a new one, and they would talk about the latest flower designs and colors. Her

Figure 6.8 Nishiwaki Hisae: Akasaka Prince Hotel Kimono Fashion Show, 2012.

Photo: Kumagai Takura.

Figure 6.9 Nishiwaki Ryuji: Akasaka Prince Hotel Kimono Fashion Show, 2012.

Photo: Kumagai Takura.

Figure 6.10 Group in new styles of wafuku created by Nishiwaki Ryuji, Hisae: Tango Kimono Fashion Show, 2013. *Photo:* Kumagai Takura.

summers are remembered as days of endless pleasure, and *yukata* is an important part of her memory of growing up.

At fifteen, she wanted to buy her own kimono, and she went into town to buy a wool kimono and *haori* ensemble. At the time, it was popular to wear an ikat design in dark blue, but Mrs. Nishiwaki came back with a bright red one. The family was in uproar. She was told that she couldn't possibly go out in that, so she was sent back to the shop to exchange it for a more conventional color. She begged her mother to let her go and have her hair done up in the Japanese style, so her mother paid for it. Then she could not lie down to go to sleep, so she slept all night sitting at a low table with her head resting on it. She found a friend to go with her to the first visit to the shrine at New Year wearing kimono. Her mother felt sure that her daughter was a little different from the other girls.

Mr. Nishiwaki's grandmother always wore kimono and insisted that one should wear a *haori* with a crest when going into Ginza. It was a special place not only for shopping and entertainment but also for parading one's kimono. Ginza was a stage for dressing up, and everyone who went there was beautiful. Mr. Nishiwaki wore *yukata* for *matsuri* and *ochigosan,* a kind of religious celebration of children. His grandmother was a teacher of flower arrangement, and just before New Year the *Katsugi-Ya* would come to the house. *Katsugu* means to carry, and the kimono seller had all the bolts piled up on his back. He would bring them to the house and then lay them all out on the tatami mats for everyone to see. All the women who studied flower arranging would be there, choosing new bolts of cloth that they would sew into kimono for the New Year. He had the impression that kimono were important and special, and they made one beautiful. The kimono bolts and cloth they had in store as a couture clothing business were also very valuable. When the war came and everyone was short of food, farmers would not sell food, but they would exchange it for bolts of cloth, which they knew would be valuable again after the war, when people wanted to make new clothes.

Mrs. Nishiwaki started working in fashion design at twenty-one, making costumes for dance, and with her very first salary, she ordered a *houmongi* kimono which she paid for in installments. She had nothing to wear with it, but a friend lent her an obi, and she wrote to her mother, who realized that she was serious, so she sewed her a *nagajuban,* under kimono. Then she went to a *kitsuke* school so she could learn how to wear it. There were other women around her who liked kimono, so they would meet for lunch wearing it. She bought an *oshima tsumugi* and a *hakata* obi to go with it. They are traditional, high-quality goods. At this point in time she had not thought about kimono as fashion. Then one of her seniors at work had an experience that really made Mrs. Nishiwaki think. The senior was on a train wearing kimono and an older woman who saw her invited her to go to her home, and look at kimono. There was something about the senior that inspired this stranger to invite her to her house. This senior told Mrs. Nishiwaki about the Ikeda Shigeko collection of kimono, which was being shown around Tokyo in major department stores. Mrs. Nishiwaki went to see this collection and was astounded by the amazing fashion sense embodied in the late nineteenth and early twentieth century kimono. She had been working away in fashion because she loved the styles of other countries, and then she suddenly encountered an amazing fashion experience right under her nose.

Mr. Nishiwaki would go and choose kimono with his wife and then started to wear them himself around 1993, partly to accompany his wife and also because he was interested in tea ceremony. He also realized that he had grown, and he could not get into his tuxedo anymore, so he decided that he would wear kimono on formal occasions, which would save him having to buy new things if his size changed. About this time there was a group of men meeting in Tokyo to wear kimono, which eventually became the kimono wearing group *Kimono De Ginza.* He began to wear kimono with these men, but he had some differences with them. He found them to be rather overconcerned with quality, and wanting the finest *tsumugi,* etc., but the look was still very safe and conservative. For Mr. Nishiwaki that was not fashion. He felt rebellious. He wanted to wear more interesting kimono, even if they were cheap and poor quality. He preferred the style of some rock musicians who wore kimono. He also looked at books about the Edo period and saw that they wore it in a more free and playful way. He thought that kimono was very broad, and that not only silk but other kinds of kimono were important. In Edo, they did not wear polyester or wool because they did not have it. They wore what they had, what fitted the age. We should wear what we have and what fits the age. He doesn't feel that silk really fits our age or lifestyle, especially not for men's underwear which needs to be washed regularly.

About twelve years ago, Mr. and Mrs. Nishiwaki were interviewed about wearing kimono by *Seinken Shinbun,* a newspaper for the textile industry. The editors of the newspaper were interested in holding an event to promote kimono and asked the Nishiwakis and two other people to organize it. This was the beginning of *Kimono Biyori* organization and events. They created posters, flyers, a webpage, and name cards and gathered volunteers as dressers. The first Kimono User show was held. They had no idea if anyone would turn up at all, but over two thousand people came, and there were many games, events, and booths selling kimono. They gathered donations from sponsors, from advertising spaces in the leaflets and from the booth spaces. For the first three years, the event was very successful financially, and some large kimono companies gave gifts and kimono, but when the economic crisis came, industry support vanished. They couldn't get sponsors, and the gifts from the kimono organizations disappeared. Mr. Nishiwaki was a part of a three-way partnership in the graphic design industry at that time, and his partners told him to quit the company or the kimono events. He was using too much company time and equipment. He quit the company.

In 2008, the event lost over two million yen, and Mrs. Nishiwaki thought they should give up. In 2009, they also lost money and were preparing to stop planning the event. However, they were fortunate enough to meet with the then manager at Gajoen, an exclusive hotel in Meguro on the south west side of Tokyo.

Gajoen was founded in 1931, by a man with a large collection of Japanese art. At that time, the surrounding people were lucky if they had running water or electricity, and Gajoen was like a fairyland of art and culture. Originally a restaurant, it grew to have a shrine, church, guest and banquet rooms, a beauty salon, and photo studio. With this heritage, the present manager wishes to capitalize on the cultural history of the venue, making it a space for promoting Japanese culture. The year 2010 was the first Kimono User Show at Gajoen Hotel, and the show has continued annually at New Year. It has proved popular, not only entertaining the guests, but locals too. There are exhibitions with flower arranging and calligraphy, music, and Japanese games and performances. When this event proved successful, *Kimono Biyori* was also invited to participate in the People's Culture Festival in Tango and also in the Black Ships Festival in Shimoda. These relationships continue. Images from fashion shows are shown in Figures 6.8, 6.9 and 6.10.

In the future, Mr. and Mrs. Nishiwaki would like to share kimono wearing with non-Japanese too because they think it can be enjoyed by anyone. They would like non-Japanese to experience how kimono feels. It is the shape that they feel is important, not the cloth. It can be made of anything and worn by anyone. It covers almost the whole body, but it reveals the body line subtly, through the cloth. In this way, it is attractive and erotic. Some people have laughed at them and said that they will never be successful if they do not court celebrities. But they are not doing events to make a business out of kimono. The importance of the event is not making money, but providing a space where new ideas can be shown and where ordinary people showcase kimono wearing for other ordinary people to enjoy.

Ishioka Kumiko—Kimono Volunteer Ambassador

Figure 6.11 Ishioka Kumiko wearing Rumi Rock kimono and obi.
Photo: Ishikawa Mao.

Figure 6.12 Ishioka Kumiko and her kimono wardrobe.

Photo: Todd Fong.

Kumiko was a children's clothing shop owner for fifteen years, and from 2010, she worked part-time in a used kimono shop, so that she could have more chances to wear kimono. In 2015, she closed her own shop so that she could devote more time to working with kimono. She not only worked at the used kimono shop, but also started to work as event staff for Rumi Rock sales. She continues this but has moved on from the used kimono store to working in a specialized shibori shop. Kumiko wears Rumi Rock in Figure 6.11.

Kumiko learnt to dress at a kimono school in her early twenties, because it was a "good thing to do," but she wasn't very interested in it. When she was around forty, she saw the new magazine *Nanaoh* featuring ordinary people in ordinary kimono that were not expensive. Usually, kimono magazines were full of doctors' wives and actresses wearing the most expensive formal wear. She discovered used kimono stores and started buying kimono. A few are gifts from relatives. Now she has over a hundred kimono piled up on the shelves she brought home from her old shop. She is experimenting with styles as she does not trust her eye yet. When she has decided on her taste, she would like to have a kimono made-to-order.

Apart from being cheap, Kumiko was attracted to kimono because she had grown tired of the constant changes of fashion that quickly render clothing useless. If kimono was only fashion, she would have become bored with it by now. She likes silk not polyester, the colors, and patterns, and the fact that there is no waste in the construction of kimono. "Once you start to look into kimono, you bump into some interesting history. It is fascinating because everything has a meaning," she says. For example, indigo was not used for farming clothes only for its beautiful color, but because it has insect repellent qualities, so it protects the wearer. Sometimes the meaning is symbolic, such as hemp plant designs being put on baby kimono, because hemp is a fast growing plant. She is amazed by *e-gasuri,* picture ikat, because it is very difficult to make, but people persevered because they had such a strong desire to make their clothing beautiful as well as functional.

When she first started to wear kimono, Kumiko needed friends and a place to go, so she joined the kimono wearing group, *Kawagoe Sanpo,* a group that walks around the historical city of Kawagoe. At first, she was nervous, but she made friends and gained confidence. She no longer needs a kimono wearing group now. She got her job in a used kimono store because she could be paid to wear kimono. She did everything wearing kimono; cleaning, carrying boxes, etc. The other staff members were knowledgeable so she could learn from them. She says that it is no longer true that older people have more knowledge. Older people get nervous when they first wear kimono. She wore kimono in the snow and rain, and talking about this experience helped other people who wanted to do so. Sharing her experiences has given her confidence. She feels that she has something to give when she dresses or helps someone, and this is very important for her. She sometimes wishes she had daughter to share kimono with.

Kumiko thinks it is very important that kimono is cheap. If it isn't, people will not wear it, so it is inevitable that it is made in China where labor is cheap. She met a craftsman in the dyeing town, Ochiai, who told her that actually everything could be done by machine now, so young people do not want to make kimono by hand. She is worried about the problem of Japanese crafts dying out, but she cannot buy expensive craftsman-made kimono. She feels that all she can do is to encourage more people to wear kimono more often. She hopes that among those people are some who have money, who will want to buy expensive craftsman-made kimono. Kumiko and her kimono can be seen in Figure 6.12.

Kumiko has started to do several volunteer activities in order to spread kimono wearing among the non-Japanese community. She runs casual classes which are not part of a long course, where she teaches people to dress in kimono, in English. For only 500 yen they can take part, or for a 1,000 yen they can borrow a kimono and take part. She advertises this on her Facebook network. She also goes into a foreign embassy and gives power-point talks and gives dressing experiences to the women there. In summer, she takes a group of the embassy women to buy *yukata* and then teaches them how to dress. She would like to go to other embassies and continue this activity. Occasionally, she has guiding work dressing non-Japanese through a travel agency, and she also takes people on a guided tour of dyeing workshops in the Nakai area once a year.

Kumiko is not only doing volunteer work to spread kimono knowledge and wearing, she also wants to continue to improve her own dressing skills. She sometimes has private advanced dressing lessons with a teacher who is experienced in dressing for period dramas and for TV shows and films. She is learning the dressing styles from different ages, and for brides. Kumiko is already a skilled dresser, but she wants to be confident that she can tie many obi when asked and can put on all sorts of different garments for people. She is really an ambassador for kimono culture.

Otomo Chisato—Dancing Free Spirit

"It's just clothes and it makes no difference whether its western clothes or kimono," says Chisato, who has been wearing kimono since she was a small child. Her father was occupied with his business so her mother, busy with two small girls, looked for a local class for the girls to attend after school once a week. Chisato was two years old, and the class could have been abacus, piano or anything, whatever was closest to their house would do. It happened to be a *nihon buyo,* a Japanese dance class. *Nihon buyo* usually costs a lot of money, but this teacher is unusual because she believes that everyone should be able to afford to do Japanese culture, so the price was reasonable. She also wanted to keep alive the old traditional folk songs and dances that ordinary people had shared over generations. She always encouraged students to perform, but performances cost a lot, so when the student couldn't pay, she would let them pay in installments to make it easier, and she charged much less than other teachers.

By the time she was eight, Chisato was wearing a *yukata* at dance practice which she put on herself. At this time, however, business was not so good, and her mother told the two girls that they could either stop their dance classes or pay for them themselves with their New Year gift money (which is the equivalent of Christmas presents for Japanese). Her sister gave up at that time, but Chisato enjoyed her classes and wanted to continue, so from eight years old she paid for her dance classes out of her own pocket.

When Chisato graduated from fashion school, she wanted to make trends in the Japanese fashion industry and traveled regularly to Los Angeles and Hawaii, gathering material and ideas, designing clothes for young girls and becoming a buyer. She didn't do Japanese dance between twenty and thirty years old, but she took up jazz and hip-hop and later flamenco and enjoyed night life and partying. She was interested in black culture and went to tanning salons until she looked really dark skinned. She saw the fashion industry in both the United States and Japan, and gradually the draw of Los Angeles began to lose its power. Japanese paid attention to materials and workmanship, but the US industry seemed sloppy to her. Orders were not always counted properly, and only parts of deliveries arrived. She also saw inside sewing factories in the United States, Korea, and Japan, and thought that Japanese practice and workmanship was far superior to what she was seeing abroad.

At this point, she became disillusioned with flamenco. She wondered why she was putting effort into a dance that seemed like a kind of prostitute's dance. She didn't like the words of the songs, or the suffering expressed on the face of the dancers. It was not a happy dance. She was also dissatisfied with her flamenco teacher's character. She kept trying to sell things to the students, and they became annoyed about it. Her flamenco classmates even asked her why she was studying flamenco when she had such a great *nihon buyo* teacher, and Chisato realized that she had been stupid. She went back to her dance teacher and simply said, "I'm back." Her teacher replied that she had been waiting and was expecting her.

Chisato looks back on those ten years without dance and kimono and says that even though she mixed with some rough and low life types, she always felt that she was not like them. She knew that she had

Figure 6.13 Otomo Chisato dancing.

Photo: Sasaki Kazuhiro.

Figure 6.14 Otomo Chisato and her kimono wardrobe.

Photo: Usami Haruhisa.

studied something special and that that culture was still inside her. She remembered as a very small child, watching her teacher dance *Renjishi,* which is a famous lion dance in kabuki. The actor wears a huge wig with long hair trailing across the stage and swings the head of long hair around. The dance depicts both the love and severity of a parent lion training a cub. The image of this spectacle never left her; she knew she had seen something very special. Chisato dancing is in Figure 6.13.

Once she returned, Chisato trained hard, took her license, and opened her own class. Her teacher is the second generation of the Hosokawa branch and will make Chisato into the fourth generation, the third generation being already established. Chisato started to invest in kimono; some formal ones which she needed as a dance teacher, and some which are especially for Japanese dance. She scoured second-hand shops because she couldn't find kimono she really liked in the kimono shops. Usually, she buys *komon,* everyday wear, which she uses for dance classes. As a dancer, she most often uses half-width obi as a full-width one gets in the way. Chisato is seen with her kimono in Figure 6.14.

She teaches three or four classes a week and is also studying *Bando Ryu kabuki* dance at the moment. She wants to keep her teacher's commitment to the folk dances though, and she also wants to prioritize relationships and warmth above the making of money. Several of her students have personal problems and coming to her classes cheers them up. They trust her, and she is always happy and laughs a lot. She does a dance class and then socializes, often drinking with the girls. As she grows older, she is more fascinated by kimono than western dress. She now takes a more advisory role in the fashion industry, and in the future she would like to design a kimono brand and start a kind of Japanese culture center which is not based on a master and apprentice system, but a place where you can try lots of different Japanese arts freely. Kimono would be one of those. She runs dance workshops for those who would like to learn some dances for events, such as flower viewing, but who cannot commit to regular weekly dance classes. She laughs and says that kimono has survived two thousand years. It has looked after her so far, and it will never see her wrong.

Yuuki Yukari—Classical Kimono Beauty

Yukari insisted that her first photograph was taken from the back, see her in Figure 6.15. Fashion shots are always taken from the front, but she believes that the most beautiful kimono shots are taken from the back. The kimono image has not only the face of the wearer but another face on the back, the obi. Yukari is a homemaker with two grown-up daughters and a son. She was born in Australia because her father worked in the foreign office as an ambassador, and she stayed there until she was three. When they went there, they were told to take lots of kimono, for parties. At an embassy party when Queen Elizabeth the Second was in attendance, her mother was pushed forward to meet her, because she was in kimono. Her mother discussed kimono with the Queen, but her father did not get to talk to the Queen. If they had two parties in one day, her mother would take two obi and change her obi in the car.

As far as Yukari can remember, her mother always wore kimono. She has a deep love and strong warm feelings about the kimonoed image of her mother. She remembers the first time she herself wore kimono. She was about seven, and the kimono was red, a hand-me-down from her sister. She remembers the time well because everyone said how cute she was wearing it. She used to wear her sisters' hand-me-down kimono at New Year. Her older sisters studied Japanese dance. She learnt to dress from her mother. First her mother dressed her and then gradually she could do it herself.

When she was in her forties, Yukari decided to take some dressing lessons at *kitsuke* schools. She wanted to make sure that the way she was wearing kimono was correct. She took her dressing license at one of the schools, and she picked the best techniques from the different schools. She began to have a large circle of friends who were interested in kimono. They went out together for lunch and to art and floral exhibitions,

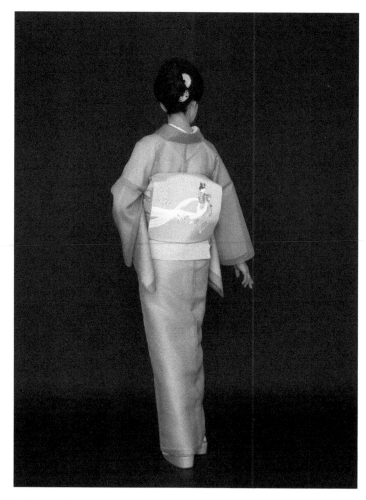

Figure 6.15 Yuuki Yukari, back view.
Photo: Baba Michiharu.

and they had a lot of fun. After a while though, Yukari realized she was always seeing the same people in the same kimono, and she wanted to widen the circle.

Yukari began to plan and arrange lunch parties at high-class hotels, to which people can invite their friends. Then she started to plan fashion shows at the parties, giving a chance for people to show off their favorite kimono. Yukari is the master of ceremonies and reads out a description of each kimono. People can listen to the description and take photographs of the kimono. In this way, the guests become familiar with new types of kimono that they did not know about and also get ideas for their own coordination. Yukari also works part-time wearing kimono. Before marriage she used to work as an announcer, and now she uses this skill and is a kimono wearing master of ceremonies for weddings and special company parties. She does kimono styling work, sometimes for TV and for films. Sometimes she is hired by the parents of a girl who is getting married or who is making a special kimono, and she finds out the budget, the taste of the customer and her exact needs, and then she acts as an advisor helping the customer to find the right kimono wardrobe using the budget provided.

Figure 6.16 Yuuki Yukari with a kimono by Yamamoto Yuki.

Photo: Hojo Hiromi.

First Yukari wanted to wear her mother's kimono, but they were too small, so she had to have her own kimono made. She has many different kinds of kimono, but she wears it on many formal occasions, so she needs a lot of formal and semiformal wear. She usually wears kimono about twice a week. She buys kimono from various sources and kimono made by various different artists. She is collecting kimono by the *yuzen* artist Yamamoto Yuki. Figure 6.16 shows a Yamamoto Yuki kimono. Her aim is to collect one of his kimono for each month of the year. She has four kimono chests with about seventy or eighty kimono in them and numerous accessories and underwear. Yukari says that buying expensive kimono is just the same as a guy buying an expensive car because he likes it. It is not a necessity as an old car would get one around almost as well, but there is satisfaction in having something high quality that was expensive. She feels the same way about her kimono. Also, if no one buys them, the kimono will die out, and she does not want that to happen.

Yukari first wears kimono because of that warm memory she has of her mother in kimono. Second, she wants to look and feel beautiful and hear people tell her that she looks lovely. She feels happy that others express happiness when she wears kimono. Third, she says that kimono improves her posture and also means that she can wear comfortable zori rather than painful high-heeled shoes. Fourth, she believes that wearing kimono affects communication.

Yukari says that people start to communicate more easily when wearing kimono. They can feel a common ground. Kimono also command a certain amount of respect. People treat you kindly when you wear one. She senses that people are more likely to give you a seat on a train, are more polite to you in shops and restaurants, and generally show more respect. Kimono also causes her to slow down, to actually listen to the sounds of the wind and leaves and even smell the smells one doesn't notice if rushing around. Her five senses are awakened by wearing kimono. She says one becomes more sensitive to the seasons. Yukari hopes that she can pass on her love of kimono to the next generation by inspiring them to wear kimono. She is a classical kimono beauty embodying the exquisite loveliness that people associate with Japanese beauties. She would look quite at home on the pages of *Utsukushii Kimono*.

Kimono Boundary Breakers

In this section, I explore the kimono in relation to persons and places beyond Japan in order to present it in a wider context. As history has shown, the kimono has always been subject to influence from other cultures, the importation of weaving and dyeing techniques, of fabrics from abroad and exotic and interesting patterns. The kimono was probably seen by many in the West for the first time in the Great Exhibitions of the late nineteenth century. These large exhibitions of industrial design and artworks from various locations were held in many countries around the developed world in the Victorian period. The first major one in Britain was at Crystal Palace in 1851, and there was a second large one in 1862. There were also important ones in Paris in 1855 and 1867. These exhibitions brought Japanese design to western audiences with far reaching results. The impressionist and post-impressionist schools of painters were strongly influenced by *ukiyoe* and the Rimpa school of design. Monet, Renoir, Tissot, Whistler, and Van Gogh are leading artists who incorporated Japanese images, items, or stylistic elements in their artwork. Japan became a destination for writers and painters, such as the American writer and painter La Farge, and Loti, who wrote the romance *Mme. Chrysanthemum* which became the opera *Madame Butterfly*. Scottish painter Hornel took two trips to Japan, and Dresser, the British designer visited on the invitation of the Japanese government, which was, and still is, eager to know what kind of Japanese goods sell abroad. The Anglo-Japanese school of design developed from 1851, as British designers became fascinated by Japanese goods such as blue and white Arita pottery, lacquer-ware and kimono. Japanese items or Japanese-inspired items became essential elements in middle class, domestic interior design. Kettles, fans, pictures, lacquer-ware, scrolls, and other goods were all bought enthusiastically by the middle classes in Britain.

As the Meiji period was one of reform and rationalization, old samurai family collections and goods acquired from Buddhist temples came onto the international market. According to Milhaupt (2014:154), this was the period when some of the great collections of Japanese textiles were started in the United States, by collectors such as Bigelow, Morse, and Fenollosa. Nomura, collector and historian, dealt with Japanese textiles internationally, and kimono were in great demand throughout the western world. Milhaupt notes that western people were often unable to distinguish between Japanese and Chinese goods. The paintings done by western artists show that kimono were used to drape the female form, often naked underneath, with no reference as to the original status or function of the real garment. Out of context, the kimono become objects, along with the women they adorn, that are part of the orientalism discussed in Chapter 1. In 2015, at the Boston Museum of Art, an *uchikake,* made and provided by Nippon Hoso Kyokai (NHK), was made available for visitors to try on, in front of a Monet painting of his wife in kimono. There was an outcry about whether or not this was continued orientalism. The *uchikake* had been used successfully in the same show in Japan, and no one had suggested that there was anything wrong with trying it on. The purpose was to understand the weight and feel of the garment. Such discussion leads to the understanding that not all locations and positions are equal, and there are those who feel that white people have no business to "appropriate" the kimono. The debate raged for several weeks but was underreported in Japan.

Hayward and Kramer (2007) write that Hornel's paintings of women in kimono did not change after his second visit to Japan, twenty years after his first, although real kimono certainly would have. Both Hornel and Dresser knew that there was a discrepancy between the kimono in collections and paintings, and what they actually saw women wearing on the streets of Japan. The paintings created an exotic and colorful Japan of the imagination, and it had little to do with real Japan, as it was going through the processes of industrialization. Kramer (2006) says that Japanese wearing western clothing was seen by these artists as very negative, as a sign of Japan losing tradition and that the kimono "served as a potent visual sign of Japanese identity." The adoption of western dress "shattered the romantic image of Japan" (2006:207). There is a paradox in the figure of Dresser, the innovative industrial designer who praised handcrafts, especially the textiles, of Japan but seemingly rejected its modernization or industrial growth. More well known for his glass, pots, and metal design, he also designed many textiles and wallpapers strongly influenced by Japanese floral designs.

Kimono arrived in Europe as antiques which were sometimes taken apart and tailored into dresses, as bolts of silk, and also as special kimono made for the export market. Liberty was one of the first importers in Britain. Milhaupt says that kimono for the export market had extra side panels to widen the skirt area and had loops for hanging the garment. Takashimaya had a collection of kimono designs for foreigners, some of which include tassels on the sleeves. According to Milhaupt, "Favoured motifs in this design book include what came to be considered quintessentially Japanese motifs thought to be especially desirable to foreigners: wisteria, butterflies, cherry trees, birds and maples leaves" (Milhaupt 2014:158). One hundred and fifty years later, thanks to various museum exhibitions, a well-known film about *geisha* and eBay, Yahoo, and YouTube, the kimono is travelling abroad again.

There is a large and steadily growing network of kimono lovers outside Japan. Due to social media networks, these people are increasingly known within Japan through Facebook, Twitter, YouTube, blogs, and other sites. Some of them can be considered to be experts in kimono culture. As these experts are from outside Japan physically, they can provide new and influential viewpoints, seeing things in kimono which appear to them to be fresh and interesting, which someone brought up with kimono might never have noticed. Until about 2010, this group could largely be characterized by an interest in art and design as well as Japanese textile culture. Now a new generation of kimono lovers is developing that is more interested in game, *manga,* cos-play, and in *kawaii* culture, which differs from the earlier group, though there is some overlap of interest between them.

At the time of writing, the kimono boom shows no signs of stopping. Kimono was high street taste in the summers of 2014 and 2015, but the western interpretation from mainstream fashion stores proved to be extremely superficial, about V necks, big sleeves, silky polyester fabrics, and floral prints, employing the word kimono in the loosest sense possible. It referenced a few stylistic features, without any solid understanding of the actual garment. Perhaps to say that such occurrences are a continuation of the orientalist project 150 years ago would be too harsh, but they are at least good examples of the way the fashion industry continues to plunder other cultures' clothes as random influences in the production of western garments. The wearers introduced here are more serious about the kimono than the mainstream fashion brands and high street shops. They are women who understand the kimono as both a dressing system and as a fashion inspiration. Their use of antique and used kimono in undeniably fashionable ways demonstrate that the dichotomy between fashion and tradition is really meaningless.

Berber Oostenbrug—Dutch Kimono Artist

Berber and kimono go back a very long way, even before she knew the word. As a child, Berber loved fairy stories, especially ones about princess with beautiful dresses. She was particularly interested in princesses from the East. Both her parents were interested in Japan. Her father as an architect and builder was interested in Japanese design, and her mother was interested in macrobiotics and shiatsu. Her family watched the TV series *Shogun* in the 1980s, and as Berber was only ten she did not know the garment names, but she loved what the girls in the program were wearing. Throughout school, she was interested in Japanese art and also religion, and she tried to make sumi-e like paintings and wrote short stories about zen and bonsai.

She acquired her first kimono when she and her boyfriend walked into a Japanese antique shop in Belgium. She said it was love at first sight and her boyfriend bought it for her. Soon after this she discovered Yamanaka's *The Book of Kimono* and she realized that what she had bought was a *kurotomesode*. As it was formal, she did not feel it was appropriate for lounging around the house, and so she went back to the shop to buy an informal *komon,* and accessories that she needed for kimono wearing. By 1996, she had become completely hooked on kimono. In the Amsterdam Hotel Okura, there was a bookshop run by some Japanese, and they helped Berber to get books from Japan. She bought everything in English that she could find on kimono, and anything Japanese, textiles and history, and even novels. At this time, she even found an article I published in *Daruma* art and antiques magazine, which was our first meeting (unbeknown to me), and this inspired her and made her realize that it was possible for a non-Japanese to wear kimono. Berber taught herself to dress from *The Book of Kimono,* and after a year, she could dress herself without too much difficulty. She now realizes that this was a very formal and stiff way of doing *kitsuke,* according to the Sodo dressing school.

Since the late 1990s, Berber has been buying kimono online. In 2001, *Ichiroya* opened up on eBay and became her favorite kimono shop. In 2001, the *Immortal Geisha* online forum was started. She joined it the following year, because she loved the styles of old kimono there, and the *susohiki,* trailing kimono. Through this forum, she was able to make friends and discuss kimono, and she started to discover more about kimono history through it. Her biggest inspiration is TV dramas. She loves period dramas, especially of the Edo period, but also of Meiji and Taisho. Berber's kimono inspired art appears in Figure 6.17.

Figure 6.17 Autumn by Berber Oostenbrug.

Photo: Berber Oostenbrug.

Figure 6.18 Berber Oostenbrug and her kimono wardrobe.
Photo: Berber Oostenbrug.

In 2007, Berber started a kimono group in the Netherlands, originally with just one and then two other women. Then she started to work in a shop selling Japanese goods, and so sometimes they arranged outings together. She decided that she was not very talented at organizing events though, and later Linda Kentie organized the group under the umbrella of Kimono Jack. For a small country, they have a large membership, around a hundred people, of whom about twenty meet regularly. Berber prefers to concentrate on making art. Since art school she has been making work concentrating on dreams and also work based on girls in romantic dresses. Later, she began to dress herself in Edo-styled kimono, and uses these photographs in her art works, which are photographic and sometimes also painted. She says that since the release of the film, *Memoirs of a Geisha,* people have mistaken her image for a *geisha*. She does not cut up kimono or obi, but she uses motifs from them in the backgrounds of her artworks.

Berber is interested in the long relationship between Japan and the Netherlands, especially in how it relates to textiles. She noticed that there was a lot of chintz in old Dutch fabrics, and that there was some in Japan too, probably imported by the Dutch. She likes to incorporate both countries into her artwork in various ways, such as using figures in kimono standing in front of iconic Dutch imagery, such as windmills or tulips. She has a kimono blog which she started in 2005, but she had a website before that too, and she says that now she can no longer separate her art and her kimono work. They are a part of the same thing. She has given up work in the shop and now does *kitsuke,* speeches, and events, when she has the chance. She has become great friends with the kimono designer *Mamechiyo* who is interested in European, particularly Dutch designs. *Mamechiyo* recommends using casual kimono for everyday dress, so she has taught Berber a more relaxed style of *kitsuke.* Berber sometimes helps her with *kitsuke.* She describes *Mamechiyo* as her kimono sister. Berber continues to be fascinated with textiles and the process of *kitsuke,* so we can expect more kimono inspired artworks and activities coming from Berber, who is one of the foremost kimono researchers in the Netherlands. Berber and her kimono are featured in Figure 6.18.

Lyuba Johnson—Kimono de Jack UK

In 2005, Lyuba Johnson, a Ukranian American, went on a jewelry making course at a community college and met a Japanese woman called Momoko, to whom she revealed that she was interested in learning about kimono. Momoko said that she was going to Japan and would buy a kimono for her. So Lyuba gave her a budget and Momoko came back with a whole kimono set for her, except underwear. This was the beginning of Lyuba's life with kimono. Lyuba had no idea about underwear anyway, and first Momoko helped her to put the kimono on. She went out to the movies like this with her friends, but unfortunately she

Figure 6.19 Western Girl Kimono Style 2.1 by Lyuba Johnson.
Photo: Robert Johnson.

Figure 6.20 Lyuba Johnson and her kimono wardrobe.
Photo: Robert Johnson.

lost touch with Momoko, and as she couldn't dress herself, she put away her kimono for about two years. Then she decided that she really wanted to wear kimono again, so she spent two and a half hours, with her mother and boyfriend helping her, to put it on. They were still not sure if it was right. She tried *yukata* too, and this looked better.

As she was working at a bookshop at the time, she looked for kimono books to help her, and she came across Yamanaka's *The Book of Kimono.* She wasn't sure if it was a good beginner's book, but it seemed to be the only one available, so she bought it, and gradually became more skilled with her dressing, though she continued to need help with the obi. In 2008, she joined the *Immortal Geisha Forums,* and things began to be clearer for her. She also had two kimono loving friends in North West Florida, and they would go out together on kimono wearing dates. Lyuba was the main motivation that kept these friends practicing dressing each other, and going out in kimono, which helped her to understand it better. She began buying kimono on eBay. She had worked out her size but not her style but was now wearing kimono regularly. She began to build up her collection with anything that took her fancy. She feels weird looking at photos from this time, as she dressed very traditionally, and not like she does now.

Looking online she came across *Kimono Hime, Mamechiyo,* and *Okimono Kimono,* and she loved this non-traditional look. Under their influence, she began to add western accessories such as hats and shawls to her outfits, but she still felt that they looked traditional. As the wife of a military man, Lyuba has to get used to moving around. It was after relocation to the UK that she really started to experiment and find her own style. She cut her hair short in a 1920s' bob, and the cold British weather made her want to wear boots with her kimono. Then she realized that for it to be comfortable she would be better off shortening the kimono. She liked this 1920s style, and she played around with hats, scarves, and gloves in addition to the boots. However, wearing her best kimono shorter meant she had a huge and uncomfortable lump of fabric in the middle. So to avoid this, she started to look again for older and shorter kimono. She doesn't like having the fold of cloth, *ohashiori,* in the middle, but even so, shorter and smaller kimono worked better for her purpose, which was to wear kimono with western footwear. Originally, she had a lot of small patterned floral kimono, but now she prefers bold patterns, especially stripes. She likes the freedom from the seasons that geometric patterns give her. She also enjoys the longer sleeves of the older kimono. She dresses for comfort and does not worry about padding anymore.

She first found out about Kimono Jack in 2010, from Ichiroya's online newsletter. She thought it would be great to start one where she lived, so she immediately contacted the organization's founder and got permission to make a group. She made a blog, a Twitter, and ordered business cards. She and her UK friends decided to have a meeting in Trafalgar Square. This was the first Kimono Jack outside Japan. It was not only a fun experience. She learnt that it was hard to run such a group and that many people who said they would come, never turned up. People traveled long distances, but only the core members could be relied upon to keep attending. They regularly went to the Hyper Japan event and a Christmas market. Although Lyuba has left the UK now, the group continues without her. She herself would think twice about starting another one. She thinks such a group needs to be in a big city with many events, and preferably a Japanese population which has events too. The Japanese community in Northwest Florida was more proactive than the Japanese she met in the UK.

Lyuba has now turned her talents to other projects though. She has her own kimono blog, *Strawberry Kimono,* on which she posts her *kitsuke* on a regular basis. She has also turned this into her own *Strawberry Kimono* website, where she explains her style, her use of short kimono and western accessories and offers styling and *kitsuke* services. The website is bilingual in English and Russian, and she has made some short videos too, explaining kimono in Russian. She believes that interest in kimono in Russia and Ukraine is growing, but there is not a lot of information in their language. She posts on Instagram too, and she says that the majority of her fans there, and on her blog and website, come from Japan. She also is heavily involved in the administration of the *Travelling Kimono Project,* with Naomi Hormozi. Recently, using her computer skills she also started her own online mini magazine called *Western Girl Kimono Style* which can be seen in Figure 6.19. Through this, she shows her kimono styling and also puts in useful information for those who are starting to wear kimono or want to make accessories for their kimono. She hopes to start publishing this in Russian too. She would like it to develop into enough material to publish a physical book. Not only a skillful stylist and administrator, she is also able to use the computer to communicate her ideas about dress and style in a positive way, in English and in Russian too. Lyuba is known as a great kimono stylist and activist among both the Japanese and non-Japanese kimono community. Lyuba and her kimono are featured in Figure 6.20.

Naomi Hormozi: Immortal Geisha

Naomi Hormozi, an Australian resident of California, has a long-term interest in kimono, especially in Meiji and Taisho period kimono and textiles, particularly those worn by *geisha* and *maiko*. She has a large collection of old postcards of *geisha* and *maiko,* and also of historical kimono sewing magazines from the Meiji period on. Not only does she enjoy sewing, but she learns about trends in kimono from these magazines and books. She has been sewing since she was five years old, and she also collects old sewing books and patterns. She doesn't consider herself a cos-player but frequently makes historical costumes for other people, including her two small daughters.

Naomi was a prolific kimono wearer and introduced Taisho fashion to an international audience. She also proposed alternative ways of wearing antique garments. Recently, she has been wearing

Figure 6.21 Naomi Hormozi and the Immortal Geisha logo.

Photo: Arian Hormozi.

Figure 6.22 Naomi Hormozi and her kimono wardrobe.
Photo: Karl Mueller.

kimono less because her antique kimono are precious to her, and she is busy taking care of her children. There are no services available for cleaning or repair of kimono, outside Japan. Synthetic kimono do not appeal to her Taisho aesthetics, and rather than compromise her personal style, she has chosen to abstain for a while.

Naomi uses social media to promote her interest in kimono. She has a blog, *Naomi's Kimono Asobi*, where she writes about antique kimono and related ephemera. However, Naomi is most well known for her kimono community, a forum for kimono information in English called *Immortal Geisha Forums.* The forum was kept going for over ten years and had over 4,000 members, many of whom were totally dependent on this site for their kimono information. It was the most well-known meeting place for discussion of kimono in English and had links to related kimono sites on the web. She also produced a kimono wiki page as a resource for kimono information. Naomi is mainly interested in kimono, accessories, and memorabilia, but other members who were keen *geisha* fans gathered at this site to share information. For the sake of user convenience in communication, there is now also a Facebook group. Naomi and her Immortal Geisha logo can be seen in Figure 6.21.

In addition to this project, Naomi was the instigator of "The Travelling Kimono" project. Inspired by the novel by Anne Brashares, *The Sisterhood of the Travelling Pants,* in which four friends share a pair of jeans which magically fit all of them and cause extraordinary things to happen, the traveling kimono is sent around the world, from one kimono wearer to another, and participants post pictures of themselves in the kimono, with their own obi and accessories. The result is a Facebook album of how many different ways one kimono can be coordinated. Lyuba Johnson helped with the organizing, recruiting, and administration of the project and together they launched the "Travelling Kimono 1" and then the "Travelling Kimono 2." The "Travelling Kimono 1" went missing somewhere in central Europe, but the "Travelling Kimono 2" is still on its global journey having passed through Japan, Hong Kong, Australia, and the United States. Naomi is a style expert of both western and Japanese clothing, and her forum and blog have been fundamental to the spread of kimono outside Japan. Naomi and her kimono appear in Figure 6.22.

Kimono and Memory

Several times, the topic of memory has been mentioned. For Mr. Nishiwaki, the image of his stylish kimonoed grandmother was important, and the fact that he remembers her putting on a crested *haori* when going into Ginza. He also remembers the scene just before New Year, with the kimono seller bringing the bolts, which were carefully laid out and examined, and after purchases were made, were sewn into new garments for the New Year. For his wife, the passing of the years was realized through the increasingly long limbs sticking out from *yukata,* necessitating the letting out of tucks and finally the choosing and purchasing of new, larger *yukata*. She also remembers affectionately the kimonoed image of her mother dressed to go into town, rather than in her rough work clothes in the fields or kitchen. Yukari lovingly remembers the image of her mother, beautifully dressed for embassy parties in Australia, being presented to the Queen of England and changing her obi inside the car. These are precious, personal memories associated with family members, and they have the effect of increasing the importance of kimono. It is something that is associated with making loved people and occasions beautiful. Berber remembers watching Japanese samurai films with her parents and being fascinated by the clothing in them. This kind of memory is partly about spending a good time with her parents, but it is also about nostalgia for an imagined place and time, as Berber herself was not alive in Edo period Japan.

Heike (2013) distinguishes memory from nostalgia. Nostalgia, apparently originally meaning pain from an old wound, has come to mean a longing for another time, rather than its original meaning, which was more closely associated with another location. Contemporary fashion, as well as other media, can instill in us a longing for periods in time that we have never experienced in reality. This is imagined nostalgia, and this kind of nostalgia can be an important source of inspiration for dressing. Clothes have their own histories, and it is possible to partake in them, by incorporating old clothes into new looks. Berber, Lyuba, and Naomi cross both geographic and temporal boundaries to find sources, which result in new and fashionable looks, and in the case of Berber, art works. None of them have memories of their own relatives wearing kimono, but they have all searched out a kimono past, and used it as a resource. In Naomi's case, the sewing books that she has collected over the years have been a strong influence. In our world of media communications, the past of one country has become an available resource for those in other countries. While the fashion industry tends to plunder indiscriminately, there is always a choice to search for authenticity or depth, as these women have done.

Memory has a profound effect on people and can strongly influence their clothing practices. Woodward found in her wardrobe studies that women have an average of 12.2 percent inactive clothing, and some women have up to 40 percent. Clothes are sorted, and some are remembered and some forgotten. Items associated with a bad experience are disposed of, and items associated with a time that we want to remember are carefully kept. Clothes that have been gifted remind us of a particular person. Clothing has the ability to hold memory; the smell, the feel, and even the shape of another person. For this reason, and because they have often been passed down, kimono are difficult to throw away. They have a role similar to the family jewels.

The Wearer Message

The interviews revealed diverse reasons for wearing kimono. Conspicuously absent was any mention of the three reasons commonly given for not wearing kimono, as found in Yano's research. These were that kimono was difficult, expensive and there is nowhere to wear it. Wearers did not mention any of these opinions, with the exception of one wearer who purposely buys kimono at the higher end, supporting the crafts industry and enjoying the pleasures of the haute couture of kimono. Apparently, there is a gap between perceptions of non-kimono wearers and the kimono wearing public. There are perceived health benefits including improved posture and breathing. Some wearers enjoy the seasons through kimono motifs, there are others who believe that abandoning that connection provides more options for fashionable dressing. The kimonoed image of a mother was an important one for several women, and an attractive aspect of kimono is the concept of interconnectedness. One can be close to people through wearing their kimono. Interconnectedness can be seen in the importance of childhood memories too, long summers in *yukata,* or people gathering to choose new fabrics for New Year. It can also be seen in the desire that through wearing the kimono of someone who has passed on, one becomes closer to ancestors.

Also important to some was that through kimono they could express Japaneseness. However, this was not in the sense of a high culture that was untouchable, or a national symbol, rather as a way into meaningful discussion about each other's culture, a sign of respect. For one person, this meant living a simpler, more natural lifestyle, for another, it meant showing his Japaneseness when traveling in other cultures. The fashion and design aspects of the kimono were important to both Japanese and non-Japanese.

Of course, Japaneseness means something different for non-Japanese kimono wearers. The kimono becomes a way to create a different kind of connectedness for them. They are visualizing an interest in Japanese culture by wearing the clothing. The non-Japanese kimono wearing community is marked by an interest in the visual, the designs, and art of the kimono, as well as its potential as a fashion option. The fact that many of them have invested considerable time, money and learning into collections and into meeting together or making kimono based projects is remarkable, and it shows the dedication and commitment they have to kimono wearing.

These fans are so interested in kimono that makers are beginning to see this community as a potential new market. Since 2009, a Facebook community page has grown from 400 to over 9,000 fans. Such a page is a group in the loosest sense of the word, requiring no commitment whatsoever, but as it can easily be unsubscribed to, it provides a barometer of the level of interest in a topic. By stated gender, about three quarters of fans are female and a quarter male, and the vast majority of them are between eighteen and thirty-four. The peak group is somewhat younger than the peak of kimono fans who participate in kimono wearing groups in Japan, but this may be due to the demographics of Facebook users, rather than the nature of kimono wearers. Japan has the largest group of fans by nationality providing about a quarter of the fans, but Indonesia and the United States also have over a thousand fans each. Muslim women appear to be interested in kimono, perhaps because it satisfies their desire for a garment that covers most of the body, which explains large numbers of fans from Indonesia, Vietnam, Malaysia, Saudi Arabia, and Turkey. France and Italy also have several hundred fans. Japanese kimono makers and wearers have become increasingly interested in this page, and interaction between Japanese and non-Japanese kimono fans is growing.

The Kimono Jack movement has also spread to many countries in Europe, the United States, and Asia, and there are also other kimono wearing groups who get together on a regular basis, to share their experiences of wearing kimono together. In the UK, although the Kimono Jack members live far from each other, they invest considerable time and money in getting together to wear kimono in a group. They stay at each other's houses and cooperate together in doing dressings at events. The community provides meaningful connections to the women involved and a place for discussion, sharing information, swopping kimono, and indulging in fashion talk. Some aspects of Japanese kimono culture interest them, but others they choose to ignore. When they cannot find goods they need, they are creative and make their own versions, and they also have made YouTube videos of ways of tying obi that they have developed. They are generally not concerned with the critical or curious gaze of other people. Some kimono fans put on lectures or events, and others raised money or even volunteered in the Great East Japan Earthquake and Tsunami disaster.

Only one of the Japanese interviewees confessed to buying and wearing high-end craftsman-made kimono. This woman is involved in many formal events, and therefore her experience is very different from the majority of kimono wearers. For the majority of people, reasonably priced kimono in easy to care for fabrics appear to point to the way of the future. Kimono as fashion is more important for most wearers than is kimono as a luxury item. However, there are still those who support this end of the market, just as there are those who support the high end of the western fashion market. It seems inevitable that this will become a small part of the market though, and it is not clear from the interviews that I conducted, whether there will still be a market for hand-loom weaving.

The non-Japanese market mostly comprises used formal kimono, which are bought up cheaply on the internet. New goods that are reasonably priced are also purchased there. That it is possible to become an accomplished dresser, and even a kimono style leader outside Japan, raises interesting questions about the future of kimono. An Australian in America, a Ukrainian in America, and a Dutch woman in the Netherlands are becoming the teachers of a new generation of kimono wearers outside Japan. With increasing interest in various aspects of contemporary Japanese culture, this creates the possibility that there is a future for kimono that is not even located inside Japan.

Bibliography

Assman, S. (2008). "Between Tradition and Innovation: The Reinvention of the Kimono in Japanese Consumer Culture." *Fashion Theory*. Vol. 12. No. 3. pp. 359–76.

Belk, R.W. (1995) *Collecting in a Consumer Society*. Abingdon, New York: Routledge.

Campbell, C. (2005) "The Craft Consumer: Culture, Craft and Consumption in a Postmodern Society." *Journal of Consumer Culture*. Vol. 5. No. 23. pp. 23–42.

Guy, A.E. Green and M. Banim. (2001) *Through the Wardrobe: Women's Relationships with Their Clothes*. Oxford, New York: Berg.

Hayward, M. and E. Kramer. (2007) *A Paradise of Pretty Girls: The Kimono and Perceptions of Japan*. In Textiles and Text. Postprints. London: Archetype.

Hebdige, D. (1979) *Subculture, The Meaning of Style*. London and New York. Routledge.

Heike, J. (2013) "Cross-Temporal Explorations: Notes on Fashion and Nostalgia." *Critical Studies in Fashion and Beauty*. Vol. 4. No. 1 and 2. pp. 107–24.

Johnson, L. http://www.strawberrykimono.com (Accessed February 1, 2015).

Kawamura, Y. (2006) "Japanese Teens as Producers of Street Fashion." *Current Sociology*. Vol. 54. pp. 784–801.

Kramer, E. (2006) "Master or Market? The Anglo-Japanese Textile Designs of Christopher Dresser in Context." *Journal of Design History*. Vol. 19. No. 3. pp. 197–214.

Milhaupt, T.S. (2014) *Kimono: A Modern History*. London: Reaktion Books.

Miller, D. (1987) *Material Culture and Mass Consumption*. Oxford: Blackwell.

Miller, D. (2010) *Stuff*. Cambridge, Malden: Polity.

Morace, F. (2010) "The Dynamics of Luxury and Basicness in Post-Crisis Fashion." *Critical Studies in Fashion and Beauty*. Vol. 1. No. 1. pp. 87–112.

Narumi, H. (2010) "Street Style and Its Meaning in Post War Japan." *Fashion Theory*. Vol. 14. No. 4. pp. 415–38.

Tseëlon, E. (2001) "Ontological, Epistemological and Methodological Clarifications in Fashion Research: From Critique to Empirical Suggests." In Green Guy and Banim. Eds. *Through the Wardrobe*. Oxford, New York: Berg.

Woodward, S. (2007) *Why Women Wear What They Wear*. Oxford, New York: Berg.

Yamanaka, N. (1982) *The Book of Kimono: The Complete Guide to Style and Wear*. New York, Tokyo, London: Kodansha.

7 Returning Kimono to the Streets

Historical Review

The hegemony that continues to state either directly or indirectly that fashion is a product of European society is facing increasing challenges, and we appear to be in the midst of a paradigm shift. The story of the kimono can be considered one of these challenges. Clothing history in Japan shows an obsession with self-presentation going way back to early historical records. While accomplishment in all the arts was desirable for the Heian period woman, the most important accomplishment was certainly the ability to dress with keen attention paid to the exquisite subtlety of colored layers. It was equally as important for a gentleman of the court to cut a fine and colorful figure. Self-presentation was a serious business for Heian courtiers. According to noble women's writings, there were trends among certain groups, and already there was evidence of an uncomfortable speed of change. As is true of so many fashionable garments, form led function for women, and the clothing made mobility almost impossible.

By the Edo period, there was an urban working class of traders and workers, whose wealthier members had effectively become a middle class, through acquiring more economic power than the farming and samurai classes who were their social superiors. This discrepancy between social status and income resulted in great expenditure on extravagant dress which came to be seen as a social and moral problem by those in authority. The sumptuary laws were harsh and reflected the importance that the government put on dress as a marker of social status. Though the government continually issued regulations, there was considerable difficulty in enforcing them in the face of a fashion obsessed and wealthy urban population. While true social climbing was not possible, that reality did nothing to stop people dressing up in splendid style if they could afford to do so.

In the Edo period, not only urbanization and strict laws but also the development of various industries was closely connected with sartorial behavior. The start of the production of domestic cotton led to increased availability, reduced cost, and hence increased the popularity of indigo-dyed cottons. Improvements in stencil dyeing contributed to the shape that patterns took. Developments in printing helped to spread both literacy and trends around urban areas at a greater speed than had been known before. *Yuzen* trends were spread in the form of *hinagata bon,* pattern books. For the most part, people wore domestically produced goods, but there was also a taste for the rare and exotic which was periodically provided for in the form of the few foreign ships that were permitted the rights to trade during this largely closed period. Goods imported from far-away countries had cachet and were highly desirable as fashion accessories in spite of, or perhaps because of, the high prices they commanded.

With its opening up to western powers at the end of the nineteenth century, industrialization came to Japan. An initial fascination with western dress changed the sartorial landscape somewhat, but with the exception of men's working wear and military uniforms, such clothing did not affect the majority of women until much later. Industrialization started with the textile industry and drew thousands of girls from impoverished farming families to the cotton and silk mills. These unsung armies of women were a key part in helping to make silk one of the most profitable exports for Japan through the early twentieth century. In spite of the depression and the Great Kanto Earthquake of 1923, the period saw a great blossoming of everyday kimono styles due to increasing mechanization; the influence of worldwide art movements; and the spread of radio, magazines, and department stores.

The Second World War and the period immediately following it mark the real changeover from Japanese to western clothing for ordinary women. This was eighty years after western styles first hit Japanese shores. The changeover, however, was never as complete as documents have made it appear. It is more accurate to think of the history of Japanese clothing in the twentieth century as two continuous parallel lines, one of western styles and one of Japanese, rather than as one line, which suddenly changes from Japanese to western style. Although the kimono has been sidelined, it has never disappeared and therefore cannot be framed as reinvented tradition. After a long slide at the end of the twentieth century, starting with the break after the war when the natural pattern of mothers teaching daughters was broken, and then the breaking of the economic bubble at the end of the 1980s, toward the end of the century, the kimono began to make a comeback.

This history makes it clear that although changes and trends might appear to be random at the time at which they occur, hindsight reveals that they are systematic and are in an inseparable relationship with technological developments, and the social and political milieu of the time. It also shows that a fashion system does not have to be about changing shape. Though the look of the clothing may be completely different from that of western clothing, it is the similarities between the systems that are most notable. Like fashion in the West, kimono has the ability to mark birth or rank, but equally has the ability to subvert the social system of the society. Japanese fashion is all about personal expressions, group behaviors, eroticism, gender, and, above all, the importance of the newest trends. In other words, it functions in exactly the same ways that fashion does in European and other societies. However, there are some additional elements in Japanese fashion that are not found in other fashion systems. First, it is flat but conversely three dimensional. Its concern with inner layers and with hidden surfaces means that it has depth. Second, it marks the natural world and nature more closely than other fashion systems, meaning that it is bound into place and seasonal time securely. Third, it is long lasting which makes it not only perhaps more sound ecologically but also it means that there are connections forged with people through the kimono. The fact that by itself it is an unfinished garment also means that it is ideal material for those who enjoy the crafting aspects of self-presentation and image creation.

Publishing Review

Just as the kimono has demonstrated change on both macro and micro scales throughout its history, publishing on kimono can also be shown to have continually been developing over time. From simple pattern books, which themselves developed along with changing trends, the kimono came to have a major role in advertising, from the Meiji period. Not only were kimonoed images advertising kimono but also a whole range of consumer goods that were used in the home and for health and beauty products.

There has been a move from museum or archive style history books, which frame the kimono as a costume, often a theatrical one, to more sociological histories which relate kimono to social, political, and technological factors. Particularly interesting are the two English language beginner kimono guides, which show a change in the way that kimono knowledge is framed and taught, as well as the necessary knowledge areas for kimono wearing. Conversely, there is also a trend for visual books, which, in Japan is satisfied by colorful *mooks*. These are now popular enough to rival the standard kimono magazines in their circulation and popularity. Indeed, as younger readers are appropriating them and using them as guides and inspiration for their kimono wearing practice, it could be argued that they are actually more influential now than the standard magazines.

New kinds of publishing and the diffusion of new kimono images are not confined to print media. Several people featured in this book are making their impact through the online publication of kimono images. *Akira Times* magazine covers have sent people off searching the bookshops for the "real" magazine. The numbers of kimono aficionados logged into Naomi Hormozi's Immortal Geisha Facebook page continues to expand, with discussions about wearing, seasonality, kimono care, and the posting of attempts at dressing are enjoyed by a large number of kimono fans. Linda Kentie and Lyuba Johnson also have large numbers of followers for their online activities.

In Japanese book shops at the time of publication, kimono books are filed with other Japanese arts, such as tea ceremony, incense and books on wrapping and tying with *mizuhiki,* Japanese paper ties. In the magazine section, kimono have until recently been filed in the women's magazine section, lying uncomfortably with the hand-sewing and knitting magazines, next to cooking and interior design ones. In the spring of 2016, I first saw the kimono magazines filed with other fashion magazines, indicating a recognition that kimono has a changing role in society.

Marketing Review

The kimono world has, in a sense, a lot of catching up to do. It is necessary for it to outgrow and discard old ways of educating and training new artisans, in order to attract young people who can carry on the crafts. It is also necessary for those who are involved in creating high-end craft goods to be able to market their works and also diminish the perceived and real distance between themselves and their customers. Survival is not assured for all who work within traditional craft production. The traditional apprenticeship system is not providing artisans with successors to carry on kimono making. Craftsmen are increasingly an older and forgotten generation. This market is likely to suffer from competing cheaper models. The handwoven casual kimono is the ultimate in everyday luxury, but it is likely that the market will remain small because of the high cost of these labor intensive items. Because of the many roles that kimono plays in Japanese life, it is unlikely that the skills will all completely disappear, but change is necessary for survival.

Jotaro Saito was critical of the industry and commented that the market was wide open for innovators. He sees a very positive outlook for the kimono, but as an innovator, he is out on a limb, not fitting easily within any publication. It is his problem, and also the proof of his position as the first kimono designer to bring kimono to the forefront of the fashion world. The growing number of new kimono related businesses and the rise in the industry marketing data also suggest a positive future for the kimono.

Contemporary Social Roles

Many Japanese people like to enjoy large and gorgeous weddings and continue to celebrate various life stages with rites of passage that almost always entail wearing Japanese clothing. After a boom in western style weddings, a return to Japanese style has been taking place, in spite of the higher charges involved in this style of wedding because of the expensive nature of the clothing and dressers required. University graduation ceremonies have also been the sites for kimono revival over the past twenty years. Twenty years ago, few female graduates wore kimono to their graduation ceremony, whereas at the time of writing, almost 100 percent of students are wearing rented polyester kimono, or kimono from their family chests. Arriving at certain ages is also celebrated with the ceremonial wearing of kimono. The kimono as formal dress is still alive and well.

Kimono is also actively worn as an essential part of many Japanese arts. It is de rigueur in the worlds of Japanese dance and various kinds of music. Specific types of costumes are assigned to specific characters in the world of the theater, and Japanese traditional dances are designed to show off the kimonoed figure in the most alluring way. Players of Japanese instruments such as the *shamisen, koto,* or *shakuhachi* typically perform wearing kimono. The worlds of flower arranging and tea ceremony also call for the wearing of kimono on formal occasions.

In the hospitality industry, the wearing of kimono signifies a commitment to good Japanese style service. *Ryokan* Japanese style inns will have innkeepers, maids, and waitresses in kimono. High-class Japanese restaurants follow this tradition, as do some drinking establishments, hostess bars, and other night life locations. The *geisha* are a tiny part of the entertainment business, but as they have captured the imagination of the West over generations, they are the most well-known of all professional kimono wearers, to the extent that the West associates all kimono wearing with *geisha*. The social roles of an iconic garment such as the kimono are enduring, though not unchanging, as a history of Japanese wedding kimono would show. These forms of kimono continue to change slowly.

Significance of the Worldwide Kimono Community

The high-street version of kimono popular in 2014 and 2015 was certainly less authentic than the kimono for foreigners that were made by Takashimaya in the Victorian period. Kimono is apparently equivalent to a wrapover top with a belt, often featuring florals. The fashion industry continues to plunder other cultures seemingly at random, and it seems no better now, than the way in which Europeans or Americans in Victorian times felt entitled to appropriate kimono in any way they wished. They chopped it up into tailored dresses or used it in art works apparently randomly, with no regard for the propriety of their actions in terms of Japanese culture. There was no interest in authenticity other than for the unity of their own concepts of dress or interior decoration. The superficiality of the high street fashion brands is enduring, in spite of the ease of access to real information, that is available today in comparison with the Victorian period.

Kimono is now spreading beyond the geographical borders of Japan, and today's group of non-Japanese kimono fans are fundamentally different from the superficial high street fashion brands and those who appropriated kimono in Victorian times. The non-Japanese women introduced in this book can be considered to be the leaders of the non-Japanese kimono community, but there are many others also who are inherently interested in the culture behind kimono. It is at the edges of the kimono system where it is most permeable, and non-Japanese wearers can be considered to be on the edge because of their physical locations outside Japan, and their lack of a kimono history. There is freedom provided by the lack of historical knowledge and kimono background or rules. Along with the freedom, however, many of these kimono fans have a desire for authenticity and a spirit of respect for kimono rules and its parent culture that drives them to seek out such information. These creative non-Japanese wearers, with their artistic skills and computer expertise are powerful purveyors of kimono culture to a new generation of kimono wearers located outside Japan.

An important aspect of this is activity is the social connections provided by kimono. Assman (2008) described *Kimono de Ginza* as a postmodern group, as it is relatively unstructured in comparison with kimono dressing schools. Groups in other countries are also unstructured and allow for varying levels of commitment. They offer a sense of community not bound by age, work, family, or country. They are a democratizing force where information and know-how is freely shared. Some people will never meet but nevertheless share meaningful relationships. Others meet and share the pleasure of being in the gaze and discuss their kimono purchases, experiences, and their creative dressing practices. Some groups, such as that in the Netherlands and in Britain, show high levels of commitment to each other, beyond what is required just to share information about a simple garment.

Figure 7.1 The calligrapher.
Photo: Okumoto Akihisa.

Until relatively recently, the takeover by western clothing as everyday wear was perhaps seen as an inevitable result of westernization. But with small signals appearing in the late 1980s and the 1990s, the first kimono wearing group starting in about 2000, the renaissance of kimono as everyday dress took off at the beginning of the twenty-first century and is now in full swing. There is something about the present zeitgeist that calls Japanese, and even non-Japanese, to the kimono. This desire for kimono can be framed in relation to global fashion trends and movements. Anthropologist Polhemus, in his revised version of *Fashion and Anti-Fashion,* argues that, "we live in a post-modern supermarket of style, where creative consumers do their own thing" (2011:8). Kimono wearers are creative consumers in that they invest considerable time and money in collecting kimono; create new looks with their coordination of items; mix the old and the new, sometimes the West and the East; tailor and construct new kimono, obi, and accessories.

In 2005, Campbell argued that consumers have been framed as "dupes, rational heroes or postmodern identity seekers" but he identified a new group whom he called "craft consumers" who need to be framed differently. These consumers tailor their products. He says that the real difference in industrial or craft production is in whether the machine controls the worker or the worker controls the machine, and he argues that the crafter is a kind of cocreator. She exercises control over the product and transforms it and its meanings by how it is used.

Kimono purchases are raw materials, and considerable skill, knowledge, love, and passion go into the customization of garments and collections, which bring originality and personalization to looks and to wardrobes. Creative kimono wearers can be aligned with street fashionistas such as teddy boys or punks who created their own styles rather than buying ready-made looks.

Figure 7.2 Mother and son at night.
Photo: Okumoto Akihisa.

Figure 7.3 Mother and son looking at flowers.
Photo: Okumoto Akihisa.

Campbell argues that a rise in craft consumption, as evidenced in the popularity of home cooking, gardening, DIY, and creative dressing, could represent a reaction against increasing commodification, and that the two phenomena go hand-in-hand. He also argues that it is fun and an expressive form of recreation for people who have decreasing chances to obtain creative satisfaction within their work situations.

Kimono Renaissance—The Kimono as Street Fashion

Trend forecasting expert Morace of Future Concept Lab in Milan agrees that there is a rise in crafting. After various global crises, starting with 9/11, he argued that there was the beginning of a renaissance rather than a trend. This renaissance comprises the filtering of luxury into everyday life. He also sees a spread of "creativity, authenticity and a spirit of craftsmanship" (2010). He describes this as being a return to "true qualities," substance, and authenticity, rather than surface and image. This implies that true quality is more important than communicative ability. Consumers, he says, have "unmasked the game, and the toy has broken." According to Morace:

> Fashion that makes original use of materials and available resources, and puts into circulation critical projects in which the originality of style, comfort and sensorality are not in contradiction with sustainability, is popular, as are clothing garments and accessories that distance themselves from the rules of short-lived fashion and present a "natural life cycle." (2010:105)

Figure 7.4 Boy cooking.
Photo: Okumoto Akihisa.

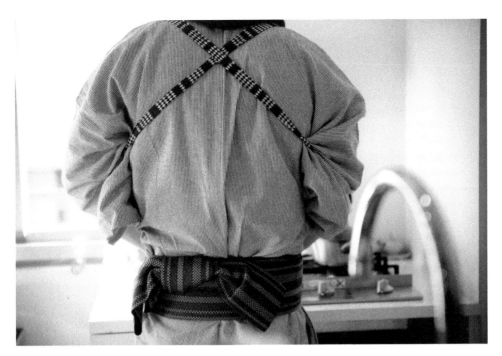

Figure 7.5 Back of boy cooking.
Photo: Okumoto Akihisa.

Figure 7.6 Detail of boy cooking.
Photo: Okumoto Akihisa.

Figure 7.7 Girl in furisode.
Photo: Okumoto Akihisa.

Creative and innovative kimono wearers are in the forefront of such global fashion developments. Kimono is by its nature about depth, quality, sensorality, and long-lastingness.

Japan looks toward holding the Olympics in 2020, and Japanese people are once again considering how to present themselves as a nation. Several projects centering on the kimono have already started. *Kimono One World Project* coming out of Kyushu is a group of *yuzen* dyers who are making a kimono representing each country in the Olympics. A kimono school has had the idea of going into schools and teaching children to wear kimono, so that they can teach their parents, in a reversal of traditional teaching and learning patterns. There are many other individual plans ahead, and there is a large movement toward not only welcoming people by wearing kimono but also providing opportunities for them to wear it themselves. The Olympics has provided a chance for people to think about the future of kimono, and what it will be like. In addition to this, the kimono is moving abroad in a more prominent way than before. In spring of 2016, *geisha* and *maiko* performed in Perth, Australia, and Auckland and Wellington, New Zealand. There were tea ceremonies held around the world. The year 2016 saw the first runway show of kimono at New York fashion week, a collaboration between Asai Hiromi and Kyoto Artisan. This was taken up by media outlets around the world and was extensively featured in written and online media platforms. Modern Antenna, a modern Kyoto brand that is highly popular with young women, also put on a highly successful exhibition in New York. With an increasing number of Japan festivals, and popularity of Japanese culture, perhaps 2016 can be seen as the year when kimono brands, creators, and organizations started to take notice of markets outside Japan and present kimono exhibitions and live fashion shows in major capital cities around the world.

In the nineteenth and early twentieth centuries, western clothing began to take over kimono. Now it seems that kimono is crossing boundaries in the other direction. It is the return of kimono from the rule governed school to the freedom of the street that has made this possible. This speaks not only of the incompleteness of the takeover of western fashions in Japan, the history of which is surprisingly short, but also of a rejection of the kimono as a status symbol or a national costume. Kimono is becoming increasingly democratic and widespread among those who are not necessarily affluent. It is being reclaimed by ordinary people, even non-Japanese.

Perhaps the kimono schools, which dominated the postwar kimono scene, could be seen as a kind of equivalent to the rise of style and color consultants in western countries, with a similar agenda of rules, formulas, and regulations. But they have had their day, and the tide has turned toward more natural flows of information and more expressive ways of dressing. The photographs in this chapter embody kimono as envisioned in the ordinary world. This is where kimono belongs and where it must be in order for it to continue its fashion journey.

New publishing, new start-up businesses, and people who use new fabrics and materials in new ways are proving that kimono not only remains a fine vehicle for self-representation and a relevant fashion

Figure 7.8 Boy on a bridge.
Photo: Okumoto Akihisa.

Figure 7.9 Gathering chestnuts.
Photo: Okumoto Akihisa.

Figure 7.10 Couple in the countryside.
Photo: Okumoto Akihisa.

Figure 7.11 Girl on a river bank.
Photo: Okumoto Akihisa.

option for Japanese and other people but also that it is possible to make a living in a kimono related business.

Perhaps kimono in the future will be largely prêt-à-porter, polyester, or in fabrics not yet developed. As kimono interacts more with western fashion, it may become more about the surface and less about the layers and hidden beauty for multiple audiences, making it less able to express the *iki* aesthetic and also less able to be subversive. Perhaps kimono will be more about geometrics and less about seasonal plants, losing some of its connections with time and place, its concern with the inner and the outer world. Perhaps it will become more about youth and less about inheritance. If these processes happen, which seem very likely, then certainly something will be lost, but from the here and now, it is impossible to know what will be gained.

In contrast with the high craftsman-made end of production, there is an increasing demand for kimono to be easily available, affordable, and easy to care for. It remains to be seen whether a younger generation of kimono wearers will value the craft traditions associated with high-end luxury kimono and be prepared to pay for them. However, if there is not a base of people who wear kimono regularly, then there will also be a very small market for high-end kimono.

Perhaps more than any other garment the kimono demands the fashion skills of its wearer. The fashion-ability or otherwise of an outfit is in his or her hands. His or her ability to coordinate the kimono, obi, and accessories determine whether or not the outfit has impact. It is for those who like to take decisions and who enjoy the challenge of coordination. The kimono wearer is usually a person who enjoys the processes

Figure 7.12 Detail of girl on a river bank.
Photo: Okumoto Akihisa.

Figure 7.13 Boy in Harajuku.
Photo: Okumoto Akihisa.

Figure 7.14 Girl in Ueno.
Photo: Okumoto Akihisa.

Figure 7.15 Girl in Ueno park at night.
Photo: Okumoto Akihisa.

Figure 7.16 Girl in the street.
Photo: Todd Fong.

involved with kimono wearing: the careful folding, the sewing of collars, and the planning and the thinking which goes into getting dressed. This creative aspect of kimono dressing means that it is in line with the global trends discussed above. Kimono wearers are craft consumers who are by nature creative and dress to be in the gaze.

It is not kimono experts who are creating new kimono fashion. The movers and shakers have mostly come from outside the industry. They are people who have worked in fashion, who can utilize the publishing industry or who know the clothing industry, and they are people who understand style. Because they are on the outside, they have been able to see more than those whose eyes are blinkered from being inside the industry. Their eyes are unfettered by rules, regulations, or convention. *Akira Times* is a kimono world punk, standing on the edge, who ignores the written rules about men's or women's kimono. He has no use for stiffeners for collars or obi. He ignores rules about who can wear red, or what can or cannot be worn with kimono. He says he is just playing. The kimono industry needs to be stirred up, it desperately needs an Akira to break down the taboos. From his corner in north Japan he throws down the gauntlet, monthly challenges in the form of magazines covers on his blog and Facebook. Okumoto Akihisa has photographed his vision of cheap ordinary kimono, for ordinary people in the street. *fussa, Kimono Hime, Nanaoh, arecole* show kimono democratized for ordinary or fashionable wear. Rumi Rock brings Edo fun and sharp wit into *yukata* wearing, while Jotaro Saito brings innovative new and modern options to the high end of kimono. Slowly but surely this diverse bunch of characters are chipping away at the stony, rule-governed establishment with their tools: new vision, creative ability, and the power to market it. The high end will survive, but the new will inevitably take over the old. Such is the law and nature of the beast we call "fashion."

Figure 7.17 Bon dancing in the evening.
Photo: Todd Fong.

When speaking about the future of the kimono with the president of the Tansu-Ya chain of second-hand kimono shops, Nakamura Kenichi suggested that the kimono business is like Mount Fuji. At 3,776 meters, Mount Fuji is the highest mountain in Japan. The cauldron at the top is relatively small; it takes an hour to walk once around it. The only reason that the volcano that is Mount Fuji could rise to 3,776 meters is the immense size of its base. There are only a few people who will support the high end of couture kimono wearing, but this can only exist if there is a huge base of people who wear and enjoy kimono in everyday life. Therefore selling large quantities of cheap kimono, used kimono, and old kimono both inside and outside Japan and decreasing the distance between the makers and markets is vital to the future of the kimono.

In Japan, where fashion is perhaps faster than anywhere else, the kimono provides an alternative, an oppositional stand: slow, rooted, and authentic as opposed to fast, anonymous, and ephemeral, an option that is beginning to look transnational and also embodies Japaneseness. Longer lasting, rooted in time and space, kimono is the quintessential art for wearing. Kimono wearers have always known that fashion is all about how you put yourself together, and it is this knowledge that puts them and their kimono style at the heart of what fashion is all about. Let the kimono revolution roll on!

Bibliography

Assman, S. (2008) "Between Tradition and Innovation: The Reinvention of the Kimono in Japanese Consumer Culture." *Fashion Theory*. Vol. 12. No. 3. pp. 357–66.

Campbell, C. (2005) "The Craft Consumer: Culture, Craft and Consumption in a Postmodern Society." *Journal of Consumer Culture*. Vol. 5. No. 23. pp. 23–42.

FACEBOOK COMMUNITY: KIMONO https://www.facebook.com/pages/Kimono/52376183722?ref=hl (Accessed August 9, 2015).

FACEBOOK COMMUNITY: KIMONO DE JACK INTERNATIONAL https://www.facebook.com/kdj.international (Accessed August 9, 2015).

FACEBOOK COMMUNITY: KIMONO DE JACK UK https://www.facebook.com/KimonoDeJackUk (Accessed August 9, 2015).

FACEBOOK GROUP: IMMORTAL GEISHA https://www.facebook.com/groups/ImmortalGeisha/583126085163180/?notif_t=like (Accessed August 9, 2015).

FOREVER21.COM http://www.forever21.com/Product/Category.aspx?category=top_kimonos (Accessed August 9, 2015).

Morace, F. (2010) "The Dynamics of Luxury and Basic-ness in Post-Crisis Fashion." *Critical Studies in Fashion and Beauty*. Vol. 1. No. 1. pp. 78–112.

NEW LOOK.COM http://www.newlook.com/shop/womens/tops/kimonos/_/N-9wfZg23 (Accessed August 9, 2015).

Polhemus, T. (2011) *Fashion and Anti-Fashion*. Lulu.com

Glossary

Arai hari Taking a kimono part, cleaning it, and resewing it.

Bashoufu Linen-like woven fiber.

Bingata Okinawa stencil dyeing.

Chirarizumu showing a glimpse of a garment.

Chuusen zome A dyeing technique used in making yukata.

Dangawari Blocks of pattern on kimono, which are placed alternately, like checks, on the left and right of the kimono.

Doujinshi Amateur self-published magazines or manga.

E-bira Picture flyers.

Edo komon Small dot stencil dyed.

E-gasuri Picture ikat.

E-sugoroku Ludo- or Parcheesi-like board and dice game.

Fudangi Very casual or home wear.

Fude Small brush for painting on kimono or calligraphy.

Furisode Long-sleeved kimono for a single woman.

Furoshiki Wrapping cloths.

Futomono sho A dry goods shop.

Futori Thick weaving.

Gaman suru Grin and bear it.

Geisha Entertainer trained in the arts of singing, shamisen, Japanese dance, and witty conversation.

Geta Casual wooden sandals.

Gofuku ten A kimono shop.

Hakama Trouser skirt.

Hakata A type of weaving from Hakata town in Kyushu, used for making obi.

Hake A flat wide brush for dyeing cloth.

Han-eri Kimono collars.

Haori A kimono jacket, like a cardigan, worn on casual occasions.

Haori-himo Cords to tie a haori closed.

Hikizome-Ya Ground dyer.

Hinagata Bon Kimono pattern book.

Hitoe Single-layered kimono.

Houmongi A kimono for visiting, rather formal wear.

Iida tsumugi Tsumugi from Iida town.

Iki A concept involving subtlety in style, detachment, and cool chic.

Itchin Nori A fine quality rice paste used in dyeing.

Izaribata Backstrap loom.

Jinbei Casual work wear of cotton pants and wrapover jacket.

Joufu High-quality, extremely fine and light linen-like fiber.

Juban Under kimono, like a petticoat.

Kakishibuzome Dyeing with fermented persimmon juice.

Kamishimo A samurai garment composed of a winglike vest and hakama.

Kanako shibori Fine fawn spot tie-dyeing.

Kanzashi Decorative hair pins.

Kasane Multiple kimono usually worn in different colors.

Katabira Fine summer linens worn by samurai class women.

Katasusomoyo Shoulder and hem designs.

Katazome Stencil dyeing.

Katsugi-Ya Portable kimono shop, kimono peddler.

Kawagoe Tozan Cotton striped cloth from Kawagoe town.

Kawaii Cuteness.

Kitsuke Kimono dressing.

Kitsuke gakuin Kimono dressing school.

Komon Casual kimono dyed with all-over patterns.

Koshimaki Hip-wrapping style, when two kimono are worn, but with the top one hanging over the obi, and the sleeves dangling.

Kosode Garment worn underneath in the Heian period which emerged in the Edo period, considered the kimono forerunner and used interchangeably in the Edo period.

Koto Japanese harp-like instrument.

Koukoku   Advertisement.

Kudzu   Japanese arrowroot.

Kumihimo   Braiding, braids.

Kurotomesode   Black kimono with a hem design used on very formal occasions.

Kyoyuzen   Yuzen dyed in Kyoto.

Machigi   Town wear.

Maiko   Trainee geisha entertainer.

Manga   Japanese comic books.

Miya daiku   a temple or shrine carpenter.

Mizuhiki   Decorative paper ties, made with washi paper.

Moga   Modern girl.

Mon   Crest.

Monpe   Baggy work trousers.

Mook   A cross between a magazine and a book, usually very visual in content.

Muji   Plain, unpatterned.

Nagaita chuugata   A complex stenciling process used on yukata.

Nagajuban   Long under kimono, like a petticoat.

Nassen zome   Paste-resist dyeing with dyes in the resist paste.

Nihon buyo   Japanese dance.

Nihonga   Japanese-style painting.

Nishiki-e   Colored woodblock prints.

Obi   Kimono sash or belt.

Obi-age   A scarf-like cloth that is worn to cover an obi pillow.

Obi-dome   a brooch for an obi.

Obi-jime   A braided cord that holds the obi in place.

Ohashiori   Fold of cloth under the obi when kimono is worn in the conventional way.

Oiran   Highest rank of courtesan in the Edo period.

Omeishi   A casual crepe-like cloth.

Onsen   Hot spring baths.

Oshima tsumugi   High-quality woven tsumugi from Oshima Islands.

Otaiko   Drum-bow style of tying a Nagoya obi.

Rakugo   Comic storytelling.

Ramie   Linen-like woven fiber.

Roketsu-some   Batik, wax-resist dyeing.

Ryokan   Japanese-style inn.

Sado   Tea ceremony.

Sagemono   Accessories that hang from the obi.

Sarasa   Chintz.

Sencha   Green tea.

Shakuhachi   Japanese bamboo flute.

Shamisen   Japanese guitar-like stringed instrument.

Shibori   Tie-dyeing.

Shika-Ya   Kimono producer.

Shimi nuki   Kimono stain removal.

Shina   Wisteria fiber.

Shita-e   Kimono design, underdrawing, drawn on paper.

Shita yunoshi   Steaming before dyeing.

Sokuhatsu   A soft bun, considered to be between Japanese and western style.

Susohiki   Trailing kimono used for dancing.

Susomoyo   Design on kimono limited to the hem area.

Tabi   Kimono socks.

Tan mono   Kimono bolts.

Tansu   Kimono chest.

Tenugui   Small cotton towels.

Tonya   Kimono dealer, middleman.

Tsujigahana   Tie-dyeing and ink-drawn flower patterns on kimono.

Tsukesage   Slightly less formal version of a houmongi.

Uchikake   Large padded over kimono, worn for weddings and in the theater.

Ukiyoe   Japanese woodblock print.

Wa   Japanese (style).

Wafuku   Japanese clothing.

Wakamatsu   Young pine tree design, popular in late Meiji period.

Wasai-jo   Kimono-tailoring business.

Yagasuri   Arrow pattern ikat.

You   Western (style).

Youfuku   Western dress.

Yukata   Cotton bath robe now considered summer casual kimono.

Yukata bira   Forerunner of the yukata, worn when bathing in the middle ages.

Yuki tsumugi   Tsumugi from Yuki town.

Yunoshi-Ya   Steamer.

Yuzen   Dye-resist technique, where paste lines are squeezed onto cloth, and the colors are painted in between the resist before it is washed off.

Zori   Kimono footwear.

Zuanka   Design artist.

Index